Business Contracts

Turn Any Business Contract to Your Advantage

Business Contracts

Turn Any Business Contract to Your Advantage (With CD ROM)

Laura Plimpton

EP
Entrepreneur® Press

Editorial Director: Jere Calmes
Cover Design: Desktop Miracles, Inc.
Production: CWL Publishing Enterprises, Inc., Madison, Wisconsin, www.cwlpub.com

ISBN 13: 978-15-9918072-4
10: 15-9918072-3

Printed in Canada

11 10 09 08 07 10 11 9 8 7 6 5 4 3 2 1

Dedication

This book is dedicated with love and thanks to my parents,
Carolyn Williams Plimpton and Charles E. Plimpton,
who are role models for successful entrepreneurs,
compassionate community members,
inspirational parents, and loving spouses.

Contents

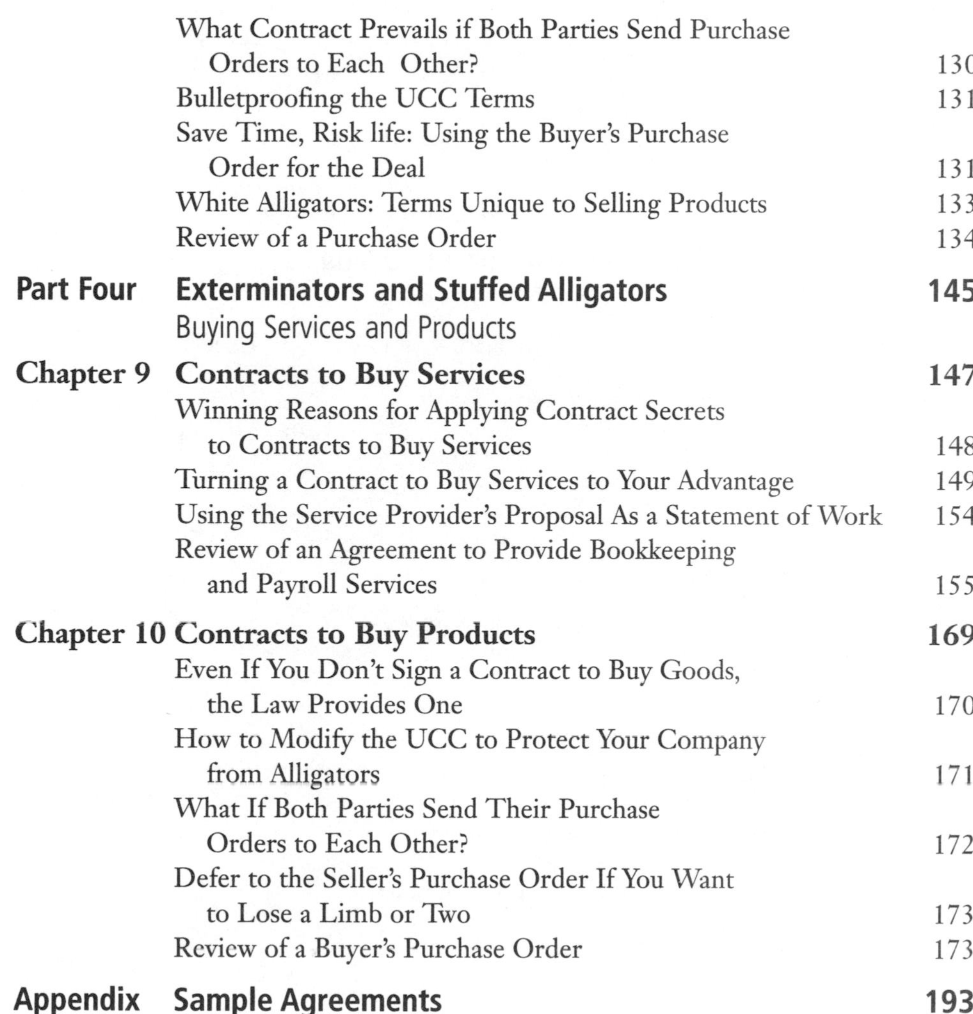

INTRODUCTION

Exercising Personal Power over Contracts

Have you ever wished you had well-written contracts that would:

- make it more likely your company would get paid for its products or services quickly
- help resolve any disputes in your company's favor
- increase the odds your company receives products or services it buys in a timely manner for a fair price?

Have you ever:

- wanted to revise a contract someone asked your

business to sign so that it favors your company rather than the company that wrote the contract
- wished you could use a form contract you found on the Internet or purchased in a book and know that it was the correct contract for your business situation
- wanted to avoid spending hundreds of dollars in legal fees to have a lawyer draft a contract?

This book answers your wishes by providing the inside secrets to drafting simple contracts, checklists for reviewing any business contract, and strategies, with examples, for turning a contract to your advantage. After reviewing and drafting over 12,000 contracts as an in-house attorney and an attorney practicing business law in a law firm, and I developed tools and techniques for quickly turning any contract into a business asset. My clients, business owners and managers, asked me to teach them how to utilize these tools to create their own contracts and be able to quickly review contracts drafted by other parties without consulting an attorney.

In one company I worked for, the sales staff never seemed to find the time or have the inclination to have the agreements they wrote documenting a sale between their company and its customers reviewed by me, their in-house attorney. In one year, 11 disputes on their way to becoming lawsuits involved these contracts. These disputes resulted from the two contracting parties having wildly different understandings of their duties under the contracts. After training the sales staff on contract drafting and review using the principles in this book, none of the succeeding contracts—all drafted or reviewed by the sales staff—were the basis of an unresolved dispute or litigation.

It helped the sales staff to think of contracts like nice peaceful lakes—with alligators under the water. If you don't know the alligators are there you are bound to eventually lose an arm or maybe get eaten all together. With some pretty simple training, alligators can be spotted in a contract and eliminated or turned on the person that pointed them in your direction. Without this training, or a lawyer to spot alligators for you, you and your business are just bait.

The following chapters offer quick, simple concepts you can immediately apply, as well as detailed analyses of contracts your business encounters every day—agreements with your customers to sell products and services and agreements with your vendors to buy services and products. The contracts that are reviewed are not perfect—some are actually pretty poor—just like the ones you may be reviewing. That way you'll get used to seeing the alligators. Each contract contains plain English explanations of each paragraph, sometimes each sentence, as well as notes about what should have been in the contract or what should be changed. A checklist for each type of contract is included in the Appendix, which can be used when reviewing a contract someone asks your company to sign or when drafting contracts your company needs to be successful.

That said, it's always better to have an attorney review or draft an agreement. They can bring knowledge of local laws and practices to the deal as well as a more detailed legal analysis than this book will discuss. This book is not legal advice. Nothing can substitute for the advice of an attorney, licensed in the state where you are doing business, reviewing your specific agreement or situation.

When you decide to skip an attorney this book will provide invaluable assistance to achieve successful business contracts, and by the time you read through Chapter 1, an arsenal of techniques for taking control of any contract.

Acknowledgments

This book is in your hands due to the careful editing of Karen Thomas and Jere Calmes at Entrepreneur Press as well as the patient and well-informed hand-holding and advice-giving talents of my irreplaceable agent, Ed Knappman at New England Publishing Associates. I am indebted to my legal mentors over the years, Gary Lowenthal, Mary Grey Hone, Monte Lee, and Mike Rooney, for passing on their wealth of knowledge. My clients get the most accolades, however, because it was they who let me practice my legal skills until I found the optimum application of legal verbiage and business strategy, especially Geoffrey Gonsher, Richard Fura, Bud Ring, Mike

Gibbons, Lisa Anderson, Michael Miller, Adam Thomas, Sara Davis, Roy Hodges, Gary Bucher, Sally Rubino, Jody Spicola, David Smith, Alberto Gutier III, Jim Carroll, Eric Rey, Steve Brandwein, Frank Flider, Scott Davis, Larry Smith, and Ethel Hoffman. And finally to my dear family and friends whose prodding and encouragement got this done—Patsy and Lee Bakunin, Randy Oakes, Virginia and Tony Migliarese, Vicki Carpel-Miller, and Jason Plimpton.

PART ONE

Protecting Your Deal from Alligators

What to Include in the Contract

CHAPTER 1

Six Secrets to Save Your Shirt (and Your Profits or Career)

John, the owner of a rapidly expanding limited liability company called Carpet Glow, buys his company's cleaning supplies from Acme. Acme sent a contract to Carpet Glow to cover an order for $100,000 in supplies. The contract seemed pretty simple, requiring half of the amount due on signing and the rest a month later, so John signed it. A month later Carpet Glow had not paid the remaining balance to Acme due to a cash flow problem. Acme sued John. John went to court and argued that he couldn't be sued because he had formed Carpet Glow as a limited liability company to protect his personal assets. The court ruled against him because of the way he signed the contract with Acme. A very simple change in the way the signature section of the Acme contract was written would have saved John from this threat to his personal assets. If you want to avoid this mistake, read on.

In This Chapter

- Recognizing the hidden contract that can hurt you later
- How a company name can be good as gold
- When signing a contract can threaten your home and savings
- The missing business point that kills a legally perfect contract
- Nailing down three hazardous deal points that are litigation hot buttons
- Deterring harmful and hard-to-detect changes to the contract after it's signed

Recognizing the Hidden Contract That Can Hurt You Later

A contracts is any agreement between two or more people. The agreement can be on behalf of individuals or on behalf of companies they represent. There are certain legal requirements that must be met for a contract to be enforceable, but they are seldom an issue in business contracts. These legal requirements include whether the person who agreed to the contract was old enough to agree (defined by state law, but usually age 18) or whether both parties had the mental capacity to enter into the agreement (for example, like being too drunk to know what was being agreed to). If your company gets into a conflict with another party over an agreement and they argue that the contract can't be enforced, yet you have a written contract signed by both parties in your hand, you need to consult an attorney.

Contracts do not have to be written. If you, on behalf of your company, make a verbal agreement and claim that the verbal agreement can't be enforced, it's possible you, and your company, will get a rude awakening when your company is sued to enforce the agreement. Contracts are enforceable in a court of law whether they are written or not.

Often verbal contracts are hidden. The verbal agreement is known to the few who were part of the agreement at the time it was made and maybe a few more who are part of fulfilling the agreement. Sometimes, because many business people believe contracts must be written, even the person making the agreement is unaware a contract exists until the other party tries to enforce it. Verbal contracts can hurt you and your company. Proving the terms of a verbal contract is always one party's word against the other. Because there is no definitive document or recording to prove what the agreement was, anything that either party can convince a judge or jury to accept as true could be determined to be enforceable. Successful business people write contracts down.

"We don't have to have that in the contract; they said they would just do it for us." "They're great guys—if the widget doesn't turn out right the first time they'll work with us." "I've been working with George for years—there will never be a problem with this company." "They're the biggest Uffelhoop provider in the world; they would never do anything to harm their reputation."

These are all actual excuses I have been given for why a contract wasn't written down or why key terms weren't included in what was written down (except "Uffelhoop" was substituted for the real product to spare the actual company embarrassment). Every excuse is attached to an agreement that resulted in an ugly conflict that could have been resolved without as much pain and suffering if the agreement—all of the agreement—had been written down.

Contracts exist for the bad times when the person you know and trust leaves the company you have done business with for eons and is replaced by your worst nightmare. They exist for when memories of what was promised in the negotiations get fuzzy. They exist for when business pressures change and what one party was just willing to do without stating it in the contract becomes too costly and because it was not written in the contract, that party decides not to do it. And they exist for when that big provider with the perfect reputation gets bought by the bigger conglomerate that must recoup its acquisition costs and stops doing everything it is not contractually obligated to do.

Drafting a contract and reducing an agreement to writing are just smart business. If you never need to look at that contract again, good for you. If there's a question or a conflict, a contract should answer it or resolve it. When the other party, or even someone on your side, suggests that everything is so friendly there is no need for a written contract—insist on one. After reading this book it will be no trouble at all to write down what you've agreed and either finalize it or send it to an attorney to be finalized.

How a Company Name Can Be Good As Gold

Well over half of the contracts I review have the name of one of the parties wrong. I don't mean spelled wrong, although that is a basic starting point, but legally wrong. The parties' names are the most basic part of the contract and they must be:

- included in the agreement
- indicated as a party to the agreement
- spelled correctly
- legally correct

What does this mean?

Miff Company, Moff Company, and Muff Company agree to share the cost and use of a booth at a trade show. They, smartly, draft a written agreement to document this. The agreement goes as follows:

> **Example A:** Miff Co., Moff, and Muff Company agree that they will split the cost of a booth at the Uffelhoop trade show. Each of us get to use it.
>
> **Signed:** *Peter Pink* *Georgia Grey* *Steven Silver*

Go back to the list above. This agreement has all the parties included. It's clear that each company named is a party to the agreement. It's not necessary that you specifically state "The parties to this agreement are …," but the parties to the agreement should be obvious from the context. It seems like the names are spelled correctly. But are these the real names of these companies? Probably not.

Most companies have an official legal name stated on a "birth certificate." Sole proprietorships will not have birth certificates; partnerships may or may not have them; but every other type of company will. A company's birth certificate is the form filed with the state where the company was started, which states the company's name, the type of company it is, and its ownership. These forms may be called "Articles of Incorporation," "Articles of Organization," "Certificate of Limited Partnership," "Statement of Qualification," or other similar titles. The name stated on these forms, as filed with the state agency overseeing formations of companies (usually the Secretary of State or

Corporation Commission) is the company's real name. Whenever you use your company's name or the name of a company you are contracting with it should be the exact name stated on the company's birth certificate. For example, let's say Miff Company was incorporated as "Miff Company Inc. of Boston." That would be its legal name.

It's possible to have a legal name that differs from the name your company is conducting business under. For this to be legally effective, often a notice must be filed with the state where the company is doing business that indicates that the real name of the company is one thing but the company is doing business under another name. These are usually called "DBA" filings, which is shorthand for "doing business as" filings. If your company is doing business under a name different from its legal name, contracts it enters into should state the legal name of your company followed by the DBA such as Miff Company Inc. of Boston DBA Harry's Pillow Shop.

Why is it important to state the legal name of the company? Because if you do not, it can be used as evidence that it was not the company that entered into the agreement but the individual who signed the contract. If you sign the agreement, your personal assets could be tapped to pay contract damages. Whether you are the owner of the company or an employee of a business signing a contract on behalf of that business, you probably don't intend to risk your personal assets when you sign the contract. Failing to use the company's real name could jeopardize your intentions.

Incorporated businesses must act as entities separate from the people that run them, and evidence of that is consistent use of the actual legal name of the company. This is a simple step that can save controversy in a lawsuit. Determine the correct legal name of your company and use it consistently in contracts.

Is it good enough for the agreement above to state "Miff Co." if the legal name is Miff Company Inc. of Boston"? It's always best to use the exact official legal name of the company as reflected on its birth certificate. Otherwise it creates the opportunity for disputes, and the whole point of a contract is to avoid disputes and create rules for resolving controversies. Use your company's actual correct legal name consistently in contracts.

What if Peter Pink, the purchasing officer for Miff Company, drafts and signs the following contract:

> **Example B:** Joan Miff and Miff Co., Moff, and Muff Company agree that they will split the cost of a booth at the Uffelhoop trade show. Each of us gets to use it.
> **Signed:** *Peter Pink Georgia Grey Steven Silver*

By including Joan Miff in the list of parties to the agreement, the agreement may be enforceable against Joan Miff's personal assets, as well as the assets of Miff Company, Moff Company, and Muff Company. Do you think Peter Pink has a long career in purchasing at Miff Company? Draft your contracts to avoid controversies—they should state very clearly who has agreed to what. If Joan Miff does not intend to be personally responsible for this contract her name should not be there.

To meet the basic name requirements above we would revise this agreement as follows:

> **Example C:** Miff Company Inc. of Boston, Moff Inc., and Muff Company LLC agree that they will split the cost of a booth at the Uffelhoop trade show. Each of us get to use it.
> **Signed:** *Peter Pink Georgia Grey Steven Silver*

When Signing a Contract Can Threaten Your Home and Savings

Refer to Example C. The signature section contains three names, presumably one name associated with each company. By signing the contract this way, a controversy lies in wait. Were these individuals signing for the companies? Or were they really signing on behalf of themselves, even if the agreement itself contains the correct legal names of the companies? Because the way they signed the agreement makes it appear they signed on behalf of themselves, the signers' personal assets could be at risk.

The purpose of signatures on contracts is to memorialize the party's agreement to what is written down. Signatures, or signature blocks as you will often see them referred to in legal discussions, should clearly indicate who is agreeing. In this case its not Peter Pink but Peter Pink on behalf of a company.

The signature block should start with who is agreeing to the contract. If it's Miff Company of Boston, that's how the signature block should start. If it's a person, the signature block would start with that person's name. This is how the Uffelhoop contract should be drafted:

Example D: Miff Company Inc. of Boston, Moff Inc., and Muff Company LLC agree that they will split the cost of a booth at the Uffelhoop trade show. Each of us gets to use it.

Signed:

Miff Company Inc. of Boston

____

Peter Pink, Purchasing Officer

Moff Inc.

____

Georgia Gray, Officer

Muff Company LLC

____

Steven Silver, Treasurer

These signature blocks start with the names of the parties agreeing to the contract, then follow with evidence of the agreement (an actual signature), and then documentation of who belongs to the signature and that person's status with the contracting party.

It's important to think this through. Who or what do you want to enforce this agreement against if there is a conflict? Is it the company? Is it the company's rich owner? I have seen the signature block used to "capture" an unknowing person or business as a party to a contract. If you want to potentially have access to the owner's personal assets in a contract dispute then draft the signature block like Example C above—it's likely the person signing won't realize the legal implications. If Peter Pink was a billionaire and had signed the agreement in Example C it's possible his personal assets could be used to satisfy a judgment issued against Miff Company resulting from a dispute over the contract. But if you are the one signing a signature block like the "Peter Pink" example and you do not want your assets to be at risk, then don't sign. If it is your intention to bind only your company's assets in the contract then make sure that the signature block is drafted to reflect that the company is the one signing the contract.

Who can bind a company to a contract? This differs according to state law, but in general if the person signing appears to have the authority to sign on behalf of the company, as evidenced by business cards, title, and other "trappings of authority" conferred by that company, the company will have to stand behind whatever is signed. If you intend only certain people in your company to be able to bind your company to a contract, then make sure that is stated on invoices, purchase orders, and other forms and contracts. It's common to see statements like "Only the signature of the President of Moff Inc. will bind the company to an agreement. Any other signature has no binding effect."

If you are concerned that the person signing a contract on behalf of the other party may not have the authority to bind the company, check to see if that company's purchase orders or other contractual agreements indicate that only an officer or some other designated person can execute the agreement, or changes to the agreement. Call the owner or president of the company and ask who has the authority to bind the company. Does the person signing appear to the have the authority and title that you would give someone in your company whom you would authorize to sign contracts?

You can ask that the agreement be signed by an officer of the company, if the company is a corporation, by the managing member, if the company is a limited liability company, or by the general partner if the company is a partnership. State law gives these individuals authority to bind a company. You can often determine who is designated in these capacities for the company you are dealing with by calling the state agency that regulates business entities in the state where the company was formed. Sometimes the state agency's web site has this information.

What if the business entity is a sole proprietorship or a partnership? If it's a sole proprietorship, the sole proprietor must sign. In community property states the sole proprietor's spouse may also have to sign in order to allow recovery of any damages against the community assets. You may want to consult an attorney about this. If a partnership is involved, the general partner should sign for the partnership. An example of both types of signature blocks follows:

> **Example E:** Piff Partnership and James Elliott agree that they will split the cost of a booth at the Uffelhoop trade show. Each of us gets to use it.
>
> **Signed:**
>
> *Piff Partnership*
>
> ________________________
>
> June Ellis, General Partner
>
> ________________________
>
> James Elliott, Sole Proprietor

The Missing Business Point That Kills a Legally Perfect Contract

Lack of specificity can kill a legally perfect contract. The basic terms of the contract need to be accurate and detailed to the smallest degree. The best way to look at this is that someone completely unfamiliar with your company, the other contracting party, and the subject of the contract should be able to pick up the contract and understand what is being contracted for, the criteria the product or service must meet to be satisfactory, when the service or product is to be delivered, how it is to be delivered, and for what cost. There should be no chance that the subject matter of the contract can be confused with any other service or product than the one the parties to the contract intend to contract about.

Review Example D, which has correct company names and signature blocks for the Uffelhoop contract.

Example D: Miff Company Inc. of Boston, Moff Inc., and Muff Company LLC agree that they will split the cost of a booth at the Uffelhoop trade show. Each of us gets to use it.

Signed:

Miff Company Inc. of Boston

____

Peter Pink, Purchasing Officer

Moff Inc.

____

Georgia Gray, Officer

Muff Company LLC

____

Steven Silver, Treasurer

Are the parties agreeing to split the cost of a booth, whatever that cost may be? Or are they intending to split the cost of a standard size booth? A booth with premium location? Is there only one Uffelhoop trade show? Or is this held every year? What if an Uffelhoop trade show is held in most major cities once a year—are they agreeing to split the booth costs for every Uffelhoop trade show in every location forever? Are they really intending to state that each of the three parties can use the booth equally at all times? Or do they mean that each of them gets to use it one day of the three-day trade show?

The agreement may in fact be that the three parties split the costs of any booth they can get at all Uffelhoop trade shows now and in the future and that they all get to use it all the time. If so, this contract does a great job of documenting the parties' agreement. If that is not the agreement, this contract contains numerous opportunities for misunderstandings and litigation.

What if the agreement is that the three companies will split the cost of a 10 × 12 booth at the 2010 Uffelhoop trade shows held in Denver and Dallas and that each of the companies will staff the booth during all times the trade show is open to the public, sharing display space equally?

Example F: Miff Company Inc. of Boston, Moff Inc., and Muff Company LLC agree that they will split the cost of a 10 × 12 booth at the 2010 Uffelhoop trade shows to be held in Denver, Colorado and Dallas, Texas. Each company agrees to staff the booth at all times the trade show is open to the public, sharing display space equally.

Signed:

Miff Company Inc. of Boston

____

Peter Pink, President

Moff Inc.

____

Georgia Gray, Officer

Muff Company LLC

____

Steven Silver, Treasurer

Example F documents the agreement of the parties. It prevents many different scenarios where the parties could conflict. What if one company was thinking they would rent a 20 X 20 booth when the other two companies were thinking a 10 X 12? What if the trade show requires the booth to be staffed at all times but two of the companies were thinking they would just be there during lunches when the heaviest traffic occurs and the third company had planned to just be there mornings when its most likely customers most often attend? This contract contains enough specifics that the likelihood for conflict is greatly reduced.

Nailing Down Three Hazardous Deal Points That Are Litigation Hot Buttons

In my experience the three contract terms that most often result in conflict are money, service or product specifications, and how a contract can be terminated.

In Example F there is no discussion of exact costs or timing of payment for the booth. If there is a reduced early payment rate, will everyone take advantage of that, or is it assumed that payment will be made at the latest possible time? It may be that the timing of payment is so clear in this case that this does not need to be a subject of the contract. Any time there is the possibility one party is assuming something that another party could be assuming differently, there is a potential for conflict. If there is a possibility that one party could be assuming, for example, that payment will be made to take advantage of early payment discounts, when others are assuming otherwise, the contract should specifically state when payment will be made by each party.

This also applies to the amount of payment. If the agreement is to rent the 10 × 12 booth whatever the costs may be, then this contract is fine. If there is a cost above which any of the parties no longer wants to participate, then a maximum cost needs to be stated in the contract. If the contract states " … agree to split the cost of a 10 × 12 booth not to exceed $10,000 at the 2010 Uffelhoop …," then if the cost is greater than $10,000 the contract would be void. Whatever the payment agreement is, it is best to document it in great detail.

Service or product specifications are another common source of conflict due to inadequate documentation of expectations in a contract. One party may assume a report they contract to have researched and drafted will cover certain subjects or be of a certain length. The other party has a different expectation. When the two expectations conflict, litigation can result unless the contract is specific enough. Every detail of the service your company is having performed or is performing, or every detail of the product your company is producing or buying should be detailed in the contract. Assume that if you do not state the specification for what your company is buying, you will get the opposite. Assume that if you do not state the specification of what your company is producing, the buyer intends to receive something else. A further incentive to be specific is that, contractually, if something is not stated as included it's likely you cannot use the contract to make the other party provide it. This will be discussed in greater detail related to independent contractor agreements for services and to purchase orders for products.

How a contract can be terminated is a provision that often results in conflicts, usually because it is not included in contracts. If there is no provision in a contract describing how the contract can be terminated, the contract lasts until each party has performed all of their duties under the contract. In the Uffelhoop contract, the contract would exist until the close of the last Uffelhoop trade show held in Denver or Dallas in 2010. This could be a bad thing if one of the companies decides to close down its Uffelhoop business. It is obligated to participate in a trade show for a product it no longer produces. In almost all cases there should be a provision stating how a contract can be terminated before the natural conclusion of the contract. Examples of termination provisions are included in Chapter 2.

Deterring Harmful and Hard-to-Detect Changes to the Contract after It's Signed

Assuming your company has a provision in all its contracts that requires any modification of the agreement to be in writing and signed by both parties, it should not be possible to change a contract after both parties have signed it unless your company agrees to the change. Yet it is possible, if your company doesn't take action to make this difficult.

I have found it not at all uncommon in a contract dispute for the other party to produce a contract with original signatures by both parties that contains different terms, invariably benefiting that party, from the contract the company I represented had in its possession. How is that possible?

It's a simple matter to retype, and change any page of a contract except the signature page. Even the signature page can be retyped if the other party can forge your company representative's signature, although I have never to my knowledge seen this. A written contract is a documentation of the agreement the parties reached on some matter. If there are two differing contracts, both signed by the parties, a court would have a difficult time using either contract to decide the dispute.

The easiest way I have found to discourage changing a contract after it is signed is to have both parties initial every page of the contract in a colored ink that is difficult to photocopy (purple seems to work well) and use that same colored ink to sign the agreement. This procedure creates a way to authenticate each page of the agreement as one that was part of the agreement at the time it was signed. It's a simple procedure that does not take much time but can save a lot of trouble later.

This chapter provided insight into the bones of a contract—the hidden structure that must be solid before the contract can become a powerful ally in getting your business deal done. The next chapter explains 23 core legal terms that, when used correctly, can significantly reduce the risks inherent in any transaction. Including these terms can save time and money for your part of the deal, while excluding them from applying to the other party can ultimately provide a very sharp sword if the deal goes bad.

CHAPTER 2

Bulletproof Terms for Every Contract

Jennie contracted with a highly recommended accounting firm to complete her company's annual tax returns. Several accountants from this firm came to her office to review her accounting records in order to prepare the returns. While idly chatting with them Jennie learned that one was a temporary employee of the firm, hired just to work during tax season, and the other was employed by another accounting firm that had subcontracted with the accounting firm Jennie hired. Jennie was incensed that her tax returns were being prepared by staff that she did not consider part of the accounting firm she hired.

Carlos's company completes tenant build-outs for leased property. After finishing a four-room office suite for a consulting business, he billed the fee agreed in the contract of $30,000. Three months later the fee still hadn't been paid. He took the consulting business to court and won a judgment for the $30,000 owed. He added up his legal fees and discovered that he had paid $35,000 to his lawyer to obtain this $30,000 judgment.

Both companies had contracts covering the work to be performed, yet neither company was able to use these contracts to achieve the results they wanted. The reason is that the contracts failed to include key bulletproof terms. Read this chapter to avoid the same mistake.

In This Chapter

- Alligator repellant: 23 bulletproof terms to prevent attacks
- Modifying terms so they don't strangle your company
- Recognizing when the term helps your company, their company, or both
- Throwing out terms that may hold your business deal back

Alligator Repellant: 23 Bulletproof Terms to Prevent Attack

Including certain clauses in your contracts will reduce risks to your company from lawsuits and misunderstandings and provide legal rights that your company might not otherwise have. In the two examples that began this chapter, including some of these clauses would have either prevented the unwanted result or provided a basis for Jennie and Carlos to seek damages for breach of contract.

Samples of these provisions are included below, along with a discussion of what each provision means, and why it's needed in a contract. The provisions without any accompanying commentary are included in the Appendix. The subject matter of these provisions is important—the exact wording is not. In fact, I recommend that in many cases you qualify the wording in the sample clauses as discussed in the following section. You may encounter clauses in contracts you review or in a contract form that cover the same subject matter but are worded differently. As long as the plain sense meaning is the same it's not critical to use the wording in the provisions presented here. It is critical to consider including these clauses in every contract your company signs, although you may decide some clauses are unnecessary in certain contracts. The important part is to decide what business risks are present in the deal your contract documents, and to remove or reduce these risks by using these clauses.

Assignment/Subcontracting: Four Alternatives

> Neither party shall have the right to assign or subcontract any part of its obligations under this agreement.

This prevents both your company and the company you are contracting with from transferring the entire agreement or subcontracting any part of it to another person or business. An assignment of the contract might occur if either your company or the company you contracted with was sold (the new owner could be assigned this contract). A subcontract might occur if an independent contractor or another company was hired to perform the work that either your company or the other company had agreed to perform. Contracts are presumed assignable unless there is a clause like this one in the agreement preventing an assignment. Including this provision in the contract Jennie signed would have assured that the accounting firm she contracted with was the one actually preparing her company's tax returns. This clause would not prevent either company from giving its consent to an assignment or a subcontract, but without such consent an assignment or subcontract would be a breach of contract.

> Neither party shall have the right to assign or subcontract any of its obligations or duties under this agreement without the prior written consent of the other party, which consent shall not be unreasonably withheld or delayed.

This prevents any transfer of the agreement to any other person or business except where the other party provides written consent. The decision on consent must be promptly provided and a decision not to consent must be based on some sound reason.

> Neither party shall have the right to assign or subcontract any of its obligations or duties under this agreement, without the prior written consent of the other party, which consent shall be in the sole determination of the party with the right to consent.

This prevents any transfer of the agreement to any other person or business except where the other party provides written consent. The decision on whether to provide consent can be based on any reason at all, even an unreasonable one.

> Notwithstanding the foregoing, either party may, without the consent of the other party, assign the agreement to an affiliate or subsidiary or to any person that acquires all or substantially all of the assets of a party.

This provision would be included with one of the provisions above that either prevents assignment or allows it with consent. This caveat to those provisions allows a transfer of the agreement without the other party's consent if the transfer is to an affiliate company (usually defined as a company with at least 50 percent of the same owners or shareholders), a subsidiary company, or to an entity that buys the company holds the contract.

If it's important to your business deal that the contract is performed by the party you are contracting with, then this clause is important to include when documenting the deal. If your company might be sold, might want to subcontract all or part of its duties under a contract, or might want to transfer a contract to an affiliate or subsidiary company, then it's important not to include or agree to a clause preventing assignment or subcontract.

Attorney's Fees

> The non-prevailing party in any dispute under this agreement shall pay all costs and expenses, including expert witness fees and attorneys fees, incurred by the prevailing party in resolving such dispute.

This clause creates a right to recover costs and expenses paid by the party that prevails *in a contract dispute. The way this clause is worded, the costs and expenses are not limited to those paid in a lawsuit—the costs and expenses incurred in any contract dispute could be recovered. It is just as common to see this clause written to apply only to costs and expenses incurred by the prevailing party in a lawsuit. Some states have laws that provide for the prevailing party in a contract lawsuit to recover its legal fees and costs from the non-prevailing party. If the state where a lawsuit occurs does not have such a law, this contract provision would provide the same right. This provision is thought to discourage frivolous lawsuits because the party filing a lawsuit risks payment of the other party's legal costs if the suit is lost. In the opening example, if Carlos had included this clause in his company contracts, his company could have recovered the $30,000 it was owed plus the $35,000 paid in legal fees.*

If the law of your state gives the prevailing party in a contract lawsuit the right to recover its legal fees, you could eliminate this clause from your company contracts. However unless the law allowed recovery in any "dispute" versus any "lawsuit" this contract clause provides a broader right to recover your costs and might be worth including anyway. If your state has no law providing for recovery of legal fees, if your company has to sue to recover a payment due, this clause will be invaluable in making the lawsuit cost-effective.

Choice of Law or Governing Law

> This agreement shall be governed by and construed in accordance with the internal laws of the State of XXX, U.S.A., without reference to any conflicts of law provisions.

This provision requires the law of the state your company designates to be used to interpret this agreement. To be legally effective, the state law your company designates must have some relationship to the parties to the contract or a relationship to the agreement. Most companies designate the state where their home office is located. This designation benefits your company because your company is operating under these laws already, is familiar with them, and has attorneys who are familiar with them. If no state law is designated, a court could interpret this agreement under the laws of the state where either business is located or was incorporated (the most likely scenario), or where the contract was performed or signed. Having this clause in a contract reduces the risk that another state's laws could be applied to the agreement with results you don't like or anticipate. If both parties to the contract are headquartered in the same state, it is unlikely that any other state law would be applied to interpret the agreement, and thus this clause could be eliminated.

In my experience, the legal departments of larger companies often dictate to their business people that this clause must name the law of the big company's state to be the governing law for the agreement. The business people are then left being able to negotiate business points like payment, quantity, and delivery date but with no flexibility on the governing law point. It's possible to use this to your company's advantage by holding out for deep concessions on the business points that benefit your company before agreeing to a governing law clause that names the big company's state. The risk, hopefully remote because your company will have such a well-drafted contract, is that the contract will end up in litigation and your company will end up litigating under the laws of another state. Whenever the other party to a contract tells you their legal department insists that the governing law be their state law you know you have an advantage. On a cautionary note, governing law is not the same as venue, so it's possible to litigate in the courts of one state while applying the law of another state. For that reason it's important to review the Choice of Venue clause.

Choice of Venue

Each party hereby submits to the exclusive jurisdiction of, and waives any venue or other objection against, any federal court sitting in the State of XXX, U.S.A., or any XXX state court in any legal proceeding arising out of or relating to this contract. Each party agrees that all claims and matters may be heard and determined in any such court and each party waives any right to object to such filing on venue, forum non-convenient, or similar grounds.

The choice of law or governing law provision determines what state law is applied to the contract, while this clause determines what state court system can resolve the dispute. Each party will want to file a lawsuit in the state they are headquartered or do the most business in. That's usually because their lawyers are familiar with those courts, their employees will not have to travel to participate in the lawsuit, and it is generally thought that courts favor local "residents." This provision creates an enforce-

able agreement between the parties that lawsuits can only be determined in the courts of the named state. The same considerations apply to this clause as to the Choice of Law clause. If the risk of litigation is remote, your company might want to use a concession on this clause to obtain concessions on business terms that provide more short-term benefit to your company.

Compliance with Laws

> Each party shall comply in all respects with all applicable legal requirements governing the duties, obligations, and business practices of that party and shall obtain any permits or licenses necessary for its operations. Neither party shall take any action in violation of any applicable legal requirement that could result in liability being imposed on the other party.

This clause may seem redundant because both parties to the contract have to comply with the law for reasons independent of the requirements of this contract. What this clause does is to make a failure to comply with the law a breach of contract. Without this clause, violation of the law would have no effect on the contract. If a violation of the law would have a negative effect on your company, either because your company might be jointly liable or might experience bad publicity, this clause is important to include so that you can terminate the contract and/or receive damages for the harm.

Conflicts

> The terms of this Agreement shall control over any conflicting terms in any referenced agreement or document.

Any time a contract is created that incorporates or refers to another document, there is the possibility that a provision in one document will conflict with a provision in the other document. For that reason there should be a provision in at least one of the documents stating how such conflicts should be resolved. It's best to identify one document that takes precedence over all the others.

Cumulative Rights

> Any specific right or remedy provided in this contract will not be exclusive but will be cumulative of all other rights and remedies.

Without this provision the contract could be interpreted to mean that the exercise of one remedy in a contract prevents the exercise of other remedies. For example, a court might find that terminating the contract prevents your company from suing to recover past due payments. This provision creates a contractual right to exercise any and all remedies in the contract.

Force Majeure

> Neither party shall be held responsible for any delay or failure in performance of any part of this agreement to the extent such delay or failure is caused by fire, flood, explosion, war, embargo, government requirement, civil or military authority, act of God, or other similar causes beyond its control and without the fault or negligence of the delayed or non-performing party. The affected party will notify the other party in writing within ten (10) days after the beginning of any such cause that would affect its performance. Notwithstanding, if a party's performance is delayed for a period exceeding thirty (30) days from the date the other party receives notice under this paragraph, the non-affected party will have the right, without any liability to the other party, to terminate this agreement.

This means that if some unforeseen event prevents either party from performing their part of the contract, the non-performance will not be considered a contract breach. The party experiencing the event must inform the other party that its performance under the contract is delayed and if the delay lasts more than 30 days, the contract may be terminated by the other party. The catastrophic events listed should include those applicable to your business, the notice period should be long enough to allow the affected company to provide the notice, and the time period giving rise to the right to terminate should be fair to both parties.

Indemnity

> Each party shall indemnify, defend, and hold the other party harmless from and against any and all claims, actions, suits, demands, assessments, or judgments asserted, and any and all losses, liabilities, damages, costs, and expenses (including, without limitation, attorneys fees, accounting fees, and investigation costs to the extent permitted by law) alleged or incurred arising out of or relating to any operations, acts, or omissions of the indemnifying party or any of its employees, agents, and invitees in the exercise of the indemnifying party's rights or the performance or observance of the indemnifying party's obligations under this agreement. Prompt notice must be given of any claim, and the party who is providing the indemnification will have control of any defense or settlement.

This means that one party (the indemnifying party) will pay the damages, claims, expenses, and other types of payments listed in this provision if the other party (the indemnified party) as well as those related to the indemnified party listed in the provision, incurs damages as a result of something the indemnifying party does related to the agreement. The things the indemnifying party could do that would result in liability to the indemnified party are listed at the end of the provision (essentially acts or omissions under the agreement). This provision requires that the indemnified party promptly notify the indemnifying party of a claim and allow that party to control the defense or settlement of the claim.

An indemnification provision addresses the risk that your company might be liable for damages resulting from something the other party does related to the contract. For example, let us say your company has a contract to buy ground beef from another company, which it then incorporates into its frozen lasagna product. If the ground beef is tainted and results in sick consumers, this provision in the contract requires the ground beef supplier to defend any action against your company resulting from the tainted ground beef and to pay all costs and damages. If this provision were not in the contract, your company would have to sue the other company to obtain a judgment for the damages and costs it incurs as a result of the tainted ground beef.

Insurance

> Each party agrees to maintain insurance in commercially reasonable amounts calculated to protect itself and the other party to this agreement from any and all claims of any kind or nature for damage to property or personal injury, including death, made by anyone, that may arise from activities performed or facilitated by this contract, whether these activities are performed by that company, its employees, agents, or anyone directly or indirectly engaged or employed by that party or its agents.

This clause requires each party to maintain insurance to protect itself and the other party from damage claims that might result from performing a required action under the contract. If there is a damage claim and no insurance and the party that causes the damage can't pay the claim, the damaged party is likely to sue your company (the one that did not cause the damage) on the theory that, as the other party to the contract, your company had some culpability for the damage. With an insurance payout, your company is more likely to be insulated from such a claim.

I have underlined a section of this clause that turns the clause from one that reduces risk to one that creates an almost impossible burden to fulfill. The underlined section requires that the amount of insurance be enough to protect both parties from all claims. It's impossible to know how much insurance would protect anyone from all claims that could be filed. For example, when asbestos was first manufactured, it had to have been impossible to foresee the size of the personal injury claims later filed against asbestos manufacturers.

It's also unlikely that one party (Business A) would know enough about the other party (Business B) to fulfill the duty to purchase enough insurance to cover claims against both Business A and B for something Business A does under the contract. The underlined section requires just that.

An insurance clause that requires your company to maintain insurance in amounts sufficient to cover all claims against either party should be revised to require insurance in reasonable amounts. The clause above would meet this requirement if the underlined section were removed and replaced with a transition word like this: "Each party agrees to maintain insurance in commercially reasonable amounts ~~calcu-~~

~~lated to protect itself and the other party to this agreement from any and all~~ covering claims of. . . .”

Integration Provision or Entire Agreement

> This agreement sets forth and constitutes the entire agreement and understanding of the parties with respect to the subject matter hereof. This agreement supersedes any and all prior agreements, negotiations, correspondence, undertakings, promises, covenants, arrangements, communications, representations, and warranties, whether oral or written, of any party to this agreement.

This means that the contract containing this provision is the only agreement that a court will examine to determine what the “deal” or agreement between the parties was. No other written documents or verbal statements can be used as evidence in a dispute over the agreement.

This is a very important provision to have in all contracts. Without this, the written agreement could be considered just one piece of evidence in determining what the deal between the parties was. E-mails, notes, conversations, and anything else related to the contract could be used to interpret the agreement. One of the key reasons to have a written contract is to document the agreement the parties to the contract reached concerning the business deal. Without this provision, the contract would not be considered a complete documentation of the deal—only one piece of that documentation. Be certain that this provision lists every document that is part of this agreement. If a schematic, drawing, blueprint, statement of work, or other supplementary statement is needed to understand the contract, then that document must be referenced and incorporated into the agreement. Otherwise the other documents will not be considered part of this contract because of this paragraph.

Limit of Liability

> IN NO EVENT SHALL EITHER PARTY BE LIABLE TO THE OTHER OR ANY THIRD PARTY IN CONTRACT, TORT, OR OTHERWISE FOR INCIDENTAL OR CONSEQUENTIAL DAMAGES OF

ANY KIND, INCLUDING, WITHOUT LIMITATION, PUNITIVE OR ECONOMIC DAMAGES OR LOST PROFITS, REGARDLESS OF WHETHER EITHER PARTY SHALL BE ADVISED, SHALL HAVE OTHER REASON TO KNOW, OR IN FACT SHALL KNOW OF THE POSSIBILITY.

If one party to this contract causes damages to the other party, the injured party has the right to recover the cost of the damages from the party causing the injury. Damage costs that could be recovered include direct damages, which are damages that are a direct result of what happened, like medical costs or property damage, and indirect damages. Indirect damages are those that are not directly caused by the other party but that are incurred because the party was injured. For example, if Business One manufacturers and delivers a widget with a loose flywheel to Business Two and the flywheel comes off injuring Business Two's customer, the injury to Business Two's customer would be direct damages resulting from Business One's faulty widget. The damage to Business Two's business reputation from the accident would be indirect damages to Business Two.

This provision means that an injured party cannot recover the costs of indirect damages resulting from an injury. It has no effect on either company's liability for direct damages. Indirect or consequential damages can be huge, so disclaiming them is a way of reducing risk in the contract. Some states have laws that require a disclaimer of liability in a contract to be conspicuous within the contract to be enforceable. For that reason these provisions are seen in all capital formats, bolded, set in a larger font than the surrounding text, or otherwise distinguished from the rest of the contract.

IN NO EVENT SHALL EITHER PARTY BE LIABLE FOR ANY INCIDENTAL OR CONSEQUENTIAL DAMAGES. SELLER'S LIABILITY AND BUYER'S EXCLUSIVE REMEDY FOR ANY CAUSE OF ACTION ARISING IN CONNECTION WITH THIS CONTRACT OR THE SALE OR USE OF THE GOODS, WHETHER BASED ON NEGLIGENCE, STRICT LIABILITY, BREACH OF WARRANTY, BREACH OF CONTRACT, OR EQUITABLE PRINCIPLES, IS EXPRESSLY LIMITED TO, AT SELLER'S OPTION, REPLACEMENT OF, OR REPAYMENT OF THE PURCHASE PRICE FOR THAT PORTION OF THE GOODS WITH RESPECT TO WHICH DAMAGES ARE CLAIMED. ALL CLAIMS OF ANY KIND ARISING IN CONNECTION WITH THIS CONTRACT OR THE SALE OR USE OF THE GOODS SHALL BE DEEMED WAIVED UNLESS MADE IN WRITING WITHIN SIXTY (60)

DAYS FROM THE DATE OF SELLER'S DELIVERY, OR THE DATE FIXED FOR DELIVERY IN THE EVENT OF NONDELIVERY.

This provision might be included in a seller's purchase order or sales agreement. It disclaims liability for consequential damages on behalf of both parties. It limits the seller's liability for any other type of damages to the two options listed in the provision, at seller's election, and it establishes a contractual statute of limitation for any action arising from the agreement. This is a short time frame in which to make a claim under the contract, which would greatly decrease the likelihood of a claim being filed. If your company is likely to be the one having the claim filed against it (in this case the seller) this would be an advantage. If your company is likely to be the one filing the claim (in this provision, the buyer) the short time frame in which to do so represents a significant concession because most states allow contract claims to be filed four or more years after the claim arises.

Notices

All notices shall be in writing and shall be delivered personally, by United States certified or registered mail, postage prepaid, return receipt requested, or by a recognized overnight delivery service. Any notice must be delivered to the parties at their respective addresses set forth below their signatures or to such other address as shall be specified in writing by either party according to the requirements of this section. The date that notice shall be deemed to have been made shall be the date of delivery, when delivered personally; on written verification of receipt if delivered by overnight delivery; or the date set forth on the return receipt if sent by certified or registered mail.

Contracts typically require one party to provide notice to the other party in the event one party thinks the contract was breached, when termination of the contract is desired, or in other instances specific to each contract. This provision sets out the requirements for how and when a notice must be made to be legally valid. It states that a legally valid notice must be in writing and be sent to a designated address. It also defines when a notice is deemed to have been received, which is important if some time period starts on the receipt of a notice. This might be the case where a party to the contract has to make a late payment within five days of receipt of a late payment notice or otherwise the contract terminates.

If the agreement omits this provision, a dispute could arise concerning whether a notice was given at all ("Harry said he told you the payment was late"), whether it was received ("You sent it to our warehouse, not our corporate office"), and when it was received, rather than a date and time easily verified or calculated according to the contract provisions. Including an address where notices must be sent is good practice to assure they are received where your company can best react to them.

Relationship of the Parties

The relationship of the parties under this agreement is that of an independent contractor and the company hiring the contractor. In all matters relating to this agreement each party hereto shall be solely responsible for the acts of its employees and agents, and employees or agents of one party shall not be considered employees or agents of the other party. Except as otherwise provided herein, no party shall have any right, power, or authority to create any obligation, express or implied, on behalf of any other party. Nothing in this agreement is intended to create or constitute a joint venture, partnership, agency, trust, or other association of any kind between the parties or persons referred to herein.

This provision defines the relationship between the contracting parties. Some business arrangements create the legal right for one party to bind the other party to contracts and other obligations. Some relationships create the potential for employment-related liabilities for the other company's employees. Courts will sometimes find that a joint venture, partnership, agency, trust, or other association exists where none was intended by the parties. These types of relationships mean that one party may have the right to incur liabilities on behalf of the other party, or otherwise act on the other party's behalf. To avoid the possibility one of these relationships may be inferred where it was not intended, this provision should be included in a contract.

Severability

> If any provision of this agreement shall be declared by any court of competent jurisdiction to be illegal, void, or unenforceable, the other provisions shall not be affected but shall remain in full force and effect. If the non-solicitation or non-competition provisions are found to be unreasonable or invalid, these restrictions shall be enforced to the maximum extent valid and enforceable.

If the law changes, making a term in a contract unenforceable or even illegal, the entire contract may be void because it contains the now illegal or unenforceable term. A provision such as this may allow the court to simply delete the term, leaving the rest of the contract to stand as it is. Whether a court will do that is a matter of state law, but it's wise to have this sentence in case the state court does allow striking only the offending provision. In cases where the contract includes a non-solicitation or non-competition provision, this provision would allow a court to interpret those provisions to comply with the law. For example, a non-competition provision may state that the former owner of your business cannot open a similar business within 50 miles of the old business. If a law were passed that stated that a non-competition provision restricting creation of a new business within 10 or more miles of the old business was unenforceable, the severability provision would allow a court to interpret the non-competition provision to restrict businesses within 9 miles rather than the 50 stated in the contract.

Successors and Assigns

> This agreement shall be binding on and inure to the benefit of the parties hereto and their respective heirs, legal or personal representatives, successors, and assigns.

Generally contracts are only binding on the parties that sign them. Even when they are assigned from one party to the contract to a new party, the assignment is a contract between the assignor and the assignee and doesn't require the other party to the assigned contract to go along with the assignment. There are other instances where the

other party to the contract could change, such as when the company is sold or if the individual that owns it dies. In those instances, the contract might not be binding on the new owners or the heirs without this clause. If your company wants to enforce its bargain for the full duration of the contract, this clause should be included.

Survival

All provisions that logically ought to survive termination of this agreement shall survive.

If an agreement ends, every provision in it is no longer effective. There are some provisions your company will want to continue to be effective after the termination or expiration of the agreement, such as Indemnification, Limitation of Liability, and Governing Law and Forum. The Survival provision allows provisions that logically are intended to govern events related to the agreement that could occur after the agreement ends to continue to govern those events.

Termination for Cause

If either party breaches any provision of this agreement and if such breach is not cured within thirty (30) days after receiving written notice from the other party specifying such breach in reasonable detail, the non-breaching party shall have the right to terminate this agreement by giving written notice thereof to the party in breach, which termination shall go into effect immediately on receipt.

This means that the contract may be terminated only when the other party breaches the agreement and then, only when the non-breaching party sends a notice of breach to the other party and allows the breaching party 30 days to cure the breach. After 90 days, another notice must be sent to actually terminate the contract. If this procedure were not followed exactly, there would be no right to terminate the contract. Any attempt to do so without following this procedure would be a breach of the agreement. An alternative is to provide for immediate termination on a breach, but if this is a provision applying to both parties, consider the effect on your own company if it is the one missing the payment deadline by one day, for example.

There should always be a provision for terminating a contract before each party's agreed-on duties have been completed. Once both parties have agreed on a termination procedure such as the one set forth here, think through the effects on your company and allow for them in the termination provision. For example, if the contract were terminated early, should there be provisions for payments to cover work completed but not yet paid for?

Termination for Convenience

> This agreement may be terminated by either party on thirty (30) days advance written notice effective as of the expiration of the notice period.

The previous provision requires the contract to be breached before the other party can move to terminate it. The non-breaching party would never have an opportunity to terminate the agreement. This provision allows either party to terminate the contract for any reason and no reason once the party desiring to end the contract sends a notice to the other party and then allows 30 days to expire. This provision provides the maximum flexibility to both parties, with the corresponding risk that if your company does not want to terminate and the other party elects to, your company will have lost the benefit of its bargain.

Termination on Insolvency

> Either party has the right to terminate this agreement where the other party becomes insolvent, fails to pay its bills when due, makes an assignment for the benefit of creditors, goes out of business, or ceases production.

This provision provides an automatic right of termination if the other party has financial problems or is no longer a going concern. Without this provision, a contract with no other termination provision would continue in force.

This could be a problem in many contractual situations. An example would be where your company has an exclusive agreement with a distributor to place your product in stores. If the distributor closed its doors, your company would seek another dis-

tributor and sign another exclusive distribution agreement. If the original distribution company reopened a year later it could sue your company for violating the exclusive contract your company had with it.

Many of these types of provisions in form agreements state that if a party declares bankruptcy, the agreement can be terminated. Most of the companies I have seen go out of business do not declare bankruptcy but simply shut down. This provision allows termination in that situation.

It's also important to address the situation in which it is widely known in the industry that a business is in dire financial straights, but your company has a contract to provide the company with products or services. Your company would not want to do this knowing the other company is unlikely to pay its bill to your company. This provision would allow your company to terminate its contractual obligations in the event the other company was insolvent or failed to pay its bills.

Waiver

> Failure of either party to insist on strict compliance with any of the terms, covenants, and conditions of this agreement shall not be deemed a waiver of such terms, covenants, and conditions, or of any similar right or power hereunder at any subsequent time.

This means that failure to enforce a term in the contract does not mean that your company has elected not to ever enforce that term. For example, this provision retains the right of your company to ignore or forgive one contract breach and still enforce a breach of the same term at a later time. If this provision is omitted, your company runs the risk of having a court find that waiving a term in the contract results in that contract term being unenforceable during the term of the agreement. For example, if your company accepted a payment one day late it might be found to have waived any right to enforce a contract provision requiring payment on a certain date or within a certain time.

Warranty Disclaimers

> EXCEPT AS EXPRESSLY STATED IN THIS AGREEMENT, THE SELLER EXPRESSLY DISCLAIMS AND NEGATES ANY IMPLIED OR EXPRESS WARRANTY OF MERCHANTABILITY, ANY IMPLIED

OR EXPRESS WARRANTY OF FITNESS FOR A PARTICULAR PURPOSE, AND ANY IMPLIED OR EXPRESS WARRANTY OF CONFORMITY TO MODELS OR SAMPLES OF MATERIALS.

Certain warranties are automatic or implied unless they are specifically disclaimed in a written agreement. To avoid the possibility of providing an implied warranty, your contracts must include a disclaimer like this in a conspicuous manner. A conspicuous manner means that the disclaimer is set off from the rest of the contract by all capital letters, perhaps bold type, or a different color type. The type cannot be smaller than the surrounding type in the contract.

Implied warranties could include a warranty of title (seller owns the goods and has the right to sell them; no creditor will interfere with buyer's purchase of the goods; and the goods are free from copyright, trademark, or patent claims of third parties), a warranty of merchantability (goods are reasonably fit for the ordinary purposes for which such goods are used; of average-, fair-, or medium-grade quality; adequately packaged and labeled; and conform to the affirmations of fact on the label), a warranty of fitness for a particular purpose (seller has reason to know of the purpose for which the goods are bought and knows that the buyer is relying on the skill and judgment of the seller to select the goods) and a warranty arising from course of dealing or trade usage (a court presumes both parties have knowledge of trade custom and presumes that custom is intended to apply to the contract). Although I have described these warranties in terms of goods, they apply equally to services.

Express warranties can be made through promotional material, brochures, proposals, and ads. They can arise through verbal statements and do not have to include words like warranty or guarantee. Generally any affirmation of fact or promise, description of the goods, or use of samples or models by the seller will create an express warranty. The provision above disclaims any express warranty that the goods or services conform to models or samples.

Without this provision, the goods or services provided under the contract will be warranted with the express warranties arising from what your company said or gave the other party and with the implied warranties provided under state law. To reduce the uncertainty that this creates, a warranty disclaimer is common in contracts.

Written Modification

> This agreement may be amended or modified only by a writing executed by both parties.

This provision means that only a written signed agreement will be enforceable to amend or modify the agreement. Otherwise, for example, one company can say that payment was agreed to be double what the contract states, and it's possible a court could find this alleged verbal modification of the contract enforceable.

Modifying Terms So They Don't Strangle Your Company

The terms presented above are written to be absolute—meet the criteria set forth in the term or the contract is breached. For example:

> Compliance with Laws: Each party shall comply in all respects with all applicable legal requirements governing the duties, obligations, and business practices of that party and shall obtain any permits or licenses necessary for its operations.

When this term is in a contract your company signs, it means that if your company breaks a minor law, the contract is breached. For example, if delivering goods is part of your business and one of your drivers receives a speeding ticket while on company business, your company has not complied "in all respects with all applicable legal requirements governing the duties, obligations, and business practices" of your company. The other party could use this minor traffic ticket to claim a breach of contract and if the contract allows, immediately terminate the contract. Clauses like this that are absolute and easily violated are often used as a pretext to terminate a contract when one party wants out because they have found a better deal.

The way to prevent this is to modify any requirement that is absolute. This is done by adding the words "reasonable" or "material" to the clause. If it's your company that is being required to do something, inserting the words reasonable and/or material to the requirements is a good business practice.

For example:

> Compliance with Laws: Each party shall comply in all <u>material</u> respects with all applicable <u>material</u> legal requirements governing the duties, obligations, and business practices of that party and shall obtain any <u>material</u> permits or licenses necessary for its operations.

In another example:

> The non-prevailing party in any dispute under this agreement shall pay all <u>reasonable</u> costs and expenses, including expert witness fees and attorney's fees, incurred by the prevailing party in resolving such dispute.

Adding "material" to a legal requirement modifies the legal requirement to apply only to matters that would have a significant effect on the bargain between the parties. In the example concerning compliance with laws, adding "material" to the contract clause means that if your company's truck driver received a ticket it would not breach a contract for unrelated consulting services. If the contract were for catering a 1,000-person dinner and your company kitchen had its health permit suspended, it would be material non-compliance with the law, triggering whatever consequences the contract provided.

Adding "reasonable" to a legal requirement means that whatever is required must be what a reasonable person would do. If the legal requirement is that an amount must be reasonable, it could not be significantly above or below what is average or common in the industry.

In the example above, agreeing to pay "all costs" means that if the prevailing party paid their attorney the highest hourly rate known on earth, if your company were required to pay the costs as the non-prevailing party, you must pay those costs. If the clause stated that the non-prevailing party is required to pay "all reasonable costs," then, if the average hourly rate for attorneys in the field required for this lawsuit were half the rate the prevailing party paid their attorney, it's likely your company would be required to pay an hourly rate closer to the industry average.

Recognizing When the Term Helps Your Company, Their Company, or Both

Contract provisions that are not general in nature (statements such as "The terms of this agreement shall control over any conflicting terms in any referenced agreement or document") are always slanted to benefit someone. They can be slanted to benefit your company, the other company, or both. It's important to assess the advantages and disadvantages of drafting a provision to benefit one party or the other and negotiate accordingly.

Often in contracts drafted by the other party, all the requirements are drafted to apply only to your company. For example, your company may be required to indemnify the other party but the other party provides no indemnification to your company. Your company may be required to comply with all laws but the same requirements are not placed on the other company. In these cases there is no reasonable excuse for the other party to refuse to make these provisions apply to both parties. You just have to have the awareness and knowledge to recognize the one-sided contract clauses and insist they be made bilateral.

On the other hand, you can use this to your company's advantage. If your company contracts include the 23 bulletproof terms described above written to benefit your company only and the other company doesn't request any changes, your company has a huge advantage throughout the contract, and even after its termination if there is a survival provision.

The bulletproof terms in the prior section are all written to apply to both parties. They describe mutual responsibilities and duties. Here is the first provision:

> Neither party shall have the right to assign or subcontract any part of its obligations under this agreement.

This is the same provision drafted to apply to the other company only where the other company is referred to as "consultant":

> Consultant shall not have the right to assign or subcontract any part of its obligations under this agreement.

If your company were referred to as "company" in the contract, this provision would preclude only your company from assigning or subcontracting the agreement.

> Company shall not have the right to assign or subcontract any part of its obligations under this agreement.

Here is the insurance provision written to apply to both parties, just the consultant and just your company.

> Each party agrees to maintain insurance in commercially reasonable amounts covering claims of any kind or nature for damage to property or personal injury, including death, made by anyone, that may arise from activities performed or facilitated by this contract, whether these activities are performed by that company, its employees, agents, or anyone directly or indirectly engaged or employed by that party or its agents.
>
> Consultant agrees to maintain insurance in commercially reasonable amounts covering claims of any kind or nature for damage to property or personal injury, including death, made by anyone, that may arise from its activities performed or facilitated by this contract, whether these activities are performed by the consultant, its employees, agents, or anyone directly or indirectly engaged or employed by that party or its agents.
>
> Company agrees to maintain insurance in commercially reasonable amounts covering claims of any kind or nature for damage to property or personal injury, including death, made by anyone, that may arise from its activities performed or facilitated by this contract, whether these activities are performed by the company, its employees, agents, or anyone directly or indirectly engaged or employed by that party or its agents.

Throwing Out Terms That May Hold Your Business Deal Back

Some business deals may get bogged down when a contract is drafted that includes all 23 of the bulletproof terms. In deciding what to include or exclude, your company has to weigh the risks that omitting the provision will have against the potential that negotiating the deal will take much longer than you had planned or that the deal will be lost altogether.

If your company believes the risk of a litigated dispute occurring is low you could omit:

- Attorney's Fees
- Choice of Law/Governing Law
- Choice of Venue

If your company has no business reason to require the following provisions they can be omitted:

- Assignment/Subcontracting (where assigning would be fine)
- Compliance with Laws (where compliance doesn't effect your company)
- Conflicts (where there are no other agreements)
- Insurance (where there are no significant risks)

Notices (where no notices would need to be given)

- Relationship of the Parties (where the relationship wouldn't be questioned)
- Severability (it's unlikely a law would change affecting the contract)
- Successors and Assigns (where binding a successor or assign would not be needed)
- Warranty Disclaimers (where no warranty could arise)

The following provisions are critical and are recommended to be included in all instances:

- Cumulative Rights (allows all remedies to be applied, not just one)
- Force Majeure (excuses non-performance if a catastrophic event occurs)
- Indemnity (requires one party to cover the other party for damages)
- Integration (makes the contract the only evidence of the business deal)
- Limit of Liability (limits liability to direct damages)
- Survival (allows contract terms to cover events after the contract ends)
- Termination (allows termination of the contract before it's fully performed)

- Termination on Insolvency (allows termination where a party is bankrupt, broke, or closes)
- Waiver (prevents one waiver of a contract provision from negating that contract provision entirely)
- Written Modification (requires any modification of the contract to be in writing)

The quick, easy review system in the next chapter provides a framework for reviewing contracts to determine if any of these bulletproof terms are missing, which party they benefit, and if other key sections of the contract are satisfactory. The system can be used to draft a contract or modify a form agreement so that it provides the greatest benefit for your company while reducing the most risk. The system uses checklists so you don't have to keep all this in your head. The tools in the next chapter will allow you to get those contracts off your desk and generating money for your company.

CHAPTER 3

The Quick, Simple Review System

Deepak, who owns a pet grooming business, has a simple system for reviewing contracts. When someone hands a contract to her she scans and immediately signs it or shoves it to the bottom of her work pile to read later. This system got her into some bad contracts that cost her some of her profits and caused her to miss some opportunities that were in contracts that got lost in the work pile. Signing a contract drafted by the opposing party without reviewing and modifying it is like swallowing a bottle of aspirin and hoping you won't throw up. Putting off reading the contract is equivalent to hiding a piece of cheese at the bottom of your file drawer for a month in hot weather.

The solution is to apply a checklist to the contract to determine if the contract has the bones and most of the muscle for a good business deal. This chapter focuses on how to use a checklist to quickly analyze a contract, with step-by-step examples.

In This Chapter

- A 15-minute strategy for conquering a contract
- A map to the where the monster alligators live
- Making a contract form into a useful agreement
- Step-by-step practice with a service contract
- Step-by-step practice with a contract for goods

A 15-Minute Strategy for Conquering a Contract

Checklists are routinely used by lawyers when reviewing contracts and completing sale or purchase transactions. Lawyers use them to make sure they have addressed the most important issues in a contract or deal. They can be used for the same purpose by you.

Each type of contract discussed in this book has a corresponding checklist in the Appendix. In 15 minutes you can determine your contract goals, read through the contract, compare it to the appropriate checklist, and determine what needs to be revised to get your company a better deal and to reduce legal risks.

The first task when reviewing a contract is to identify the top five things you want to achieve with the contract. For example, Deepak placed an order for various electronic parts he needs to stock in the computer repair store he owns. The supplier confirmed the order by mailing a purchase order contract to Deepak. The first thing Deepak did when he received it was to determine his top five goals for the purchase. These were to:

- receive the correct parts
- have delivery occur within one week of the order
- obtain a replacement for a defective part within a week of returning the defective one
- pay for the order no sooner than 15 days after its receipt

- be able to order more of the same parts at the same price for at least six months.

When Deepak read the purchase order he noticed there was no mention of when delivery would occur, the remedy for a defective part was a credit against future orders, and there was no provision for placing future orders at the contract prices in the current purchase order. He knew that when negotiating the revisions to the purchase order he might give in on other points, but that these three points would be the ones he would work the hardest to get.

After identifying the contract goals Deepak reviewed the contract using the purchase order checklist. He found eight missing issues that he decided were important to his business deal. These were the secondary issues he would negotiate for inclusion in the purchase order. This whole process took Deepak less than 15 minutes, after which he knew exactly what risks and rewards were in the purchase order.

A Map to Where the Monster Alligators Live

There are contract terms that are always monsters. Your company needs to watch out for them.

Automatic renewal—These provisions state that the contract automatically renews for another term when the current term expires. Usually they include the right to cancel if you provide written notice some period of time before the current term ends. The deadline for indicating your company doesn't want to renew is usually way before the contract ends. Rarely do companies remember to cancel the contract prior to the deadline. Then the contact automatically renews and your company is stuck another year, or maybe longer depending on the renewal term. I don't recommend agreeing to an automatic renewal provision. If your company must agree to a contract containing this provision, set up some system to remind a responsible person in your company (who will be sure to still be working there) when the deadline is coming up and then management can determine if it wants to renew or not. Creating this reminder can be as simple as writing it on every calendar in your company.

Time is of the essence—This means that every date or deadline in the contract is absolute. The failure to meet the deadline, whether it be early or late, is a contract breach. This is a very difficult standard to comply with over the life of a contract. If your company agrees to this provision in a contract, negotiate to make it mutual. Often the other company will not want to agree to the same standard and will agree to drop the provision altogether.

Best Efforts—Best efforts is a legal standard of the highest magnitude. Boiled down, it means your company will move heaven, earth, and all the alligators to get done whatever the contract is requiring your company's best efforts to do, even if that costs boatloads of money. There are very few contractual responsibilities companies intend to agree to devote this much effort and money to. The alternatives are to agree to diligent effort, reasonable effort, or good faith effort. Good faith effort is the least onerous standard in that it requires what amounts to an effort to try to make the agreed-on action happen. Anything that could be interpreted as "trying" is good enough. Reasonable effort is the amount of effort a reasonable person would expend to make the action happen. A reasonable amount of time and money utilized to make the agreed-on action happen would be sufficient to meet the contract requirements in that case. The level of effort just below a "best efforts" standard is a diligent level of effort. Diligent effort is an amount of effort more than reasonable but less than moving heaven and earth. When you see a standard of effort in a contract, be careful to agree to what you realistically can do.

Sole determination—When a party is contractually permitted to make a decision in its "sole determination" it means that the party can make the decision based on no reason or any reason at all. They could flip a coin or ask the next person who happens by to decide. In contrast, when a contractual provision does not include the right to make the decision in a party's sole determination it means that the decision must be reasonable under the circumstances. For example, if consent to assignment is in a party's sole determination, the party can refuse to consent because they don't like the attire of the owner of the company to whom the contract is being assigned to. If there was no right to decide whether to consent in a party's sole determination, a decision not to consent based on attire would be unreasonable and a violation of the contract. Avoid allowing the other party to make a decision in its sole determination.

Satisfactory—When the standard for whether a contract deliverable or action is "satisfactory," your company should realize that determining this is highly subjective. Anything left subjective in a contract leaves room for misunderstandings and contract disputes. The term "satisfactory" is often used in the following ways:

- in form and substance satisfactory to XXX
- mutually satisfactory
- satisfactory in all respects

These clauses can be made less subjective by qualifying them such as:

- in form and substance customary for deals of this type
- reasonably satisfactory
- substantially in the form used in transactions of this type

Any time you see the word "satisfactory" in a contract, make sure the determination of what is satisfactory is not subjective.

Making a Contract Form into a Useful Agreement

Form contracts can be downloaded from many Internet sites as well as purchased in books or from stores. In many ways they are riskier to use than simply signing the other party's contract. At least with the other party's contract you know who the contract benefits and where to look for the alligators. With forms you won't know if they were drafted to benefit the buyer or seller, or even if they were drafted for products or services.

The starting point with a form is to determine if the form was written to document a transaction in goods or services. Reading through the contract should identify the subject matter. Then determine if the contract was drafted from a seller's viewpoint or a buyer's. This may be harder to identify. Look for the following:

- Who has the majority of the duties in the contract? (If the buyer has all the duties, then the contract was written to benefit the seller—if the seller has all the duties then it is a contract to benefit the buyer.)

- Whom do the payment arrangements benefit? (Whomever is benefited will be the party the contract is oriented towards—if payment is after services are rendered it's a buyer's contract.)
- Which party do the bulletproof terms place the duties on? (The contract benefits the other party.)

The form is a good starting point if you've determined that it is drafted to cover the same subject matter as the transaction your company is documenting, and if it is written to benefit a party in the same position your company is in—a buyer or seller.

Then apply the quick, simple review system to the form and modify it as you would any contract. Does the form have the bulletproof terms needed to protect your company? Are the terms written to meet your company's top five business goals? Are there any big alligators in the form, like terms that require best efforts of your company or a time is of the essence clause applicable to your company? Applying the review system will result in a contract form that enforces your business deal and benefits your company.

Step-by-Step Practice with a Service Contract

The following contract is between a company and a consultant. The contract was drafted by the company and presented to the consultant for review. This analysis is presented as if the consultant were the one reviewing the contract.

SERVICE AGREEMENT

This consulting agreement, dated effective March 1, 2009 ("Agreement"), is made and entered into by and among Dancing Theater, a Nebraska corporation ("Company") and Mary Public Relations, a Wyoming limited liability company ("Consultant").

SCOPE OF WORK

1. Services—The Company has engaged Consultant to provide the services described in Exhibit A ("Services").

2. Hours—Consultant will devote 10 hours per month in performing services for Company. Consultant shall have discretion in selecting the dates and times it performs services in any given month, giving due regard to the needs of Company. If Company deems it necessary for Consultant to provide more than 10 hours of services in any month, Consultant is not obligated to undertake such work until the Consultant and Company have agreed on a rate of compensation.
3. Reports—Consultant shall periodically provide Company with written reports regarding the consulting services. On the termination of this Agreement, Consultant shall, on the request of Company, prepare a final report of Consultant's activities.

COMPENSATION

4. Fees—Company shall pay Consultant $1,000 per month for performance of services. This monthly fee shall be paid on the first of the month following the month in which the services were provided.
5. Expenses—Company agrees to reimburse Consultant for all actual reasonable and necessary expenses that are directly related to the services. These expenditures may include, but are not limited to, expenses related to travel (i.e., airfare, hotel, temporary housing, meals, parking, taxis, mileage, etc.), telephone calls, and postal expenditure. Expenses incurred by Consultant will be reimbursed by Company within 15 days of Consultant's proper written request for reimbursement.

TERM AND TERMINATION

6. Term—This Agreement shall be effective as of April 1, 2009 and shall continue in full force and effect for 12 consecutive months. Company and Consultant may extend the term of this Agreement and the terms and conditions under which the relationship shall continue.
7. Termination—Company may terminate this Agreement after giving Consultant 30 days advance written notice. Any equipment, samples, or information in any form provided by Company to Consultant in connection with the services shall be returned to Company prior to termination of the Agreement.

CONTRACTOR STATUS

8. Independent Contractor—Consultant is an independent contractor and is not an employee, partner, or co-venturer of Company. The manner in which services are pro-

vided shall be within Consultant's sole control and discretion. Consultant is not authorized to represent, speak for, or obligate Company in any manner without the prior written authorization from an officer of Company. Consultant and Consultant's employees will not be eligible for, and shall not participate in, any employee pension, health, welfare, or other fringe benefit plan of Company. No workers' compensation insurance shall be obtained by Company covering Consultant or Consultant's employees.

9. Taxes—Consultant shall be responsible for all taxes arising from compensation and other amounts paid under this Agreement, and shall be responsible for all payroll taxes and fringe benefits of Consultant's employees. No payroll tax of any kind shall be withheld or paid by Company on behalf of Consultant or its employees. Consultant understands that it is responsible to pay, according to law, Consultant's taxes and Consultant shall, when requested by Company, properly document to Company that any and all federal and state taxes have been paid.

CONFIDENTIAL INFORMATION

10. Definition—"Confidential Information" means information, not generally known, and proprietary to Company or to a third party for whom Company is performing work, including, without limitation, information concerning any patents or trade secrets, confidential or secret designs, processes, formulas, source codes, plans, devices or material, research and development, proprietary software, analysis, techniques, materials, or designs (whether or not patented or patentable), directly or indirectly useful in any aspect of the business of Company; any vendor names, customer and supplier lists, databases, management systems, and sales and marketing plans of Company; any confidential secret development or research work of Company, or any other confidential information or proprietary aspects of the business of Company. All information that Consultant acquires or becomes acquainted with during the period of this Agreement, whether developed by Consultant or by others, which Consultant has a reasonable basis to believe to be confidential information, or which is treated by Company as being confidential information, shall be presumed to be confidential information.
11. Duties of Confidentiality—Consultant may be exposed to and will be required to use certain confidential information of Company. Consultant agrees that Consultant will not and Consultant's employees, agents, or representatives will not, use, directly or

indirectly, such confidential information for the benefit of any person, entity, or organization other than Company, or disclose such confidential information without the written authorization of an officer of Company, either during or after the term of this Agreement, for as long as such information is confidential information.

OWNERSHIP OF INFORMATION

12. Data from Services-All drawings, models, designs, formulas, methods, documents, and tangible items developed as part of the services belong exclusively to Company and are works made for hire ("data"). To the extent that any data may not, by operation of law, be works made for hire, Consultant hereby assigns to Company the ownership of copyright or mask work in data, and Company shall have the right to obtain and hold in its own name any trademark, copyright, or mask work registration, and any other registrations and similar protection that may be available in data. Consultant agrees to give the Company or its designees all assistance reasonably required to perfect such rights.

CONFLICT OF INTEREST AND NON-SOLICITATION

13. Conflict of Interest—Consultant shall not consult or provide any services in any manner or capacity to a direct competitor of Company during the term of this Agreement. A direct competitor of Company is any individual, partnership, corporation and/or other business entity that engages in the business of live theater performances within 30 miles of Dancing Theater.
14. Non-Solicitation—Consultant will not, directly or indirectly, through an existing corporation, unincorporated business, affiliated party, successor employer, or otherwise, solicit, hire for employment, or work with, on a part-time, consulting, advising, or any other basis, other than on behalf of Company any employee or independent contractor employed by Company while Consultant is performing services for Company and six months thereafter.

GENERAL PROVISIONS

15. The terms of sections 10, 11, 12, 13, and 14 are reasonably necessary to protect the interests of Company, are reasonable in scope and duration, and are not unduly restrictive. A breach of any of these sections will render irreparable harm to Company for which a remedy at law is inadequate. Company shall therefore be entitled to seek any

and all equitable relief, including, but not limited to, injunctive relief, and to any other remedy that may be available under any applicable law or agreement between the parties. An award of damages to Company does not preclude a court from ordering injunctive relief.

16. Survival—The provisions of sections 10, 11, 12, 13, 14, and 15 shall survive the expiration or termination of this Agreement.
17. Standard of Conduct—Consultant shall not use time, materials, or equipment of Company without the prior written consent of Company. In no event shall Consultant take any action or accept any assistance or engage in any activity that would result in any university, governmental body, research institute, or other person, entity, or organization acquiring any rights of any nature in the results of work performed by or for Company.
18. Subcontracting—Consultant shall not use the service of any other person, entity, or organization ("Subcontractor") in the performance of the services without the prior written consent of an officer of Company. Where Company consents, no information regarding the services shall be disclosed to Subcontractor until an agreement has been executed between Company and Subcontractor to protect the confidentiality of Company's confidential information and to vest Company's absolute and complete ownership of all right, title, and interest in the work performed under this Agreement.
19. Severability—If any provision of this Agreement is held unenforceable by a court of competent jurisdiction, that provision shall be severed and shall not affect the validity or enforceability of the remaining provisions.
20. Governing Law—This Agreement shall be governed by and construed in accordance with the internal laws (and not the laws of conflicts) of the State of Nebraska.
21. Complete Agreement—This Agreement constitutes the complete agreement and sets forth the entire understanding and agreement of the parties as to the subject matter of this Agreement and supersedes all prior discussions and understandings in respect to the subject of this Agreement, whether written or oral.
22. Modification—No modification, termination, or attempted waiver of this Agreement, or any provision thereof, shall be valid unless in writing signed by the party against whom the same is sought to be enforced.

23. Waiver of Breach—The waiver by a party of a breach of any provision of this Agreement by the other party shall not operate or be construed as a waiver of any other or subsequent breach by the party in breach.
24. Successors and Assigns—This Agreement may not be assigned by either party without the prior written consent of the other party; provided, however, that the Agreement shall be assignable by Company without Consultant's consent in the event Company is acquired by or merged into another corporation or business entity. The benefits and obligations of this Agreement shall be binding on and inure to the parties hereto, their successors and assigns.
25. No Conflict—Consultant warrants that Consultant has not previously assumed any obligations inconsistent with those undertaken by Consultant under this Agreement.

IN WITNESS WHEREOF, this Agreement is executed as of the date set forth above.

Dancing Theater Inc. Mary Public Relations LLC

Company Consultant

By: ______________________________ By: ______________________________

Its: ______________________________ Its: ______________________________

EXHIBIT A SERVICES

Consultant shall place at least two articles of at least 1,000 words each in newspapers, magazines, or other periodicals with readership located within 100 miles of Lincoln, Nebraska. Each article shall positively represent and promote, as reasonably determined by Company, some aspect of Dancing Theater. Each article shall be reviewed and approved prior to dissemination by Dancing Theater.

The consultant, Mary Public Relations LLC, starts by defining its top five goals for the contract. These are:

- Getting paid $1,000 per month
- Receiving payment promptly after the client approves each article
- Making sure both parties have the same understanding of what the services will include
- Being able to use the client's name and a brief description of the work in promotional literature

• Having a long-term relationship with the client

Along with the items in the appropriate checklist, Mary Public Relations LLC will be reviewing this contract to see if the terms accomplish these goals. Because the contract was drafted by the client, it's likely that the contract reflects the client's goals, not the consultant's.

The correct checklist for reviewing this contract is the one for services where the reviewing party is the one selling the services, in this case the consultant. If the client were reviewing a contract presented by the consultant, the correct checklist would be the one for buying services. The checklist for this contract is presented below with annotations indicating how the contract above conforms to the checklist. It will be apparent when applying the checklist that some contract terms are written in ways that don't affect the consultant but do negatively affect the consultant's client, Dancing Theater. Because it's the consultant reviewing the contract, the consultant won't be concerned with this—it's up to the client to protect its interests.

Checklist for Service Agreements Where Your Company Is the Service Provider

❑ Correct legal name of parties (*Appears to be correct*)

❑ Effective date of contract (*Has two conflicting dates. Because the contract lasts 12 months from the effective date, this must be resolved so that it's clear when the contract starts and stops.*)

❑ Date work starts, if different (*Maybe one of the two dates is the date work starts? This must be resolved.*)

❑ Definitions for capitalized terms (*Included*)

❑ Term of contract (*Included, but does this meet the consultant's goal of a long-term relationship?*)

❑ Detailed description of duties:

- What is to be done (*Included*)
- How is it to be accomplished (*Not necessary—left up to consultant*)
- When is it to be done (*Included*)
- What are final products or deliverables (*Included*)

- ❑ What are the specifications for the final products or deliverables (*Included*)
- ❑ Deadlines for deliverables and project milestones (*Included*)
- ❑ What cooperation or assistance is required from the other party (*Included, but to prevent client from delaying approval of articles there should be a limit to how long the client can review them before they are automatically deemed approved for publication.*)
- ❑ Designate specific person from customer to be key contact or otherwise involved (*Not included*)
- ❑ What specific labor and materials are supplied by your company (*Included*)
- ❑ Quality standards (*Included [standard is client's approval]but make sure approval is required to be reasonable and not delayed*)
- ❑ Payment terms:
  - Will your company require a retainer or deposit *(Consultant should consider this because he or she is getting paid after work is performed)*
  - Will consultant keep this as security or bill against it *(Should be considered)*
  - When is payment due and how is this calculated *(Consultant wants to be paid after articles are approved. This should be one of the change requests made by the consultant.)*
  - Is an invoice sent or amount due automatically *(Included)*
  - If invoice, what are the invoice intervals *(Not applicable)*
  - What is payment amount *(Included)*
  - In what currency *(Not included)*
  - How is payment to be made—cash, check, electronic funds transfer, or other *(Not included)*
  - Late fees assessed and if so how *(Consultant should include this)*
  - Out-of-pocket expenses reimbursable—if so on what basis and when *(Included)*
  - No right of set off or deduction *(Not applicable because payment is one monthly fee.)*
- ❑ If a repair agreement, is there a deadline for the customer to pick up the repair *(Not applicable)*
- ❑ What happens if not picked up *(Not applicable)*
- ❑ If a repair agreement, does customer sign acceptance of the terms and con-

ditions *(Not applicable)*

- ❑ Does customer sign for repair quote *(Not applicable, but consultant might consider having company provide a written indication of article approval)*
- ❑ Does customer sign for return of goods *(Not applicable)*
- ❑ Return of confidential information on termination *(Included)*
- ❑ Destruction of confidential information on termination *(This is company's issue because the confidential information being protected is the company's. The company needs to assure that the contract requires the information to be destroyed at the contract's end.)*
- ❑ Confidential information:
  - How defined *(Included)*
  - What are acceptable uses and disclosures *(Included but make sure the clause allows for all the uses the consultant needs.)*
  - Term of confidentiality obligations *(Included—in this case it's the company's issue because this provisions protects only the company's confidential information; and because the duty of confidentiality ends with the contract, the company is allowing the consultant to expose confidential information after that time. This is poorly drafted from the company's viewpoint but that's not the consultant's problem.)*
  - Duties towards confidential information *(Included)*
  - Exceptions to duties of confidentiality *(Not included, but may not be an issue for the consultant)*
  - No solicitation of employees *(Included for company, but does consultant need to make this a mutual duty so that company cannot hire away consultant's staff?)*
- ❑ Length of restriction *(Included)*
  - Non-compete *(Included but is it too restrictive for consultant?)*
  - In what geographic area *(Included)*
  - For how long *(Included)*
  - In what markets *(Included)*
- ❑ Alternative dispute resolution *(Not included)*
  - Negotiation *(Consider requiring before a lawsuit can be filed.)*
  - Mediation *(Consider requiring before a lawsuit can be filed.)*

- Arbitration *(Consider requiring before a lawsuit can be filed.)*
- Is alternative exclusive or required before litigation? *(Not included)*
- Who pays for alternative? *(Not included)*
- Who specifically is required to participate in alternative? *(Not included)*
- Required qualifications of neutral party officiating over the alternative *(Not included)*
- What is the timeframe for alternative? *(Not included)*
- Where does alternative dispute forum occur? *(Not included)*
- What rules govern alternative dispute forum? *(Not included)*
- If neutral party renders a decision, is it binding? *(Not included)*

❑ Alligators applicable to your company *(None)*
- Satisfactory standard
- Time is of the essence
- Best efforts
- Automatic renewal provision
- Sole determination standard

❑ Assignment/subcontracting permitted *(Included—consultant subcontracts with consent, client assigns if merger)*
- Preclude partial or complete assignment but allow subcontracting *(Not applicable)*
- Preclude subcontracting but allow partial or complete assignment *(Not applicable)*
- Allow subcontracting with consent not to be withheld unreasonably *(Included but with no reasonableness standard, which consultant should include)*
- Allow subcontracting with consent at other party's sole discretion *(Not applicable)*
- Allow subcontracting if a party is sold *(Included but applies only to client)*
- Allow subcontracting if a party is transferred to an affiliate or subsidiary *(Included but applies only to client)*
- If subcontractors permitted, will they be required to maintain confidentiality of all confidential information? *(Included)*

❑ Recovery of prevailing party's expenses in litigation *(Not included)*
- Attorney's fees *(Not included)*

- Legal costs *(Not included)*
- Expert witness fees *(Not included)*
- Investigation costs *(Not included)*

❑ Choice of law to interpret agreement *(Included as law of client's state)*

❑ Choice of venue for litigation *(Not included)*

❑ Compliance with laws *(Not included)*

❑ If required, specify material compliance with laws applicable to this contract

❑ Conflicting language between agreements is resolved in what manner *(Not applicable)*

❑ Rights provided in contract are cumulative or exclusive *(Included)*

❑ Force Majeure—consider inclusion of fire, accident, acts of public enemy, terrorism, severe weather, acts of God, labor disruption, flood, failure of suppliers to deliver, difficulty obtaining supplies, epidemics, nuclear strike, government intervention, government or freight embargo, quarantine, difficulty obtaining transportation *(Not included)*

- Notice required if event occurs *(Not included)*
- Right to terminate if event lasts specified amount of time *(Not included)*
- Indemnity *(Not included)*

❑ Who provides indemnification *(Not included)*

- To your company, officers, employees, consultants, directors, agents, parent company, subsidiary *(Not included)*
- For claims, liabilities, losses, damages, costs, charges, attorneys fees, legal costs, liens, death, personal injury, accidents, property damage. *(Not included)*
- Arising out of actual or alleged negligence, gross negligence, breach of the contract, claims of liens, or encumbrances *(Not included)*

❑ Integration (or Entire Agreement) provision *(Included)*

- All documents making up the agreement referenced *(Not applicable)*
- Requirement to obtain and maintain insurance *(Not included)*
- Insurance certificates required to be produced *(Not included)*
- Your company a "named insured" if insurance requirement is on other party *(Not included)*

- ❑ Limitation on liability *(Not included)*
  - Consequential damages—special, indirect, incidental, exemplary *(Not included)*
  - Limitation on remedies and, if so, is word "exclusive" included? *(Not included)*
  - Limitation on amount of damages *(Not included)*
  - Limitation on liability provision conspicuous *(Not included)*
- ❑ Notice provision *(Not included)*
  - Is address for notices included? *(Not included)*
  - Acceptable ways to make delivery specified *(Not included)*
  - Time that the other party is deemed to have received the notice specified *(Not included)*
- ❑ No joint venture, agency, partnership, trust, or association *(Included)*
- ❑ Relationship is that of independent contractor *(Included)*
- ❑ Severability—illegal or otherwise unenforceable provisions can be severed *(Included)*
- ❑ Successors and assigns—agreement binding on *(Included)*
- ❑ Survival— certain terms of the agreement survive termination or expiration *(Included)*
- ❑ Termination provision *(Included, but does this meet the consultant's goals for a long-term relationship with the client? Perhaps require termination only for cause?)*
- ❑ How much notice is required before contract terminates *(Included)*
  - For cause *(Not included)*
  - Is right to cure default provided *(Not included)*
  - Any breach or material breach *(Not included)*
  - For convenience *(Included)*
- ❑ If elected by either party, does any party have a right to damages *(Included)*
  - Insolvency *(Not included)*
  - Bankruptcy *(Not included)*
  - Assignment for benefit of creditors *(Not included)*
  - Receiver appointed *(Not included)*
  - Initiates reorganization *(Not included)*

- Closes business *(Not included)*
- Stops operating *(Not included)*

❑ Waiver—waiver of breach not agreement to waive all breaches *(Included)*
❑ No third party beneficiaries *(Not included)*
❑ Publicity *(Not included)*

- Allow with other party's written consent not to be unreasonably withheld *(Not included)*
- Allow for your company at its discretion *(Not included)*
- Prohibit entirely *(Not included)*
- Allow use of customer's name in advertisements *(Not included)*

❑ Warranty *(Not included, but this is something the client would want so it's not the consultant's issue. Warranties are liabilities for the one giving them.)*

- How long and for what *(Not included)*
- If disclaimed, express, implied, merchantability, fitness for purpose, title *(Not included)*
- Voided for improper use or operation, inadequate maintenance, or calibration *(Not included)*

❑ If remedy limited, is the word "exclusive" clearly stated *(Not included)*
❑ If disclaimer or exclusive remedy, is language conspicuous *(Not included)*
❑ Written modification—all modifications in writing and signed *(Included)*
❑ Correct signature blocks *(Included)*
❑ Agreement signed and each page initialed by both parties *(Not applicable yet)*

The consultant can now go back through the checklist and note all the instances where something on the checklist was not included in the agreement. These are:

- Effective date of contract
- Date work starts, if different
- Term of contract
- What cooperation or assistance is required from the other party?
- Designate specific person from customer to be key contact or otherwise involved

- Quality standards
- Payment terms
- Does customer sign for article approval?
- What are acceptable uses and disclosures of confidential information?
- Exceptions to duties of confidentiality
- No solicitation of employees
- Non-compete
- Alternative dispute resolution
- Assignment/subcontracting allowed with consent not to be withheld unreasonably
- Assignment/subcontracting allowed if a party is sold
- Assignment/subcontracting allowed if a party is transferred to an affiliate or subsidiary
- Recovery of prevailing party's expenses in litigation
- Choice of venue for litigation
- Compliance with laws
- Force majeure
- Indemnity
- Requirement to obtain and maintain insurance
- Limitation on liability
- Notice provision
- Termination provision
- No third-party beneficiaries
- Publicity

The consultant can quickly go through this list and decide what, if any, of these terms need to be modified in the contract or added if they are missing. Let's say that Mary Public Relations LLC has decided these terms are ones that must be negotiated with Dancing Theater Inc. and that everything else was either not important or not applicable. The information in parenthesis indicates what needs to be changed.

- Effective date of contract (April 1, 2009)
- Date work starts, if different (same as effective date)

- What cooperation or assistance is required from the other party? (submitted articles deemed approved one week after submission to client)
- Quality standards (client's approvals must be reasonable)
- Payment terms (payment is in advance)
- Assignment/subcontracting allowed with consent not to be withheld unreasonably
- Termination provision (for cause only)
- Publicity (use of customer's name allowed in advertisements)

At this point the contract has been thoroughly reviewed, the alligators identified, and a very simple process for corralling them has started. Once the eight terms above have been decided on, the contract can be easily revised and signed.

Step-by-Step Practice with a Contract for Goods

Here is the quick review process applied to a contract to sell goods, in which the seller of the goods is reviewing an agreement provided by the buyer. Here is the agreement:

CONTRACT FOR SALE OF GOODS

Agreement made and entered into this 10th day of December, 2010, by and between Cerron Inc. (Seller), 1212 Ready Street, New York, New York, and ReadyMart, LLC (Buyer), 365 Delivery Street, New York, New York.

Seller hereby agrees to transfer and deliver to Buyer on or before December 15, 2010 the following goods:

20 cases of #310 plastic green frogs as described in Buyer's Circular 45

Buyer agrees to accept the goods and pay for them in accordance with this Agreement.

Buyer and Seller agree that acceptance of the goods shall not be deemed to have been made until Buyer indicates such acceptance in writing to Seller.

Buyer agrees to pay for the goods at the time they are delivered and at the place where goods are received. Until such time as the indicated goods have been delivered to Buyer, all risk of loss shall be on Seller.

Seller warrants that the goods are now free from any security interest or other lien orencumbrance and that they shall be free from same at the time of delivery.

____

____

[Signatures]

The seller's top five goals for the contract are:

- Get paid before shipping the goods
- Get paid $1.50 per frog
- Have a fair process for return of damaged goods
- Make acceptance of the goods automatic 14 days after receipt
- Disclaim all warranties

Here is the checklist for a seller of goods as applied to the contract above:

Checklist for Agreements Where Your Company Is the Seller

- ❑ Definitions for capitalized terms *(Not applicable)*
- ❑ Description of goods ordered—quantity, size, stock number, etc. *(Included)*
- ❑ Acceptance of order *(Included, but does not meet seller's goals)*
    - Acceptance governed by seller's purchase terms *(Not applicable)*
    - Orders must be in writing *(Not applicable)*
- ❑ Rejection of goods *(Not included)*
    - Time limit for rejection of products *(Not included)*
    - Final acceptance presumed after some period *(Not included)*
    - Payment is final acceptance *(Not included)*
    - Rejection must be in writing detailing reasons *(Not included)*
    - Remedy for rejection is at exclusive election of seller *(Not included)*
    - Remedy is repair, replace, refund only *(Not included)*
- ❑ Changes to order—process *(Not applicable)*
    - Order not cancelable *(Not included)*
    - Provision for additional charges if seller accepts changes *(Not applicable)*
    - Provision of additional time for delivery if seller accepts changes *(Not applicable)*

- ❑ Seller expressly objects to any conflicting terms between its purchase order and Buyer's *(Not applicable)*
- ❑ Technical assistance—disclaim any warranty arising from *(Not applicable)*
- ❑ How are prices for goods determined *(Included)*
- ❑ No "most favored nation" or "we promise you our lowest price" clause *(Included)*
  - If necessary, limit to orders on substantially similar terms for same volumes and substantially identical product *(Not applicable)*
  - Not applicable for promotional pricing *(Not applicable)*
  - Applies only for same period as for third party *(Not applicable)*
- ❑ Shipping *(Not included)*
  - Quantities may be up to 10 percent less and still be considered in compliance with order *(Not included)*
  - If delivery by seller rejected or delayed by buyer, buyer pays storage and insurance costs *(Not included)*
  - When does title pass *(Included)*
  - Who designates carrier *(Not included)*
  - Packaging and labeling requirements *(Not included)*
- ❑ Risk of loss passes between parties at what point *(Included)*
- ❑ Delivery date *(Not included)*
  - Seller's performance dates are estimates only *(Not included)*
  - Buyer may not reschedule delivery date without seller's written permission *(Not included)*
  - Returns *(Not included)*
  - Return material authorization number required *(Not included)*
  - Return shipping paid by buyer *(Not included)*
  - Other details of process *(Not included)*
- ❑ Warranty *(Not included)*
  - Free from defects in workmanship or materials *(Not included but implied under law)*
  - Meets certain specifications *(Not included)*
  - Remedy limited to repair, replacement, or refund at seller's option *(Not included)*

- If remedy limited, is word "exclusive" clearly stated *(Not included)*
- If disclaimer or exclusive remedy, is language conspicuous *(Not included)*
- Warranty period—period of time, period of use, period of performance *(Not included)*
- Disclaimer of implied warranty of merchantability, fitness for purpose, title *(Not included)*
- Disclaim liability for packaging and labeling, defects in material or workmanship *(Not included)*
- Warranty void if improper use or operation, modification, inadequate maintenance or calibration *(Not applicable)*

❑ Will buyer provide tooling or otherwise have its own property at seller *(Not applicable)*

- Disclaim all responsibility for damage, destruction, or return of tooling *(Not applicable)*
- Buyer provides tooling at own risk *(Not applicable)*

❑ Publicity *(Not included)*

- Allow with other party's written consent not to be unreasonably withheld *(Not included)*
- Allow for your company at its discretion *(Not included)*
- Prohibit entirely *(Not included)*
- Allow use of customer's name in advertisements *(Not included)*

❑ Taxes—included in price or additional to price *(Not included)*

❑ Patent infringement warranty *(Not included)*

- If required by buyer, limit to indemnification for U.S. patents *(Not included)*
- Require notice of claim, right to defend and settle *(Not included)*
- Seller has right to procure for buyer right to use product *(Not included)*
- Seller has right to modify product to become non-infringing *(Not included)*
- Seller has right to refund price *(Not included)*
- No buyer's right if product made to buyer's specifications, product includes buyer's parts or parts designated by buyer, products modified after purchase, or seller's products combined with another seller's *(Not included)*

- ❑ Payment terms *(Included but does not meet seller's goals)*
  - When is payment due and how is this calculated *(Included)*
  - Is an invoice sent or amount due automatically *(Not included)*
  - If invoice what are the invoice intervals *(Not included)*
  - In what currency *(Not included)*
  - How is payment to be made—cash, check, electronic funds transfer, or other *(Not included)*
  - Late fees assessed and if so how *(Not included)*
  - No right of set-off or deduction *(Not applicable)*
- ❑ Confidential information *(Not applicable)*
  - How defined *(Not applicable)*
  - What are acceptable uses and disclosures *(Not applicable)*
  - Term of confidentiality obligations *(Not applicable)*
  - Duties towards confidential information *(Not applicable)*
  - Exceptions to duties of confidentiality *(Not applicable)*
- ❑ Alternative dispute resolution *(Not included)*
  - Negotiation *(Not included)*
  - Mediation *(Not included)*
  - Arbitration *(Not included)*
  - If none of these wanted, include provision specifically rejecting *(Not included)*
  - Is alternative exclusive or required before litigation *(Not included)*
  - Who pays for alternative *(Not included)*
  - Who specifically is required to participate in alternative *(Not included)*
  - Qualifications of neutral party officiating over the alternative *(Not included)*
  - What is the time frame for alternative *(Not included)*
  - Where does alternative dispute forum occur *(Not included)*
  - What rules govern alternative dispute forum *(Not included)*
  - If neutral party renders a decision is it binding *(Not included)*
- ❑ Assignment/subcontracting permitted *(Not included)*
  - Preclude partial or complete assignment but allow subcontracting *(Not included)*

- Preclude subcontracting but allow partial or complete assignment *(Not included)*
- Allowed with consent not to be withheld unreasonably *(Not included)*
- Allowed with consent at other party's sole discretion *(Not included)*
- Allowed if a party is sold *(Not included)*
- Allowed if a party is transferred to an affiliate or subsidiary *(Not included)*
- If subcontractors permitted, will sub be required to maintain confidentiality of confidential information *(Not included)*
- Attorney's fees *(Not included)*
- Legal costs *(Not included)*
- Expert witness fees *(Not included)*
- Investigation costs *(Not included)*

❑ Choice of law to interpret agreement *(Not included)*

❑ Choice of venue for litigation *(Not included)*

Compliance with laws *(Not included)*

- If buyer requires, specify material compliance with laws applicable to this contract *(Not included)*

❑ Conflicting language between agreements is resolved in what manner *(Not applicable)*

❑ Rights provided in contract are cumulative or exclusive *(Not included)*

Force majeure—consider inclusion of fire, accident, acts of public enemy, terrorism, severe weather, acts of God, labor disruption, flood, failure of suppliers to deliver, difficulty obtaining supplies, epidemics, nuclear strike, government intervention, government or freight embargo, quarantine, difficulty obtaining transportation *(Not included)*

- Notice required if event occurs *(Not included)*
- Right to terminate if event lasts specified amount of time *(Not included)*

❑ Indemnity *(Not included)*

- Which party is providing the indemnification *(Not included)*
- To the other company, officers, employees, consultants, directors, agents, parent company, subsidiary *(Not included)*

- Claims, liabilities, losses, damages, costs, charges, attorneys fees, legal costs, liens, death, personal injury, accidents, property damage *(Not included)*
- Arising out of actual or alleged defects in material and workmanship, negligence, gross negligence, breach of the contract, claims of liens, or encumbrances *(Not included)*

❑ Integration (or Entire Agreement) provision *(Not included)*
- All documents making up the agreement referenced *(Not included)*

❑ Limitation on liability *(Not included)*
- Consequential damages *(Not included)*
- Limitation on remedies, and if so is word "exclusive" included *(Not included)*
- Limitation on amount of damages *(Not included)*
- Limitation on liability provision conspicuous *(Not included)*

❑ Notice provision *(Not included)*
- Are both parties' addresses included *(Not included)*
- Acceptable delivery methods *(Not included)*
- Time that the other party is deemed to have received the notice specified *(Not included)*

❑ No joint venture, agency, partnership, trust, or association *(Not included)*

❑ Severability—illegal or otherwise unenforceable provisions can be severed *(Not included)*

❑ Successors and assigns—agreement binding on *(Not included)*

❑ Survival—certain terms of the agreement may survive termination *(Not included)*

❑ Termination provision *(Not applicable)*
- How much notice is required before contract terminates *(Not applicable)*
- For cause *(Not applicable)*
- Is right to cure default provided *(Not applicable)*
- Any breach or material breach *(Not applicable)*
- For convenience *(Not applicable)*
- If elected by either party, does any party have a right to damages *(Not applicable)*

- Insolvency *(Not applicable)*
- Bankruptcy *(Not applicable)*
- Assignment for benefit of creditors *(Not applicable)*
- Receiver appointed *(Not applicable)*
- Initiates reorganization *(Not applicable)*
- Closes business *(Not applicable)*
- Stops operating *(Not applicable)*

❑ Waiver—waiver of breach not agreement to waive all breaches *(Not included)*

❑ Written modification—all modifications in writing and signed *(Not included)*

❑ If terms on back of a form, does the front incorporate the terms *(Not applicable)*

Checklist for Terms Not Included in the Agreement

Here are the terms on the checklist not included in the agreement:

- Acceptance of order
- Rejection of goods
- Order not cancelable
- Shipping
- Delivery date
- Returns
- Warranty
- Publicity
- Taxes
- Patent infringement warranty disclaimer
- Payment terms
- Alternative dispute resolution
- Assignment/subcontracting permitted
- Recovery of prevailing party's expenses in litigation
- Choice of law to interpret agreement

- Choice of venue for litigation
- Compliance with laws
- Rights provided in contract are cumulative or exclusive
- Force majeure
- Indemnity
- Integration
- Limit on Liability
- Notice provision
- No joint venture, agency, partnership, trust, or association
- Severability
- Successors and assigns
- Survival
- Waiver
- Written modification

These are the terms that the seller decides are to be negotiated with the buyer:

- Acceptance of order (order accepted automatically 14 days after receipt by buyer)
- Rejection of goods (goods may not be rejected but damaged goods may be returned)
- Order not cancelable
- Returns (damaged goods returned for replacement only)
- Warranty (disclaim all warranties)
- Payment terms (Payment of $1.50 per frog due prior to shipping)
- Force Majeure
- Integration
- Limit on Liability
- Survival
- Written modification

Once you have applied the checklist, identified terms that are missing or need to be revised, and narrowed this list to the terms most important to your deal, it is simple to apply the tools in the next chapter to easily modify the contract you reviewed. The next chapter discusses alternative methods of modifying a contract and the positives and negatives of doing that yourself or letting the other party do it.

PART TWO

Trading a Blue Alligator for a Red One

Strategies for Changing Contracts

CHAPTER 4

Smart Ways to Modify a Contract Already in Effect

Martin's Auto Repair has a contract with Clean as a Whistle Janitorial Service to clean the auto repair offices once a week. The contract had a one-year term and is about to expire. Clean as a Whistle has offered to clean the auto repair offices for another year if the fees it receives are increased by $25 a month. The owner of Martin's Auto Repair accepts this offer. Does an entirely new contract have to be drafted to reflect the increased fees and the additional year added to the contract?

Jennifer is an accountant and does the books for Classic Touch Hair Salon. The contract between Jennifer and Classic Touch states that Jennifer will reconcile the bank accounts for the beauty salon, prepare payroll, make employment tax payments, and maintain accounting records. Jennifer and Classic Touch agree that Jennifer will also prepare the annual federal and state tax returns for Classic Touch. Does a new contract need to be prepared to reflect these new duties?

Pasquale's Restaurant has a contract with Italian Wine Shop to deliver 10 cases of 6 wines every month. One of the wines doesn't sell well and the restaurant wants to delete this wine from the order. Will a new contract need to be drafted to reflect that 10 cases of 5 wines will be delivered every month?

In This Chapter

- Adding, deleting, changing, but keeping most of the original contract
- When and how to do an amendment
- Restating a contract and when it's a wise move

Adding, Deleting, Changing, but Keeping Most of the Original Contract

The answers to the three questions above are "no." There is no need in the situations described to write a new contract. In each case the original contract can be amended to reflect the revised business deal.

Amendments to contracts can add terms to the original contract as well as delete terms or change the ones that are there. They are commonly used to extend the term of a contract. The document that changes a contract is called an amendment, a supplement, or a modification. These are all terms for contracts that modify a contract already in effect. When the entire contract is retyped with the new terms included in place of the old ones, or the new terms added to the old ones, the document is called a restatement. Both ways of modifying a contract have in common that the majority of the original contract remains intact. If changes are made to more than a quarter of the contract, it's too confusing to try to accomplish this through an amendment or restatement. It's best to draft a new contract in that case.

If your company does elect to draft a new contract, there must be a paragraph in the new contract stating that the old contract is void as of the effective date of the new contract. Otherwise you will have two contracts covering the same transaction and for the same or similar contract lengths. An example of a clause that would accomplish this is:

As of the effective date of this agreement the Services Agreement dated March 1, 2007 between Piff Partnership and James Elliott is void and has no further force or effect.

When and How to Do an Amendment

Amendments are best used when there are no more than five or six terms that are being added, deleted, or changed. More than that gets confusing and then it's best to restate the contract as described in the next section.

An amendment to the agreement can add to the existing contract or delete outdated or offensive terms and replace them with ones acceptable to both parties. An amendment should simply state what provisions are being deleted, added to, or changed, and how.

The most important issues to get right in an amendment are:

- use of correct business names
- proper signature block
- the effective date of the amendment
- correctly referencing the exact name and effective date of the contract being amended
- specifying what is being deleted, added, or changed in the existing agreement

The reasons it is critical to use correct business names and a proper signature block in a contract are discussed in Chapter 1. Amendments are also contracts and therefore must include these important elements.

Specifying an effective date for an amendment is a necessary part of the amendment. When no effective date is included, it leaves a huge controversy brewing as to what the intent of the parties was. The amendment could be determined to be effective on the date signed (but that may not have been included either), when the existing contract ends (but what if that is years from now?), when an action mentioned in the amendment would logically need to be performed (but when that might be is subject to interpretation), or any other time anyone can argue for. The point of having a contract is to reduce the likelihood of disputes, and when the parties intend the amendment to modify the existing contract will be a subject of dispute unless it is specifically indicated in the amendment.

The title of the amendment should reference the exact name of the contract being amended as well as the date of the contract being amended. That way there will be no controversy over what contract was intended to be modified. Over time your company may end up with several contracts titled "Service Agreement" or "Purchase Order" with the same vendor. It is unlikely these would all reference the same effective date. Referencing the name of the contract along with its effective date pinpoints the exact contract the parties intend to amend.

Once it's clear what contract is being amended, the amendment must clearly state how it is being amended by referencing the term in the original contract that is being added to, deleted, or modified, along with how the term is being amended. You must specifically state that one of the following is occurring:

- something is being added
- something is being deleted
- something is being modified

Then you must define what the "something" is (what part of the contract it being added to, deleted, or modified). It's important to clearly state what is being done and to what term or section of the contract. There should be no question about what the amendment accomplishes.

Here is an example of an amendment to one of the contracts discussed in Chapter 1.

Amendment One

This Amendment deletes, replaces, and amends the following paragraphs as described below in the Uffelhoop Trade Show Agreement dated March 1, 2005 by and between Miff Company of Boston and Moff Inc.

1. Paragraph 2 "Assignment" is deleted and replaced with:
   Assignment. Either Party may assign this agreement to a successor in interest to that party's business. The party making such assignment shall give written notice to the other party within 10 days of the assignment.

[This means that what used to be in paragraph 2 is replaced with what is written here.]

2. Paragraph 4 "Forum and Legal Fees" is amended to add the following:
   Forum and Legal Fees. The parties agree that any legal dispute arising from this agreement shall be filed and litigated in the state courts of New Jersey.

[This means that whatever is in paragraph 4 of the original agreement is still effective with the addition of what is written here.]

Miff Company of Boston	Moff Inc.
____________________	____________________
Peter Pink President	Georgia Grey Officer
Date: ____________	Date: ____________

It's wise to number amendments, as this amendment shows, so that if there is more than one amendment to an original contract, each amendment can be referred to specifically.

Agreements to sell goods and purchase orders, or terms of sale, typically contain no expiration date or termination provisions. For that reason companies often don't consider revisions as amendments to an existing agreement, even though they are. The party issuing them simply issues a new version. This very often creates problems later, because no one can figure out which purchase order terms or agreement is in effect to cover a certain transaction.

A paragraph similar to the following should be included in the new purchase order terms to prevent later confusion:

These Purchase Order Terms and Conditions, effective January 1, 2009, supersede the purchase order terms and conditions dated January 1, 2000.

Another alternative is to simply title the new document:

Revised Purchase Order Terms and Conditions
Effective January 1, 2009

Both alternatives will cause the new terms to supersede the prior terms and will govern all future transactions. Your company should specify how the new terms govern any existing transactions that have not been completed when the new purchase order terms are effective. For example, do the old terms that were in effect when the order was placed still apply, or do the new terms that are in effect when the order is delivered apply to the transaction?

Restating a Contract and When It's a Wise Move

A restated contract is simply a retyped version of the original contract with revisions to some of the terms typed in place of the old versions of those terms. To understand an amendment you must reference the original contract plus the amendment. To understand a restatement you simply read the restatement.

Restating a contract is not as simple as an amendment, and if your company is not the one doing the retyping, your company must be very careful to make sure no changes are made to the original contract other than the ones agreed to. However, when more than 25 percent of the contract is being changed, doing a restatement makes it much easier to understand what the agreement governing the business deal is.

A restatement should be titled "Amended and restated ________" indicating the name of the original contract and the date of the original contract. Once the restatement is executed, it takes the place, in its entirety, of the original contract. In contrast, an amendment only takes the place of the terms referenced in the amendment.

One final warning—be careful to have both parties execute the amendment or restatement. The integration provision often titled "Entire Agreement" in many contracts requires any modification of the original agreement to be in writing and signed by both parties. Drafting an amendment or restatement and having only one party sign will not amend the original contract.

A checklist for contract amendments and restatements is included in the Appendix.

This chapter discusses changes to an executed contract. The next chapter discusses how to negotiate for changes to a contract drafted by the other party and presented to your company for review. Because the contract has not been signed, the original contract can be changed by simply redrafting it. Once it's signed, only an amendment or restatement such as described in this chapter can change it.

CHAPTER 5

Winning at Getting Changes to the Contract

Lin is a scientist who owns many patents on technology for reducing the loss of gases from soda bottles. Her company sells machines that assess seepage from plastic bottles to companies that make these bottles. Lin agrees to sell six machines to a bottle manufacturer who sends her a contract for this sale. She applies the quick review system and identifies several items that must be changed in the contract. Lin is uncertain whether a new contract has to be written, if she should just ask that certain additions and changes be made to the manufacturer's contract, or if she should present an entirely new contract to the manufacturer that she drafts herself.

In This Chapter

- Deflecting alligators—strategies for making their contract good for you
- Getting past the "we can't change the form" argument

Deflecting Alligators: Strategies for Making Their Contract Good for You

When you are reviewing a contract drafted by the other party in a business deal you should expect five things:

- The legal name of your company will be incorrect
- The signature block will be drafted to bind a person, not a company
- The bulletproof terms will be written to apply only to your company
- The terms on payment, specifications, and termination will benefit the other company, not yours
- Your company's goals for the business deal will not be addressed

After identifying your company's goals for the business deal, your next step in reviewing a contract is to apply the correct checklist, keeping in mind the five likely areas where the contract is weighted against your company. It's critical to include your company's legal name and a signature block naming the company as a party to the contract, not an individual. Having the bulletproof terms be rewritten to apply to both companies should be an easy matter to achieve, because it will be hard to argue that what benefits the other company should not also benefit yours.

Your company should identify the payment, specification, and termination provisions that will benefit it. Then identify a middle ground between what the other company's provision states and what your company needs. The final step is to identify where in the contract you will insert language addressing your company's goals for the business deal. Their contract will bind them to as little as possible, so your company must take the initiative to insert into the contract anything it wants to hold the other company to. Resources, cooperation, deliverables, or other requirements you want to legally require the other company to provide must be in the contract.

Once your company knows how it wants the contract changed, you need to determine how to change it. Sending an entirely new contract, drafted by your company, in response to a contract forwarded by the other company, will rarely result in your contract being the one that is executed. Whoever drafts and sends the first contract has claimed the contract-drafting territory. Responding to their contract with your contract necessitates explaining why their contract needed to be scuttled in its entirety, and the answer has to involve some version of "yours wasn't good enough." That is never a message that helps a business negotiation. If the other side sends their contract for review first, their contract should be your starting point.

I've found that the best way to quickly reach agreement on the final contract is to make your company's proposed changes directly on an electronic version of the contract and send it back to the other party. When doing this you should use the "track changes" feature found in word processing software to clearly indicate what has been deleted or added to the original contract and what new language inserted.

If you do not track changes, the other party is highly unlikely to bother to compare your revised contract against its proposed contract to see what changes were made. The likely result is that the other party will simply refuse to change the proposed contract in any way.

If your company receives the proposed contract in paper form, it should ask for an electronic version. If the other party refuses, or sends an electronic version in a form that cannot be modified, it's worth the effort to have the contract entered into your word processing system. Then make the proposed changes using the "track changes" feature and send the contract back to the other party for review.

It's my experience that sending proposed revisions accompanied by a detailed explanation of why each change is requested is unnecessary and often causes more problems. It gives the other side more work to do and thus an incentive to place a stake in the ground and refuse to make any changes to their proposed contract. Sometimes the explanation will reveal a deal consideration the other party hadn't considered, resulting in further negotiations that delay the contract. It's best just to revise the contract and send it back.

The other party has a significant incentive at that point to accept the changes and execute the contract just to get the deal done. To have sent your company a contract in the first place is an indication of their desire to complete the deal. Odds are that the other party will print and execute the contract with your changes.

Getting Past the "We Can't Change the Form" Argument

When your company requests changes to a contract, you may be told by the business people on the other side of the deal that the contract they sent your company is a form that their legal department has decreed can't be changed. That is often true, but it is not an impediment to getting the changes your company wants. Although the business people on the other side of the deal may not know how to modify the contract without changing the form, you do.

Form contracts always have a page where the specifics of the business deal are detailed. For example, a cellular telephone lease will be a form with a page listing the telephones and rate plans associated with the form lease. A form sales agreement will have a page listing what exactly is being sold along with the specific concerning price and delivery.

When your company is told the form cannot be changed, either obtain an electronic version of the section listing the details of the business deal, or have it entered into your company's word processing system. Then add the changes to the contract your company desires as if your company was drafting an amendment (described in the prior chapter). The business people for the other company have the authority to modify this page and will usually agree to your changes to get the deal done. Technically they have not changed the form contract in violation of their company's policy, although effectively they have. Either way your company has achieved its objective.

Here is an example of a specifications page with changes to a form contract underlined:

Appendix A

Sales, Price, and Delivery Terms

Equipment: Bivalve rotary sourcers stock 756233, new in crate

Quantity Sold: 2

Price: $12,345 each

Delivery: FBO Axea Warehouse, Stockton, California

Payment: Thirty days from delivery date

The following contract terms are incorporated into the agreement to which this Appendix is attached.

Hazardous Materials: Seller acknowledges that Buyer intends to utilize the equipment in contact with hazardous materials. Seller agrees to honor its warranty for its full term without regard to damage caused by contact with these hazardous materials.

Additional Purchases: Buyer has the right to purchase up to 10 additional pieces of equipment for the price listed herein within one year from the date of delivery of the two sourcers listed above.

Late Delivery: If the two sourcers are not delivered by November 15, 2012 this contract will be void and neither party will have any obligations to the other as a result.

When changes are requested to a contract your company drafted, your concern is not to negate the benefits you have drafted for yourself if you make changes. The next chapter covers issues and strategies when changes are requested to a contract your company drafts.

CHAPTER 6

Solutions for Changes Requested to Your Contract

Chet owns a company that rents heavy equipment to small businesses on a short-term basis. His company recently purchased several front-loaders that need to have the company logo painted on them before they are rented out. Chet interviews graphic artists and sends his company's contract for services to the artist he chooses. The artist requests that the payment terms and quality standards change, that the warranty provision be deleted, and that the limit on liability provision be made mutual. Chet has no idea if the changes will place his company at significant risk or if they are minor revisions that don't negate the benefit of the business deal. After reading this chapter Chet will know what effect the changes have and how to make them to benefit his company.

In This Chapter

- Recognizing when change requests are alligators in disguise
- Avoid getting eaten when modifying payment, specification, and termination provisions

Recognizing When Change Requests Are Alligators in Disguise

When your company sends its contract to the other party in a business deal it will usually just get signed and returned to you. If changes are requested the most common ones are requesting that bulletproof terms apply to both parties and that criteria for the three hazardous deal points from Chapter 1 (payment, specifications, and termination) be modified.

The 23 bulletproof terms in Chapter 2 are written so that they apply to both parties. In your company contracts they should be written to apply only to the other company. The reason is that agreeing to do anything in a contract creates a risk to your company, and your company should only take on necessary risks. If your company is not required to undertake a risk, it shouldn't, and if your company is the one drafting a contract it shouldn't volunteer to place itself at risk. The reason agreeing to do anything in a contract creates a risk is that if your company does not do the thing it has agreed to do, it has breached the contract and can be sued, resulting in expenditures for legal fees and perhaps money damages.

For these reasons your contracts will have provisions that require the other party to do things and that require little or nothing of your company. It's up to the other company to make sure the contract requires your company to do what it agreed to do in the business negotiation. Of course if you are reviewing a contract drafted by someone else, you can be sure they have drafted it with the same determination to place all the burdens on your company and none on themselves, so be sure you have read Chapter 5.

If the other company requests that any of the bulletproof terms be made mutual, your company will have to assess the business risk those changes present. Sometimes this risk will be minimal and other times it will be significant. Below is a list of the bulletproof terms, with considerations for changing each from applying to the other company only to applying to your company also.

1. **Assignment/subcontracting**—This prevents or limits the other party in the agreement from assigning the contract to another company and/or from subcontracting the work to another person or business. If your company might sell its business, or the part of the business this contract pertains to, a mutual provision of this type would prevent transfer of the contract to the new owner. Hiring a contractor to perform all or part of the work would be a contract breach under this provision. If your company agrees to make this provision mutual but knows that it will hire a subcontractor to perform part of the work, the provision can be written to preclude subcontracting but with the specific exception, written into the provision, that a specific named person or company will be retained to perform all or part of the contract duties.
2. **Attorney's fees**—This requires the other company to pay your company's fees and expenses if a lawsuit is decided in favor of your company. Under a mutual provision, your company would have to have a strong case, if it filed a lawsuit, to keep it from losing the lawsuit and paying the costs for both itself and the other company.
3. **Choice of law or governing law**—This identifies the state law that will be used by a judge to interpret the contract. This term can't be made mutual, but instead must name either your state's law, the other company's, or a state that has a significant connection with the contract. Agreeing to interpret the contract under the other company's state law may affect the enforceability of certain provisions, such as a covenant not to compete and a nonsolicitation provision, or may imply rights that your state's laws don't provide. You can often research laws affecting small business in a specific state by reviewing the web sites of the individual state department of commerce, chamber of commerce, and small business association. Your company may determine after this research that agreeing to use the other company's state law to interpret the contract is not a big risk.

4. **Choice of venue**—This names the state where lawsuits can be filed and decided. This cannot be mutual but must name a state with a connection to the companies or the contract. It's best if the same state is named for both a choice of law and a choice of venue provision. The risk when agreeing to change the choice of venue to the other company's state is that your company will be inconvenienced with travel costs and out-of-state lawyers in the event of a lawsuit. It's also possible that the local court will favor the local company, although courts are supposed to act neutrally. The local advantage could work against the local company if they are not perceived in a welcome light.
5. **Compliance with laws**—Making this term mutual should not be a burden on your company, because it should be complying with the law anyway. It can, however, be a contractual risk if the provision is not modified to specify that "all material laws" must be complied with rather than all laws. If the provision does not include the "material" requirement, renewing the registration for one of your company's vehicles late would constitute a breach of contract.
6. **Conflicts**—This is not a provision that would be mutual because it simply specifies which written document takes precedence over the others.
7. **Cumulative rights**—This is also not a provision that can be mutual. It allows all rights in a contract to be exercised, not just the one exercised first.
8. **Force majeure**—This provision can be made mutual in that both parties can be excused from performance under the contract in the event of a catastrophe, not just your company. When made mutual it's important to consider what effect the delay or termination of the other party's performance would have on your company. If a catastrophe did occur and the other company stopped performing, the contract should define what rights your company has to the work products, the other company's or yours, may have had in process before the catastrophe. Also look at what happens to payments for work not completed or in regards to work completed but not yet paid for, and cooperation the other company must provide to the company taking over the work.

9. **Indemnity**—Making this provision mutual means taking on significant risks. Your company is agreeing to pay whatever amount is required if the other company experiences a loss or claim resulting from something your company does as part of the contract. Your company can temper the effects of making this provision mutual by limiting indemnification to a certain dollar amount ("costs and expenses paid under the indemnification provision limited to $1,000,000") or requiring that the indemnification occur only where damages exceed a certain amount ("costs and expenses paid under the indemnification provision payable only where individual claims exceed $1,000,000"). The effect of these changes is that in the first case the maximum liability your company would have for any indemnification obligations is $1,000,000, and in the second case, the other company would be responsible to pay all claims under $1,000,000. The later alternative might reduce risk where your company believed any indemnification obligations would be claims under $1,000,000.
10. **Insurance**—Where this provision requires the other company to maintain certain insurance, perhaps provide proof of insurance and name your company as an additional insured on the insurance policy, making these requirements mutual may be an administrative hassle and may require your company to add to or increase its insurance coverage. Companies frequently forget to provide copies of insurance certificates when they have agreed to do so in a contract. If your company agrees to provide these certificates and doesn't, it has breached the contract. Sometimes companies ask that this provision be mutual for no real reason. It's often easy to negotiate out of this request by asking the other company to identify the specific contractual risks that making this provision mutual will mitigate.
11. **Integration**—This cannot be made mutual because it applies to the contract itself.
12. **Limit of liability**—Limiting liability to direct damages arising from harm caused by an action is a smart business move. The other company may know that and ask that the limit of liability provision be made mutual. Agreeing to this reduces the damages you could obtain from the other

company, but it's difficult to argue against making this mutual when the other party has already agreed to limit the damages it can obtain from your company.

13. **Notices**—This term should be mutual in that it should identify for both parties the official address where notices must be sent under the contract, how the notices must be delivered, and when it will be deemed that those notices were officially received.
14. **Relationship of the parties**—This term should state for both parties what their relationship to each other is.
15. **Severability**—This provision relates to the contract and applies to both parties.
16. **Successors and assigns**—If this provision is rewritten to make the contract binding on your company's successors and assigns, it could be perceived as a good thing to a successor or a bad thing. At the point your company agrees to make the provision mutual it will be impossible to know which. A successor or assignee of the contract may want to get rid of the contract obligations and be glad the contract is not binding or may want the benefits of the contract and be sorry it's not binding. On that basis, making this provision mutual may not be a big risk for your company.
17. **Survival**—This provision lists contract sections that survive after the contract expires or is terminated, so the possibility of making it mutual does not exist.
18. **Termination for cause**—Your contract states that your company can terminate the contract for cause. If the other party wants to also terminate the contract for something your company does wrong, make sure the "cause" or wrongdoing is precisely defined, requires written notice of the wrongdoing, and provides an opportunity to cure the default.
19. **Termination for convenience**—This is the more problematic of the termination provisions if it's made mutual. This allows a company to send written notice that the contract is terminated after a certain time period has expired. The termination could occur after little work is performed or a lot. It could be right before a payment is due or a significant deliverable is expected. For that reason, if your company agrees to make this

mutual, you must consider what effect a termination would have at each stage of the contract's timeline and then provide for the consequences in the contract. State what has to be done if the contract is terminated by the other party so that the termination has the least effect on your company. It's worth putting time and effort into thinking this through and writing it down in the contract.

20. **Termination on insolvency**—This allows your company to terminate the contract if the other party becomes insolvent, closes down, or declares bankruptcy. When made mutual it provides the same rights to the other party. This is another provision where it's hard to argue that the other party should not have this right when your company has it.
21. **Waiver**—This applies to the contract so is not subject to being mutual.
22. **Warranty disclaimers**—Warranties are implied or expressly given by the seller or manufacturer of goods. Therefore disclaiming a warranty would only be done by the seller or manufacturer. There would be no point to a buyer asking that this provision be made mutual. The buyer is more likely to request that the disclaimer be deleted, thus allowing all implied and express warranties to apply to the sale. In deleting this provision, if your company is prepared to guaranty, which is essentially what a warranty is, some aspect of its product or service, it's best to very specifically state what is being guaranteed. Then disclaim all other warranties not specifically provided. That's because warranties are implied by law and there may be warranties your company is not aware of that it is inadvertently providing by not disclaiming them.
23. **Written Modification**—This applies to the contract itself and cannot be made mutual.

Avoid Getting Eaten When Modifying Payment, Specification, and Termination Provisions

Your contracts should make the payment, specification, and termination provisions benefit your company. Where your company is the buyer of services, that usually means that payment is made after services are completed and are known to meet your requirements, that specifications are subject to your determination that they have been met, and that the contract can be terminated at your discretion for no reason or any reason. Where your company is the seller of services, the payment provision might specify that payments are due before services are rendered, that specifications are met when the services are delivered by a certain date, and that the contract can be terminated only for insolvency.

In the case of contracts to buy goods, your contracts will specify that payment is due on acceptance of the goods, that specifications must be met exactly, and that the contract can be terminated only for insolvency (because your company wants to make sure it receives the ordered products). Where your company is selling goods, the payment provision in its contracts will require payment to be made before the goods are shipped, the goods will be required to materially conform to specifications, and the contract will allow termination for insolvency or for cause.

When the other party asks for changes, your company's goal should be to stay as close to your original intentions in the contract as possible. For example, where your company is the buyer of services with a contract provision providing for payment to be made after the services are completed, if the service provider requests an earlier payment the goal is to reach a compromise in which your company is still paying for services as they are completed. Instead of payment when all the services are completed, make payment provisional on completion of steps in the services. For a janitorial contract, this could mean payment is made weekly after the weekly cleaning is done instead of monthly payments. For a consulting contract, payment could be made after interim reports are made instead of when the final project is complete.

If you are the seller of goods or provider of services, seek to get paid in advance or within days of furnishing whatever is bought when making changes to payment provisions. If you cannot reach agreement on getting paid in advance, consider including a fee if payment is not made when required, as well as interest on all unpaid amounts. Because you will have expended your time and money providing the service or product that the buyer has yet to pay for, be sure to include a provision allowing immediate termination of the contract if payment is not made. Otherwise your company will be contractually obligated to continue providing the service or delivering the goods even though it hasn't been paid.

If your company is the buyer of services or products and changes are requested to the payment provision of your contract, your company will want to pay when the services or products are delivered and determined to be acceptable. Because the definition of acceptable is often subjective, the seller of the services or products will often seek to make payment before or at delivery of the products or services. If your company agrees to delete the requirement that whatever it has bought must be acceptable before payment is made, be sure to include a provision addressing what remedies your company has in the event it pays and later determines the goods or services are not right. Remedies could include a refund, credit against future payments, replacement, or some other alternative that makes your company whole.

For changes to specifications, the issue is often the standard the specification must meet, as opposed to a disagreement concerning how the final deliverables or products should look. If the product or service does not meet the buyer's requirements during the shopping stage the buyer goes elsewhere. The contractual issue is usually which party gets to determine if the specifications were met and whether the goods or services must exactly conform to specifications or some lesser standard.

If your company is the one selling services or products it will want to determine if the specifications are met. The other company may ask for this right. A common compromise is to agree to a "reasonable person" standard, which is whether a reasonable person in the exercise of their judgment would determine that the specifications were met.

Whether your company is the seller or buyer of goods or services, it will want the specifications to be met exactly. The other party will balk at this, because failure to meet the specifications exactly will result in a breach of contract even though the nonconformity may be relatively minor. A compromise might be to require material conformity to specifications. That means that the product or service must substantially meet the requirements. If the product or service materially conforms, a breach of contract will not occur, but there must be some corresponding reduction in costs or other remedy for the failure to exactly meet specifications.

Regarding termination provisions, both parties will likely seek a provision allowing termination if the other company becomes insolvent or bankrupt. Both companies will also want to include a contract provision allowing termination for cause, although what defines "cause" may be contested. It is usually easy to agree that nonpayment, failure to provide resources defined in the contract, and failure to meet delivery dates for services or goods is cause for termination.

Termination for convenience is a wonderful right to have and a difficult one to give to the other party. If your company must provide this right to the other party, it's important to mitigate the effects of an early termination of the contract by specifying how payments, return of materials, and in-process work will be handled.

If your company is selling services, the tools it needs to maximize its contracts to reduce risk and make money are in the next chapter, including line-by-line feedback on what common provisions in service contracts mean and how to modify them to benefit your company.

PART THREE

Don't Get Eaten

Essential Customer Contracts

CHAPTER 7

Contracts to Sell Services

Deidre agreed to paint the logo and contact information for Chet's truck rental business on the new front-loaders Chet's company purchased in Chapter 6. Because the cost of this service was relatively minor—$300 per front-loader —Deidre didn't bother with a contract. Deidre completed the logos on five trucks and submitted the invoice to Chet's company. The company's equipment manager called Deidre and told her the logos were painted with the wrong color and they wouldn't be paying the invoice. Deidre told him Chet had asked for the specific color she used. The manager argued that the shade she used was not the color the company wanted. Chet refused to take Deidre's calls and she never got paid.

Looking at the same situation from Chet's perspective, Chet hired Deidre's graphic arts company to paint logos on the front-loaders he bought in Chapter 6. Because the dollar value of the painting project wasn't much, $1500 total, Chet didn't bother with a contract. Deidre painted the logos and sent Chet's company an invoice. Justin, Chet's equipment manager, advised Chet that the logos were navy blue, making them look deceptively like the logos of a rival rental company. Chet was furious because he had made a point of telling Deidre that he wanted royal blue. Chet refused to take Deidre's calls and never paid the invoice because he had to have her work painted over and redone.

Chet's company and Deidre's company both lost in this deal, all because of a misunderstanding regarding a shade of blue. If Deidre's company had a simple contract detailing what she had agreed to do for Chet's company, the outcome could have been two happy companies instead of none.

In This Chapter

- How to use a service agreement to avoid alligators
- Key issues to address in contracts to sell services
- Turning your proposal into a contract
- Review of an independent contractor agreement

How to Use a Service Agreement to Avoid Alligators

Service agreements are either specialized agreements drafted for the specific type of service being provided or independent contractor agreements. Independent contractor agreements are used for many types of services because, they are essentially form contracts with a unique statement of services to be provided or work to be performed incorporated into them. Independent contractor agreements can be used to document a transaction involving everything from consulting to wedding planning to construction. These agreements are often used when something is analyzed and a report is written, when your company builds or creates something, or when a specific project is to be completed.

Why not just write that computer program, cater that event, or build that shed without an agreement? There are several important reasons. By writing down what both parties have agreed to do, both you, on behalf of your company, and the customer will have a shared concept of what each of you is responsible for. Without describing the services, the customer may have one idea of what the final project will look like and your company may have another. Putting it down on paper will make it more likely that the vision is the same. Your company may be expecting to be paid at certain points in the process, and your customer may be expecting to write checks at completely different points. Specifying payment arrangements in the contract will make it more likely that everyone's expectations are met.

A key reason to have these agreements is to specify who owns what your company produces. If the deliverable produced by your company is something that can be copyrighted (photos, software, speeches, articles, reports, website code, drawings, or other works of authorship) it belongs to your company unless there is a written agreement specifying otherwise. Your company may use this right to its advantage by excluding any mention of ownership of the completed project, because by law, your company will own this work and therefore the right to use it again, reproduce it, or even charge royalties for its use.

Key Issues to Address in Contracts to Sell Services

As the company providing services, your company contracts should pay special attention to defining the services your company is providing. The statement of work should specify who will perform the services (identify staff levels or actual names and what specific tasks they will perform), what deliverables will be produced from the service if any (reports, drawings, designs, other written documents, physical creations all detailed by size, length, or other distinguishing features), what standards will be used to determine that the services have been performed adequately (key questions a report will answer, key attributes of something to be built, issuance of a certificate of occupancy, the return to function of a repaired piece of equipment, or some other objective measure), when the services will be performed (completion date, a specific reoccurring basis, or other specific time-based measure), and where the services will be completed (location or state, or that this is at your company's discretion).

Payment is another key issue to address. The contract should specify the total amount payable for the service and a final due date for payment of the total due, as well as the dates for interim payments (but even if there are interim payments, always include a date that final payment is due in case interim payments are missed). Include provisions for late fees and interest on unpaid amounts. Don't forget reimbursement for expenses such as travel costs, permit fees, and long-distance telephone. State what is payable, when it is payable, and where and how it should be paid.

If your company requires resources from the company retaining it in order to perform the services, these should be specified in the contract. For example, if your company is required to interview the other company's staff, the contract should require the named staff to be available during a specific week for interviews. Failure to have these staff available at that time would be a breach of contract. If your company requires an officer of the company to approve building plans before they can be submitted to city officials for issuance of a building permit, the officer's approval should be specifically required by a certain date.

As was previously discussed, ownership of copyrights, trademarks, patents, and trade secrets developed for the other company should be indicated in the contract. Ownership of some of these types of intellectual property automatically goes to the creator rather than the company paying for the creation. If your company is unclear on how ownership of intellectual property is determined, the United States Patent and Trademark Office has many useful publications that provide guidance on this issue.

Turning Your Proposal into a Contract

Many service providers seek work by submitting a proposal to a potential client. Service providers as well as clients sometimes think the proposal becomes a contract when the client retains the service provider to do the proposed work. This is not technically true. If there is a dispute over the terms of the deal in a situation where a proposal had been submitted and the service provider was performing work based on the proposal, the proposal would be just one piece of evidence a court would use to decide the terms of the actual deal consisted of. Evidence would probably be admitted concerning verbal agreements, correspondence, course of dealings, and who knows what else. In the end, it's anyone's guess what a court could decide.

To prevent this, your company should have a contract it forwards to clients who accept your company's proposal. The contract can be as simple as an independent contractor agreement with the statement of work from your company's proposal attached as the statement of work for the contract. As you'll read in Chapter 9, proposals do not make good statements of work from the perspective of the company retaining the service provider. That's because they are often written with more puffery and promises than commitments. Where having a statement of work that fails to promise much may be a bad idea for the company buying the service, it presents no problems for the company providing the service. Your company can still provide excellent service even if the statement of work is sketchy; it just won't be contractually obligated to do so.

Review of an Independent Contractor Agreement

The contract below is a detailed independent contractor agreement. As the seller of services, your company is the independent contractor. The independent contractor agreement should contain the basic legal terms discussed in Chapter 1 as well as specific provisions addressing your company's duties, the duties of the company or person retaining your company, the warranty your company will provide, if any, how your company expects to be paid, and which company will own what your company produces. What your company is doing for the other company or person must be specifically described.

In the example below, the contract wording is in Roman type, and the explanation of each part is in italics within brackets.

INDEPENDENT CONTRACTOR AGREEMENT

This Independent Contractor Agreement ("Contract") is effective on May 1, 2008 ("Effective Date")

[Your company should make a point of deciding when you want this contract to be effective. If your company starts work before the contract's effective date, your company is at

risk for all the reasons it would be if there was no contract at all. If the effective date is in a week but your company starts work today, if the company requesting this work terminates the contract immediately, your company may not get paid for what was done before the contract became effective.) by and between Moff Inc. with its main office at 12 Oak Street, Harmony, NM, *(Be sure to include each company's correct mailing address in the contract. I have seen many, many contracts that contain no address for one or both of the parties. This will be a problem if your company ever needs to send a legal notice.]*
("Contractor")
[Placing a word in quotes has the legal effect of indicating that the word in quotes is being used as shorthand for whatever description came immediately before the word in quotes. The quotes here indicate that the word "Contractor" will be used in this agreement as shorthand for Moff Inc. located at 12 Oak Street Harmony, NM. It is no longer necessary, after this point in the agreement, to use the official legal name of this company because you have legally made the association between the shorthand term "Contractor" and the correct legal name and address.]
and Miff Company LLC, with its main office at 25 Maple Street, Beauty, MT ("Company"). Contractor desires to complete the project described herein, and Company desires to retain Contractor to complete this project according to the terms of this Contract.
[Contracts must be bargains where each party does something. This sentence is stating the legal bargain being struck in this contract.]
In consideration of the mutual promises set forth in this Contract, the parties agree as follows:
[Consideration is another legal requirement for a contract, and here you are simply satisfying the legal requirement for consideration by stating that both parties acknowledge that there is consideration for this agreement.]

1. **Duties.** The work to be performed by Contractor ("Project") is described in the attached Project Description. The Project Description is hereby incorporated into and made a part of this Contract.
   [Because this is a form agreement, designed to be used over and over with as few simple changes as possible, the document containing the main changes is an attachment that can be redrafted without making changes to the main agreement.]

2. **Payment.** Company shall pay Contractor the amounts set forth in the Project Description along with reimbursement for all out-of-pocket expenses incurred by Contractor in completing the Project. Where the Project Description does not include a payment schedule, payments of reimbursable costs and Contractor's fees shall be made by Company to Contractor no later than five (5) days after receipt of an invoice from Contractor. Payment shall be made in United States dollars without set-off or deduction. Payments remaining unpaid after the due date shall bear interest at eighteen percent per year, amortized daily until the amount due is paid in full. Payments received by Contractor shall first be applied to payment of interest due, then to unpaid reimbursable costs and finally to unpaid fees for services.

   [The attachment will describe the unique payment terms and fees for this specific project. If payment terms are not included in the attachment, this provision provides for payment five days after the customer receives your company's invoice. Be sure to include a requirement that out-of-picket expenses such as travel, parking, and similar charges are reimbursable. Whether or not to assess a late fee or charge interest on past due amounts is a business decision, but if late fees or interest are not provided for in the contract the other party will have no contractual obligation to pay them . If included, your company can always choose to waive their payment if it wants to. Some states have usury laws that preclude charging interest over a certain amount. Your company should determine these limits in your state. The requirement that payments be made without set-off or deduction means that the other party cannot deduct amounts your company may owe the other company when it pays your company's bills or use amounts your company may owe to "set off" against amounts it owes. By including this in the contract, any set-off or deduction would be a breach of the contract.]

3. **Contract Term.** Unless this Contract is terminated earlier as allowed in section 4, this Contract shall be effective for the length of time stated in the Project Description or one (1) year from the Effective Date, whichever is earlier.

   [The attachment will contain the key requirements for what project is being completed, how it will be paid for, and when it will be provided or completed. If whoever drafts that document forgets to include a final completion date for the project, this provision makes the agreement automatically end in a year. Otherwise your company could have

contracts with no end dates or end dates that neither party can determine with any accuracy.)

4. **Termination.** Contractor may terminate this Contract effective on a date contained in a written notice of termination provided to Company but no less than thirty (30) days from the date of the notice of termination.

   [I recommend always including a provision for terminating the contract early. At this moment in time your company may desire to produce that software program or build that shed, but many things could come up that could change your company's plans. Perhaps the other party to this agreement proves impossible to please, or your company decides to focus on another area of business and hasn't even started this project. If you have no provision for terminating this contract the only recourse is to complete the promised project or fail to complete it and be sued for breaching the contract. Consider the amount of advance notice your company would optimally prefer to give if it desired to end the contract early. There is nothing magical about 30 days. Your company could define the notice period to be more or fewer days.

   An alternative to a provision such as this one that allows termination for any reason or no reason would be to include a provision that allows termination only if one party breaches the contract or becomes insolvent. An example of this provision is included in Chapter 2.]

5. **Company's Duty to Return Contractor Information.** On termination or expiration of this Contract, Company shall, within five (5) business days, return to Contractor any and all Confidential Information, as defined below, belonging to Contractor in the possession or control of Company.

   [If your company provides any of its confidential information to the other party this is a good provision to have. Your confidential information is more likely to remain confidential if it is not in a third party's possession. If your company's information is not returned, this provision would provide the basis for a breach of contract lawsuit. As a breach of contract lawsuit, because this contract contains a provision for reimbursement of legal fees if one party has to sue to enforce the contract and prevails in that lawsuit, your company could recover its legal fees. A lawsuit to recover this information that was not based on a breach of this contract might not result in recovery of legal fees.]

6 **Independent Contractor Relationship.** The parties intend this Contract to create an independent contractor relationship. Neither Contractor nor its employees or agents, if any, are to be considered agents or employees of Company for any purpose. Company does not require Contractor to provide services exclusively to it. Contractor shall complete the Project according to its own methods of work, which are not controlled by Company.

[This clarifies that the parties are contracting, not entering into an employment relationship. The two relationships are treated entirely differently for tax and other purposes, so it's important to clarify the relationship here. It also provides valuable evidence if a government authority questions whether this is really an employment relationship.]

7. **Indemnity.**

[Indemnification means that the party who provides the indemnification agrees to step into the shoes of the other party if the other party is sued. The party doing the indemnifying would then have to defend any claim or lawsuit and pay all the costs of doing so. Frequently a company's insurance provider will require that certain language be included in the indemnification section of all contracts a company enters into in order not to void the insurance coverage. It's wise to check on this so that your company does not find out after the fact that it has no insurance coverage because the contract failed to include the required language.]

Company shall indemnify and hold harmless Contractor and its respective officers, directors, employees, and agents,

[This clause has sought to cover anyone that might be sued based on the actions of the company doing the indemnifying here. The list should be comprehensive but include only those who logically and directly might be sued based on some action of the indemnifying party. For example, one typically would not see spouses of these parties included here.)

from and against any and all suits, claims, losses, forfeitures, demands, fees, costs, expenses, obligations, or proceedings of any kind or nature, including reasonable attorney's fees

[This clause has sought to be comprehensive in the kinds of claims the indemnifying party is responsible for. If the clause was limited to "lawsuits" then only an actual lawsuit filed in a court of law would trigger the duty to provide indemnification.

Instances where someone claims they were injured and is negotiating not to file a lawsuit would not be covered. Most injured parties attempt to receive compensation for their injuries prior to filing a lawsuit and it's frequently smarter, if there is clear liability, to settle a claim this way. For that reason, being comprehensive in the kinds of matters the indemnifying party is responsible for is advisable.]

that Contractor may hereafter incur, become responsible for, or pay out

[This clause is stating that the indemnifying party must indemnify for not only actual payments but those the indemnified party is responsible for but may not have paid yet. Therefore the indemnified party can seek payment from the indemnifying party and then use this reimbursement to pay any damages due, instead of having to front their own money.]

as a result of death or personal injury to any person, destruction or damage to any property, contamination of or adverse effects on the environment, or violation of governmental law, regulation, or orders,

[This clause seeks to comprehensively set out the possible damages the indemnifying party is responsible for. If there are potential damages not included in this clause that might arise from the transactions that are covered under this agreement, then be sure to include them here.]

arising out of or connected with (a) Company's breach of any term or provision of this Contract, (b) any negligent act or omission or willful misconduct of Company, its agents, employees, or subcontractors, or (c) a claim of lien or encumbrances made by third parties.

[This is a very important part of the indemnification provision. I frequently see clauses here that simply state "that result from any negligence of the other party." This is a hugely broad promise to pay for damages as well as legal fees for injuries that may have no relationship to this agreement. It may not be enforceable, even if it benefits your company as the party being indemnified. If it is not enforceable the entire provision might be struck by a court enforcing the contract and your company would be left with no indemnification at all. Make sure the situations that cause the indemnification provision to kick in relate to the contract. The ones here—breach of contract, negligence, and a lien placed by a party in a dispute with the other company—are typical.]

8. **Confidential Information.**

[This is a very important section of the agreement that you should put thought and detail into. Think about what is unique to your company. Is it a special customer service system? A certain assessment technique you use to hire staff? A list of sources for your products that you took years to develop? A recipe? Formulas? Computer programs your company developed? Designs? Pricing systems? Inventory management? Think about what makes your business different from others. Another way to look at this is to examine why your customers do business with your company rather than your competitors. It's likely that some of those reasons either are or arise from what is legally called confidential information—information that is not public knowledge. Your company must protect the confidentiality of this information, because once it becomes public your company is unlikely to be able to prevent an ex-employee or a competitor from using it.]

"Confidential Information" means all information and material disclosed by Contractor to Company or obtained by Company through observation of Contractor's work processes, employees or agents, property, or facilities that is marked or described as, identified in writing as, or provided under circumstances indicating it is confidential or proprietary.

[The definition in the prior sentence should apply to everything your company considers to be confidential. Put some thought into this and make sure it does. Note that the prior sentence applies only to information that is disclosed by your company to the other party. It does not safeguard anything the other party discloses. If you are reviewing another party's form agreement you will want to make sure that the definition of confidential information includes information in any form, not just written information. Otherwise something the other party sees at your facility but is not provided in writing may not be covered. Be careful of how information is deemed to be confidential. Does it have to be marked "confidential'? If so then it's unlikely that anything the company sees could be considered confidential. This provision states that information is confidential if it is provided under circumstances that indicate it's confidential. These circumstances might be statements that the process being observed or the information being reviewed is secret or proprietary, signs on doors or walls stating this, or execution of facility access agreements stating that what the visitor might observe while visiting is confidential and proprietary. It is common to see a sentence here that requires that any-

thing that is to be treated as confidential but is not marked "confidential" when it is disclosed must be documented in writing as confidential within 30 days of its disclosure. I have rarely seen a company that even half-heartedly complied with this type of provision. The reality is that sales staff, scientists, and others who disclose confidential information in the process of wooing clients or impressing colleagues rarely bother to go back and document what confidential information was disclosed. Given that this requirement is unlikely to be followed I see no reason to include it. It's better to draft this section to state with as much detail as possible what your company is protecting, whether it is marked confidential or not. Be aware that it is highly unlikely that anything that loses its status as confidential can regain that status.]

Confidential Information includes, without limitation, any trade secret, know-how, idea, invention, process, technique, algorithm, program, hardware, device, design, schematic, drawing, formula, data, plan, strategy and forecast of, and technical, engineering, manufacturing, product, marketing, servicing, financial, personnel and other information and materials of Contractor and its employees, consultants, investors, affiliates, licensors, suppliers, vendors, customers, clients, and other persons and entities.

[The prior sentence defines the types of information your company wants to protect. I would not advise just copying this sentence for your agreement. The sentence should be directly applicable to your business and be comprehensive. You can always change it as you develop new lines of business.]

For the avoidance of doubt, Confidential Information includes all analyses, compilations, forecasts, data studies, notes, translations, memoranda, or other documents or materials containing, based on, generated, or derived from, in whole or in part, any Confidential Information.

[This is a key sentence, and a similar provision should be included in your company's agreements. If it is not included, then anything based on or developed from your company's confidential information may not be considered your company's. Because what is developed is not your company's exact information, it's arguable that it does not meet the definition of confidential information above. This sentence captures information that is derived from your company's confidential information.]

9. **Duties Concerning Confidential Information.**

[This section details what the other party's duties are when dealing with your com-

pany's confidential information. Put some thought into this to be sure to include any specific duties that apply to your business.]

Company shall hold all Confidential Information in strict confidence and shall not disclose any Confidential Information to any third party. Company shall disclose Confidential Information only to its employees, consultants, and agents who need to know such information to accomplish the objectives of this Contract and who are bound in writing by restrictions regarding disclosure and use of such information comparable to and no less restrictive than those set forth here.

[This sentence provides for disclosure within the company receiving the information, but more importantly requires that company to have executed agreements with its employees, consultants, and agents that require them to maintain the confidentiality of your company's information. Not all companies routinely have these types of agreements, and it is wise to inquire if the other company has such agreements in place if you truly want to safeguard your company's information. If the other company does not routinely have their employees, consultants, or agents sign such agreements, it's a better idea to insist that they do so rather than to delete this sentence.]

Company shall not use any Confidential Information for the benefit of itself or any third party or for any purpose other than to accomplish the objectives of this Contract.

[Up to this point you have made clear that certain information that belongs to your company is secret and that it cannot be disclosed to anyone outside the other company. However you have not prevented the other company from using your company's confidential information for its own benefit. This sentence contractually obligates the other company to use your company's information only for its duties under this contract.]

Company shall take the same degree of care that it uses to protect its own confidential and proprietary information (but in no event less than reasonable care) and avoid the unauthorized use, disclosure, publication, or dissemination of the Confidential Information.

[This sentence requires the other company to protect your company's confidential information once it is in their hands. Some companies will not be familiar with handling confidential information and will not have systems in place to protect such information. In those cases it's important to have a statement that requires the company to

use reasonable care to protect your information. Legally this requires the contractor to do what a reasonable person would do when safeguarding any valuable property like cash or jewels.]

Company shall not make any copies of the Confidential Information except as approved in writing in advance by Contractor.

[Making copies of confidential information is problematic. Copies may not be marked as confidential and those receiving the copies may not be aware of your company's ownership or that the information is secret. The more copies of your information there are, the more likely the information will become publicly known.]

Any copies made shall be identified as the property of Contractor and marked "confidential," "proprietary," or with a similar legend.

[This further limits the likelihood of disclosure of your company's information through release of copies.]

These obligations shall survive and continue for five (5) years from the date of termination or expiration of this Contract. *[Your company does not want the duties placed on the company in this section to end if this contract were terminated, because the confidential information would presumably continue to have value as a secret. The duty to keep your company's information confidential must continue for as short or as long a period as is realistic for your industry and information.]*

10. **Exceptions to Confidential Information.** The obligations of this Contract, including the restrictions on disclosure and use, shall not apply to any Confidential Information if it (a) is or becomes publicly known through no act or omission of Company; (b) was rightfully known by Company without having violated any duty of confidentiality to anyone before it was received from Contractor, as evidenced by written records; (c) becomes known to Company without violating any duty of confidentiality from a source other than Contractor that does not owe a duty of confidentiality to Contractor with respect to the Confidential Information; or (d) is independently developed by Company without the use of, reference, or access to the Confidential Information, as evidenced by written records. Company may use or disclose Confidential Information if approved in writing by Contractor or Company is legally required to disclose the Confidential Information, but only if Company provides reasonable advance notice to Contractor that it must legally disclose the Confidential

Information and cooperates with Contractor if Contractor seeks to challenge or restrict the legal requirement.

[This section removes certain information from being considered confidential information that would otherwise be included. What is excluded is confidential information that becomes public without any fault of the party receiving it under this contract, information that the other party already knew that is documented in that party's written records, information that the other party learns from a third party without violating anyone's confidentiality, and information that the company receiving the confidential information develops on its own without referencing or knowing the disclosing party's confidential information. This provision also provides exceptions to the receiving party's duty to not disclose confidential information where the disclosing party gives permission for the disclosure or where there is a governmental order to disclose it. Where there is an order, there must first be notice to the party that owns the information that it is being disclosed and the party disclosing must cooperate with the owner to try to fight the order if the owner decides to do that. Without this provision, confidential information that falls within the exceptions, even though it might no longer be treated as confidential by your company, would continue to have to be treated as confidential by the other party to this agreement.]

11. **No solicitation.** Company agrees not to recruit or engage the services or employment of any of Contractor's employees during the term of this Contract and for a period of ninety (90) days following the termination or expiration of this Contract (or any renewal periods).

[This provision is included in agreements in which a company believes its employees would provide a competitive advantage to another company if the employees moved from one company to the other. The time period between an employee leaving and then joining the other party should be restricted to the amount of time in which the information the employee has would be useful to the other company. However, courts generally will not allow this time period to be greater than a year, and in many cases a shorter time has been deemed to be the maximum allowed.

If your company wants to discourage movement of staff from your company to the company you are doing work for, this provision would provide a discouragement.

However, your company has to be prepared to enforce a provision like this. In my experience, once employees determine your company does not enforce these types of provisions, they are ignored. If your company does not expect to enforce a violation of this provision, don't include it.]

12. **Entire Agreement.** This Contract including the Project Description constitutes the entire agreement between the parties concerning this subject matter and supersedes all other representations, negotiations, conditions, communications, and agreements, whether oral or written, between the parties relating to the same subject matter except where the other agreement is specifically incorporated into this Contract. *(Every agreement should have a provision similar to this—commonly called an "integration provision". The effect of this provision is that no other written documents or verbal agreements can be used as evidence if there is a dispute over this agreement. A provision like this makes any verbal agreements ["They said they wouldn't enforce that provision." "The e-mail he sent me said the fees would be lower."] unenforceable to prove what the parties' agreement consisted of. Be certain that this provision lists every document that is part of your agreement—confidentiality, fee schedule, etc.—because what is not listed will not be enforceable as evidence of what the parties agreed to.)*
13. **Conflict Between Agreements.** If the terms of the Project Description conflict with this Contract, this Contract prevails.
    [Any time your company references another document into an agreement, one or both agreements should specify how any conflicts between the documents will be decided. There should be one agreement that is stated to take precedence over all the others.]
14. **Assignment and Binding Obligations.** This Contract may not be subcontracted, delegated, or assigned in whole or in part without the express written consent of Contractor, which may be withheld or granted in Contractor's sole determination.
    [This means that the other company must obtain your company's written consent before subcontracting or delegating any part of the contract, or transferring it to another person or company. Without this sentence the other company is free to delegate performance of any tasks it must perform under the contract to others or to sell its business and assign this contract to the new company. This provision allows your company to assess a proposed party being delegated, subcontracted, or assigned this con-

tract and decide if your company wants to allow the transfer. Be careful that this sentence includes the caveat "which may be withheld or granted in Contractor's sole determination." *If this sentence simply states* "This Contract may not be subcontracted, delegated or assigned in whole or in part without the express written consent of Contractor" *the law implies that your company's consent will be reasonable under the circumstances. If, for example, the other party is sold to your company's competitor and you simply don't want to do business with that company that would probably not be a reasonable reason for withholding consent to assignment of this contract. By including the caveat that the decision to consent to a transfer of this contract is in your company's sole determination, your company's reasons for consenting or not consenting can usually not be challenged.)*

Subject to the written consent required in this provision this Contract shall be binding on the parties and their heirs, legal t representatives, successors, and assigns.

[If the owners of either party change, through transfer on the death of an owner, a sale, assignment, or otherwise, this contract may not be enforceable against the new owners because technically the new owners are not a party to this contract—the old owners are. If your company wants to be able to enforce this contract if it is transferred, this provision should be included.]

15. **Cumulative Rights/Survival.** Any specific rights or remedy provided in this Contract will not be exclusive but will be cumulative of all other rights and remedies.

    [This sentence allows your company to enforce all the rights and remedies in the contract, not just one. For example, if the other party fails to pay your company—a violation of section 2—this provision would allow your company to both terminate the contract as provided in section 4 and sue the company for damages for violating section 2.]

    If any one or more of the provisions of this Contract are held to be invalid, illegal, or unenforceable by a court or arbitrator of competent jurisdiction, the validity, legality, and enforceability of the remaining provision shall not be affected or impaired.

    [Courts have sometimes held that when the law changes, making a term in a contract unenforceable or even illegal, the entire contract is void because it contains the now illegal or unenforceable term. This sentence may allow the court to simply delete the

term, leaving the rest of the contract to stand as it is. Whether a court will do that is a matter of state law, but it's wise to include this provision in contracts in case the state court does allow striking only the offending provision.]

16. **LIMIT OF LIABILITY.** IN NO EVENT SHALL CONTRACTOR BE LIABLE TO COMPANY OR ANY THIRD PARTY IN CONTRACT, TORT, OR OTHERWISE FOR INCIDENTAL OR CONSEQUENTIAL DAMAGES OF ANY KIND, INCLUDING, WITHOUT LIMITATION, ECONOMIC DAMAGE OR LOST PROFITS, REGARDLESS OF WHETHER CONTRACTOR SHALL BE ADVISED, SHALL HAVE OTHER REASON TO KNOW, OR IN FACT SHALL KNOW OF THE POSSIBILITY.

    [I often have found that if an agreement contains an indemnification provision, it does not have a limitation of liability provision or visa versa. The two provisions are different and should both be included in an agreement. The limit of liability provision precludes the party named in the provision from responsibility for consequential damages. Consequential damages are damages that arise indirectly from an event that causes damage to someone or something. For example, if I throw a brick at you, the cut to your head would be direct damage, and the fact that you miss a presentation to an angel investor's group that might fund your new business because you're at the hospital getting stitches would be indirect damage. Consequential damages in a business context can be huge and are usually not damages your company is calculating into the risks of entering into a contract. A provision excluding them from damages payable under the agreement is almost always advisable.]

17. **Dispute Resolution/Forum.** Any and all disputes arising out of or relating to this Contract shall be subject to good faith negotiations between the parties before legal proceedings.

    [This sentence would allow your company to ask a court to dismiss a lawsuit filed by the other company if good faith negotiations had not occurred prior to filing the lawsuit. "Good faith" usually means that both parties participate in the negotiations, that those participating have the authority to come to an agreement on the issue, and that a reasonable amount of time is spent negotiating before a lawsuit is filed. Lawsuits are expensive, time consuming, and distracting from a company's business. Requiring that the parties to a dispute talk before filing one is good business. However, in a serious dispute I have found that one or both parties will no longer desire to speak to each

other. Having a contract provision that requires speaking to each other in a negotiation often bridges this hurdle and allows a resolution to occur before resorting to court.) This Contract shall be governed by and construed in accordance with the laws of the state of New Mexico, without reference to its conflict of laws provisions. *(This provision requires any legal disputes to be decided under the laws of the state where your company, the contractor, is located. This is usually advantageous to your company, because your company will be more familiar with these laws than with another state's, as will your company's lawyers.]*

Each party hereby submits to the exclusive jurisdiction of and waives any venue or other objection against, any federal or state court sitting in New Mexico in any legal proceeding arising out of or relating to this Contract.

[This provision means that all legal disputes must be decided in a court located in New Mexico, where the contractor is located. This is also advantageous to your company, because travel costs will be reduced in the event of litigation, your company will be able to retain local attorneys, and it is sometimes thought that courts favor individuals or companies residing in their home state. The other company has the right to object to litigation being filed in a court that it considers inconvenient or unfair. Including this sentence would most likely forgo that argument, because the other party would be deemed to have bargained away the right to object to the location of the lawsuit by signing this agreement.]

If any party seeks to enforce its rights under this Contract by legal proceedings or otherwise, the non-prevailing party shall pay all reasonable costs and expenses of the prevailing party.

[Some states provide for recovery of the prevailing party's attorney's fees and other costs in contract lawsuits but some do not. In the states where there is no statute governing recovery of the prevailing party's legal fees, this contract provision would allow the recovery. Having this provision in contracts is commonly thought to discourage the filing of a frivolous lawsuit or one not well grounded in evidence supporting the party filing it, because the filing party risks paying the other party's fees and costs if it loses.]

18. **Waiver.** No breach of this Contract can be waived except in writing. Waiver of any breach shall not be deemed to be a waiver of any other breach of the same or any other provision of this Contract.

[A court may find that if a company fails to enforce a provision of a contract it has waived the right to enforce that provision throughout the life of the contract. This section makes clear that your company intends to retain its right to enforce a contract provision even if it has waived a breach of that provision in the past.]

19. **Written Amendments.** No amendment or modification of any provision of this Contract shall be effective unless in writing and signed by both parties.

[This is a very important provision to include. Otherwise, for example, the company here can claim that payment for the project was agreed to be half what the contract states, and it's possible the claim would be upheld by a court. This provision means that only a written signed amendment or modification will be enforceable to effect a change to this agreement.]

"Contractor" "Company"

[By placing the names here in quotes you are indicating that these are shorthand for the official names which are included elsewhere. If you intend to use this as a form agreement to be used over and over for many different projects you will want to limit changes that have to be made. By using the quotes here you have made it unnecessary to actually type in the official legal names of your company and the other company in the signature blocks. It would only have to be done where the words in these quotes are defined (in the preamble before section 1.)]

By: ____________________	By: ____________________
Name: ____________________	Name: ____________________
Title: ____________________	Title: ____________________
Date:____________________	Date: ____________________

The Project Description should state in detail the project to be completed, the services to be provided, or the item being created by your company as well as what deliverables are expected, the fees to be paid, when they are to be paid, and how long this agreement will last. I cannot overemphasize how important it is to be concrete and specific. If someone completely unfamiliar with either company recites their understanding of what the Project Description states, neither party should be able to identify anything they expect to be done that was not included.

Consider the following:

1. What is to be done, accomplished, built, written, provided?
2. What expectations does your company or the company requesting this work have about how this will be accomplished. Examples include if the work will be done at the company's site between the hours of 10:00 a.m. and 2:00 p.m. three days per week, that five interviews will occur, that the company will provide access to observe the operations of each of its 20 chicken farms for at least five days each, that the building will be 20 feet in height.
3. What evidence does the other company expect to see indicating that the project was completed, accomplished, etc? A report? A shed? A software program? A verbally presented system for treating disease in agricultural animals?
4. What is the due date or deadline for completion of the project?
5. Are there deadlines or due dates for any steps that are expected to occur between the contract start date and the final product or result?
6. How will the final product look? If it's a shed, how big is it according to dimensions? What is it made of? What color is it painted? Is it just the shell of a shed or is it finished inside with electricity and natural gas installed? Do you expect the area surrounding the shed to be returned to the condition it was before construction? Will the building debris be hauled away? Will it have to meet certain construction standards? If the final product is a report, what sections will it have? What subjects will it cover? Will a solution to a problem be included? Will that solution include details concerning implementation such as costs and staffing? Will the report include details about what was done to reach the conclusion that was reached? How many copies of the report will be produced? How long should the report be? If the final product is that your company will lead five training sessions on contract analysis, how long are the sessions expected to be? Will handouts be provided? How long will the handouts be? Where will the training sessions be held? Will your company decide where and when the sessions are held or will the other company? What subjects will be cov-

ered in the training sessions? You should include as much specificity concerning the project as you can. Include the staff that will be utilizing the final product in this process. I have never seen too much detail in this section of the contract.

7. What cooperation or assistance do you want to contractually require from the other company so that your company can meet the deadlines and produce the project it is promising in this contract?
8. Is there a specific person working with the other company that your company wants to contractually require to work on this project with your company? If so, completion of the project should be contingent on that specific person's assistance.

In the section on payment consider the following:

1. Will your company require a retainer or up-front deposit? If so, will the retainer or deposit be held like a security deposit until the company makes all the other payments required under the contract, or will it be billed against as the contract proceeds?
2. Does your company plan to invoice the other company? If so, at what intervals? How long after an invoice does the company have to pay your bills?
3. Is the time for payment calculated from the date of the invoice? The date the other company receives the invoice? How will you know when that was?
4. If your company does not plan to send invoices, how will reimbursable expenses be billed? Are they to be paid on the same schedule as payments for performance of project?
5. If no invoices are sent, on what basis will payments to your company be made? At regular calendar intervals? After specified progress is made on the project?
6. How would your company like to receive payment—cash, check, wire transfer?
7. Will payment be made in United States dollars? Euros?

In the section on how long the contract will last, consider the following:

1. Is an effective date stated in the contract?
2. Is the effective date of the contract the same as the date your company expects to begin performing services? Sometimes your company will want to immediately bind the other company to the contract, so that your company is assured it will have the work, but the start date for the project will be a later date. In that case the contract can be stated to be effective on the date it is signed, but in the project description, it can be stated that the project will begin on a different specified date. For example, if the effective date of the contract is August 1, 2010 and the project is to start on October 1, 2010 this could be stated as follows:

   In the body of the agreement:

   This Independent Contractor Agreement ("Contract") is effective on August 1, 2010 ("Effective Date").

   In the project description:

   Performance of Project by Contractor shall begin on or about October 1, 2010.

   If no start date is stated in the project description, performance of the project will be presumed to start on the effective date stated in the contract.
3. Can the expiration date for the contract be determined with certainty? If so, state this date or perhaps a few weeks after this date to provide some leeway. Sometimes your company will not know when the project will be completed. In that case the expiration date can be linked to the occurrence of some event. If this is done, the contract must also state a final drop-dead date after which the contract ends even if the project is not completed. This is so that if the event that triggers the contract's expiration never occurs, the contract won't go on forever if elsewhere in the agreement there is no automatic end date. For example, if your company is retained to assist with 10 presentations to the other party's customers that have not yet been scheduled, the term could be as follows:

   Term: From the Effective Date through completion of the Project (*assuming you have defined the Project as assistance with 10 presentations to Moff's customers)* or December 15, 2010, whichever occurs first.

This means that the project will be performed starting on the effective date of the contract until the 10 presentations are completed, but if they have not been completed by December 15, 2010, the contract ends automatically.

Remember that under the terms of section 3 of this agreement, the contract expires automatically after one year. If that is the term your company expects the project to be performed in, you do not need a "term" section in the project description. The term is one year from the effective date.

This is an example of a project description for the independent contractor agreement just reviewed.

PROJECT DESCRIPTION

Project: Contractor shall perform phlebotomy services in support of Company's medical research. Contractor shall draw blood from 2–5 human volunteers a day between the hours of 7:00 am–8:30 am Monday through Friday at Company's facility.

[This means that your company would not be contractually obligated to draw blood from more than five volunteers a day or before 7:00 am or after 8:30 am, or on weekends.]

Term: On completion of the Project.

[There is no stated expiration date in this contract other than the one-year period included in section 3 of the main agreement. The Payment section states that no more than 50 hours can be spent on this project. Therefore, the contract would expire whenever your company reaches the 50-hour limit or a year from the effective date.]

Payment: Contractor will be paid ten dollars ($10) per hour for each hour it performs the Project. Company agrees to pay Contractor within ten (10) business days of the date of each of Contractor's weekly invoices.

[This specifies how often your company can invoice the other company, when payment is due, and how much is due. Note that because there is no provision for prorating the hourly rate for partial hours worked, your company could charge for a full hour even if only part of an hour was worked.]

As the contractor performing the services or completing the project, your company should pick and choose the language in the project description carefully. Words that are absolute will be contractually enforceable, but words like "may" or "expects to" are likely not to be. If your company does not want to be obligated to perform certain tasks but wants to mention that they might be done, use words that are not absolute like "can" and "may" rather than "shall" and "will." For example:

"Contractor can complete the shed by May 1" rather than "Contractor will complete the shed by May 1."

"The report may include detailed costs for each recommendation" rather than "The report shall include detailed costs for each recommendation."

The Appendix contains a line-by-line analysis of three additional contracts.

If your company sells products, don't be tempted to modify one of these service contracts for your company's business and stop reading here. There are state laws governing the sale of goods that either create a contract, if you and the other party haven't expressly done so, or add certain terms to a contract unless the contract specifically excludes them. If your company is selling products it needs to be aware of these laws and what they require. The next chapter covers these laws and discusses how to utilize them to your company's advantage.

CHAPTER 8

Contracts to Sell Products

John, owner of Bacchus Wines, ships 10 cases of his best white burgundy, trade price $320 a bottle, to a new hotel in town. The wine steward at the hotel agrees to taste one bottle and if she likes it, purchase the remaining bottles for use at a convention dinner the hotel will host the following week. John sends a purchase order with the delivery that contains the name of his company as the seller, the hotel as the buyer, that 10 cases of his company's best white burgundy at $320 a bottle is being purchased for a total of $38,400, and that payment is due within 10 days of delivery. Three days after John delivers the wine there is a fire in the kitchen of the hotel, destroying all 10 cases of the fine white burgundy. John contacts the wine steward to make sure the hotel intends to pay his company for the destroyed wine. The steward informs John that the hotel has no responsibility for the value of the wine, because the contract between the hotel and John's company states that the risk of loss to the wine belongs to the seller until the hotel pays for the wine. John is furious and states that the purchase order contains no such statement. John's lawyer says the wine steward is correct. How can this be when the purchase order, which John knows creates a contract between seller and buyer, doesn't state any such thing?

In This Chapter

- If you're selling goods, state law writes the contract: how to modify it
- The "implied by law" terms of your contract for the sale of goods
- What contract prevails if both parties send purchase orders to each other?
- Bulletproofing the UCC terms
- Save time, risk life: using the buyer's purchase order for the deal
- White alligators: term unique to selling products
- Review of a purchase order

If You're Selling Goods, State Law Writes the Contract: How to Modify It

There is a special set of laws just for transactions in the sale of goods. If selling or buying goods is your business you should know these laws backwards and forwards as they apply to your state. The laws are called the Uniform Commercial Code (UCC). The UCC defines the terms under which a sale of goods is made between a buyer and seller if the parties have not entered into a signed written agreement that replaces one or more terms of the UCC. Provisions of the UCC have been enacted in different versions, usually varying only slightly, from state to state.

One or both parties to a purchase often desire to change part of the contract created by the UCC. Even if your company is happy with using all the terms of the UCC, there are important contract provisions left out that your company should consider placing in a purchase order or other sales contract to protect itself from risk.

There are several ways to modify or add to the sales contract created by the UCC. The parties can draft and sign a contract, often called a sales agreement. Another option is for the party who desires to change the UCC terms to draft what is commonly referred to as a purchase order or terms of sale, which sets forth the terms under which that party is agreeing to either buy or sell goods. A purchase order is not signed by the parties. Once sent to the other party, the purchase order becomes the contract between the parties if the party receiving it does not formally object or send their own purchase order. However, even if a purchase order is sent, if it is silent on a term that the UCC covers, then that UCC provision becomes part of the agreement between the parties.

Because a sales agreement is a signed contract, it has the same enforceability as any contract. Purchase orders may or may not be enforceable depending on whether the other party sent a conflicting purchase order. If that is the case, why use purchase orders at all? Drafting contracts usually involves negotiating, which takes time. Even if your company has a form sales agreement and the other party does not try to negotiate its terms, sending it out and waiting for it to be returned signed takes time. In the meantime, revenue that could be coming in to your company is not. Many companies use purchase orders to speed the sales process and in hopes that a dispute over the sale never occurs.

The "Implied by Law" Terms of Your Contract for the Sale of Goods

Because even if your company does not issue a purchase order, the buyer does not issue a purchase order, and the parties do not draft and sign a contract regarding the sale, there will still be a contract with terms implied by the UCC, the principal terms of the UCC are summarized below.

There are entire books and courses on the UCC terms of sale, so this is not meant to be comprehensive. I will also not cover the remedies the UCC implies for contract breach. The UCC is different from state to state, so if your business principally involves the sales of goods, you should review the specific UCC provisions of state law that govern your company's contracts. The following summary provides an overview of general UCC principles governing sale of products if no signed written contract exists. Read the section on "sales on approval" for the reasons why Bacchus Wine, not the hotel, was out $38,400 for the destroyed wine.

UCC Terms of Sale for Goods

Price: If no price is discussed for the goods, the UCC implies a reasonable price at the time of delivery. If it is agreed that either the buyer or seller is to set the price, the price must be set in good faith.

Duty of Good Faith: Every contract imposes an obligation of good faith in performance and enforcement. Good faith for a business is honesty in fact and observance of reasonable commercial standards of fair dealing in the trade.

Payment: If no payment terms are agreed to, payment is due at the time and place at which the buyer is to receive the goods. The buyer can make payment in any commercially reasonable manner, but if the seller demands cash, the buyer must be given a reasonable time to obtain it.

Delivery: If no delivery terms are specified, delivery occurs at the seller's business, or if there is no place of business then the seller's residence. If the goods are not at the seller's business and both parties are aware of this, delivery occurs wherever the goods are located. If a manner of delivery is agreed to but becomes impractical through no fault of either party, a commercially reasonable substitute must be used. Delivery must be timely or it is considered a contract breach, except if due to the commercial impracticability exception discussed below.

Shipment: If time for shipment is not specified the UCC implies a reasonable time for performance.

Output Contracts: The UCC imposes a good faith limit on output contracts. The limit is what the seller produces in a normal production year.

Requirements Contracts: Under the UCC these are not enforceable if the decision to purchase is left up to the buyer or if the buyer reserves the right to buy the goods from another seller. They are enforceable if the agreement is that the buyer is obligated to buy all it needs or requires from the seller. The UCC also implies a good faith limit on requirements contracts to the amount the seller produces in a normal production year.

Option Contracts: Normally an offer to sell something can be revoked at any time by the seller before the buyer accepts the offer. If the buyer pays for the right to have a certain period of time to consider the offer during which the offer cannot be revoked (the "option"), the offer to sell cannot be revoked until the option period expires. Under the UCC, options are valid if paid for or if the seller is a business and the irrevocable offer is in a signed writing. In either instance the option period cannot exceed three months.

Acceptance of the Offer to Sell or Buy: Acceptance of an offer occurs at any time the response indicates a definite acceptance of the offer, even if the acceptance includes different terms than what the offer included. An offer to buy can be accepted by the seller by prompt shipment of the goods or a prompt promise to ship.

Terms: If either party is not a business the contract formed by the UCC is that contained in the offer, and none of the terms of the acceptance are included. If the contract to buy and sell is between businesses, the contract is composed of the terms of the offer and the additional terms of the acceptance, except if the offer expressly limits acceptance to the terms of the offer, the new or changed terms materially alter the offer, or the party making the acceptance objects to the terms of the offer in a reasonable time.

Certain Contracts Must Be in Writing: Contracts for the sale of goods priced at $500 or more must be signed by the party against whom the contract would be enforced. Terms of the contract can be proven in court by oral testimony, except for the quantity of goods, which should be identified in the written agreement. In the case of contracts between merchants, there can be an oral agreement if there is a subsequent written confirmation of the agreement sent by one of the businesses that indicates the terms of the agreement. If the business receiving the confirmation fails to object within 10 days after receipt, the confirmation is sufficient to prove the existence of the contract even if it is for the sale of goods priced over $500 and the confirmation is not signed. There are also exceptions to the requirements stated above if the goods are specially manufactured for the buyer, the goods are not for resale in the buyer's business, or the seller has already started to make the goods. In these cases an oral agreement to purchase will be enforced.

Title: Title to the goods passes to the buyer at the time and place the seller physically delivers the goods. Where this delivery occurs depends on whether the contract is a shipment contract or a destination contract. A shipment contract authorizes the seller to deliver the goods to a carrier, like the United States Post Office. In this type of contract title passes at the time and place of shipment. All contracts are assumed to be shipment contracts unless an agreement states otherwise. In a destination contract the seller has agreed to deliver the goods to a destination such as the buyer's facility. In these contracts, title passes on delivery to the agreed destination. If the goods are not to be delivered by the seller, title passes either on delivery of a bill of lading or warehouse receipt to the buyer, or if there is no such document, at the time the sales contract is made.

Risk of Loss: Risk of loss does not necessarily pass with title. If the agreement is that the seller is to ship the goods by carrier, risk of loss passes to the buyer when the goods are delivered to the carrier. In a destination contract the risk of loss passes to the buyer on delivery by the seller to the destination. Some states have older versions of the UCC that use terms such as F.O.B., C.I.F., and delivery ex-ship to determine passage of title and risk of loss. Determine if these are applicable in your state so that your purchase orders or contracts may modify what the UCC implies if necessary.

Sale and Return Contracts: Contracts in which the buyer has the right to return the goods within a certain amount of time are called sale and return contracts. When the buyer receives possession of the goods, both title and risk of loss passes to the buyer. If the buyer fails to return the goods in the stated time, the sale becomes final. If the goods are returned to the seller within the allowed period, title and risk of loss passes back to the seller on return of the goods to the seller.

Sales on Approval: If the seller permits the buyer to take the goods on a trial basis, risk of loss and title remain with the seller. Title and risk of loss pass to the buyer only where the trial period expires and the buyer keeps the goods (technically this is treated as an act of ownership inconsistent with the seller's ownership) or where the buyer expressly accepts the seller's offer to sell.

Commercial Impracticability: Nondelivery or delayed delivery is excused if due to the occurrence of a contingency the nonoccurrence of which was a basic assumption on which the contract was made. The seller must notify the buyer as soon as possible that this is the case.

Lack of Cooperation by the Other Party: If one party needs the cooperation of the other party in order to perform its duties under the contract, noncooperation results in the other party having the right to suspend its performance without liability or hold the other party in breach of the contract and continue performing in any reasonable manner.

Assurances of Performance: If one party has reasonable grounds to believe the other party cannot or will not perform its duties under the contract, that party can demand in writing that the other party provide adequate assurances of performance. These assurances must be provided within 30 days. If they are not provided, the party not responding will be treated as if it repudiated the contract, giving the other party the right to terminate the contract and seek damages.

Acceptance of Goods: Acceptance occurs if the buyer has time to inspect the goods and signifies acceptance, fails to reject the goods in a reasonable time, or performs any act inconsistent with the seller's ownership. Inconsistent actions might be selling the goods or using them.

Remedies of the Seller: If the buyer breaches the sales agreement, the seller may withhold delivery of the goods, discontinue performance of its contract duties, sell, or dispose of the goods that are the subject of the agreement, or recover the price of the goods plus incidental damages. This is a very general overview of the seller's remedies without discussion of the many nuances and conditions under the UCC. If the sales agreement contains specific remedies, these remedies will be in addition to those provided for in the UCC unless the agreement states that the remedies are exclusive.

Warranties: The UCC automatically provides for several warranties, all good for four years, including a warranty of title (seller owns the goods, has the right to sell them, no creditor will interfere with buyer's purchase of the goods, and the goods are free from copyright, trademark, or patent claims of third parties), a warranty of merchantability (goods are reasonably fit for the ordinary purposes for which such goods are used, of average, fair, or medium grade quality, adequately packaged and labeled, and conform to the affirmations of fact on the label), a warranty of fitness for a particular purpose (seller has reason to know of the purpose for which the goods are bought and knows that the buyer is relying on the skill and judgment of the seller to select the goods), and a warranty arising from course of dealing or trade usage (a court presumes both parties have knowledge of trade custom and presumes that custom is intended to apply to the contract).There can also be express warranties, which are any representation of quality, condition, description, or performance potential of the goods. Express warranties can be made through promotional material, brochures, proposals, and ads. They can arise through verbal statements and do not have to include words like warranty or guarantee. Generally any affirmation of fact or promise, description of the goods, or use of samples or models by the seller will create an express warranty. The UCC allows express warranties to be limited, or negated entirely, if there is language to that effect that is specific and unambiguous and is called to the buyer's attention. Implied warranties can be disclaimed by a specific disclaimer in writing that is conspicuous, or by inclusion of statements like "as is" or "with any and all faults." In the case of a disclaimer of warranty of fitness for a particular purpose, the word "fitness" does not have to be mentioned, but the disclaimer must be conspicuous and in writing. In the case of a disclaimer of warranty of merchantability, the word "merchantability" must be mentioned, but the disclaimer does not need to be written. If it is, the disclaimer must be conspicuous.

Remedies for Warranty Breach: The UCC allows the buyer to recover the purchase price of the goods as well as damages. Damages include those for consequential damages such as lost profits, loss of revenue, purchase of replacement goods, and injuries to people.

What Contract Prevails if Both Parties Send Purchase Orders to Each Other?

If the party receiving a purchase order sends their own purchase order to the other party, it is treated as an objection to the terms of the sender's purchase order. What happens now? There is abundant litigation over the effect of these potentially conflicting terms of sale. Generally if there is a conflict between specific terms in the two purchase orders, the individual conflicting terms cancel each other out and are replaced by the UCC's treatment of that specific issue. Any non-conflicting terms in the two purchasing orders remain part of the agreement.

There is an exception to this when the sender's purchase order states that the contract for sale of the goods is expressly conditional on the receiver's acceptance of all the terms of the purchase order. If the receiver sends their own purchase order containing even one conflicting term, it is an implied rejection to "all" the terms of the sender's purchase order. This rejection means there is no contract between the parties. Because a contract is simply evidence of an agreement, there is essentially no agreement to buy and sell between the parties. Even if both parties had verbally agreed to a deal, the clause just discussed would negate the bargain. I have often seen this type of clause in purchase orders, an example, I believe, of one party not understanding what its contract says, because I doubt that party intends to refuse to do business with the other party.

What happens if your company objects to the terms of the buyer's purchase order, but the other company doesn't send your company a revised purchase order, and your company still ships the goods to the customer? Under the UCC your company will be deemed to have consented to the terms of the other party's purchase order, because your company followed through on the transaction despite objecting to the sale terms. Your company should have either sent a conflicting purchase order, as long as the conflicting term was one where the UCC provision that would be deemed to replace the two conflicting provisions was one your company agreed with, or enter into a signed contract with the other party containing terms both parties agreed to. Of course there is always a third option of foregoing the sale.

Bulletproofing the UCC Terms

If every term in the UCC is acceptable to your company and you decide to forgo using purchase orders or sales agreements in favor of the UCC, your company has decided to swim unprotected in alligator-infested waters. That's because the UCC addresses many commercial issues but does not address most contractual legal issues. That's what the bulletproof terms in Chapter 2 are for. Relying on the UCC means your company has no assurance that the deal terms won't change, because there is no agreement that changes to the contract must be in writing. It means that your company is subject to paying consequential damages and won't be indemnified if the other company causes harm to your company. It means that your company will be responsible for fulfilling warranties of title, merchantability, fitness for particular purpose, course of dealing, and trade usage and express warranties such as a representation of quality, condition, description, or performance potential of the goods.

To protect your company, include the bulletproof terms in your purchase orders. This can be accomplished as simply as printing them in readable type on the reverse of your company's one-page purchase order. The front of the purchase order must reference, again in readable type, that the terms on the reverse of the purchase order are incorporated into the agreement to sell goods to the buyer and that the buyer is agreeing to those terms. By doing this your company has created a contract comprised of the bulletproof terms, the UCC, and the terms on the front of the purchase order, which usually contain the specifics regarding the items purchased, the price, and delivery requirements.

Save Time, Risk life: Using the Buyer's Purchase Order for the Deal

Sometimes the buyer places an order by sending your company a purchase order drafted by the buyer. There will be a very hard-to-resist order for your company's products along with a bunch of contract stuff. Many companies just fulfill the order, deferring to the buyer's terms to govern the sale. Your company is jumping into alligator-infested waters again.

Whoever drafts a contract writes it to benefit themselves. A buyer's definition of a great deal is frequently not the same as the seller's. Deferring to the buyer's purchase order means the deal will heavily benefit the buyer.

Here is an example. This clause is from a seller's purchase order:

Here is a clause covering the same issues but from a buyer's purchase order:

Buyer's Acceptance of Goods. Buyer is deemed to have accepted the goods when Buyer fails to notify Seller in writing within five (5) days of delivery of the goods to Buyer of its rejection. Notification of rejection to Seller must include reasonable detail concerning the reasons for rejection. Buyer may return a properly rejected product for credit, replacement, or refund at Seller's option. Goods not properly rejected will be deemed accepted.

As the seller in this transaction, which clause would your company rather do business under? If it's the seller's clause, it's a smart business decision to draft your own purchase orders and use them, even if it takes more effort.

Acceptance and Rejection. All products may be inspected and tested at reasonable times and places during and after manufacture and will be subject to final inspection and acceptance after delivery. Payment will not constitute final acceptance. Buyer may reject any products that contain defective material or workmanship, do not meet specifications, or otherwise do not conform to the purchase order. Buyer's inspection and acceptance does not relieve the Seller from liability for latent defects. On rejection of products, Buyer may, at its sole option (a) return the products at Seller's risk and expense for prompt issuance of a credit for the amount of previous payments, if any, (b) return the products at Seller's risk and expense for prompt replacement with conforming products, (c) halt the products for prompt correction by Seller at Buyer's facility, or (d) accept the products subject to an equitable adjustment in price. All corrective work will be performed at Seller's expense. If Buyer elects to return nonconforming products, Seller shall issue a return material authorization ("RMA") within forty-eight (48) hours of Buyer's request. If no RMA is received within forty-eight (48) hours, Buyer may return the products without Seller authorization. If Seller fails to promptly refund prior payments or replace or correct rejected products with conforming products, Buyer may at its sole option (a) replace or correct the rejected products, and Seller will be liable for all of Company's costs therefore, or (b) cancel the purchase order for cause under Paragraph 13.

White Alligators: Terms Unique to Selling Products

There are contract provisions that apply to selling products t hat are not found in contracts to sell services. The most common of these provisions are described below.

- **Shipping**—How goods will be shipped, who pays for shipping, how the goods will be packaged for shipping.
- **Acceptance of the product**—When it will be determined that the buyer cannot return the product.
- **Conflicts between purchase orders**—How conflicts will be handled.
- **Order changes**—Are changes allowed, when will they be allowed, how will any increase or decrease in cost be addressed, how will changes affect the original delivery date for the order.
- **Delivery**—Who pays for delivery, how will goods be delivered, what is the expected delivery date, what if the goods are delivered early or late.
- **Risk of loss**—Which party bears the risk of loss of the goods between leaving the seller's facility and being delivered to the buyer's facility.
- **Title** —Who owns the goods during the time between leaving the seller and being delivered at the buyer.
- **Returns**—Are they allowed, is a return material authorization required, if goods are returned what accommodation will be made such as repair, replacement, refund.
- **Favored pricing (most favored nation clause)**—agrees to give the buyer the most favored pricing the seller gives anyone else, but usually qualified to sales on substantially similar terms for substantially similar products in substantially similar amounts for the same period as the third party and does not include promotional pricing.

These terms address important issues in transactions involving goods.

Consider whether your company's business deals can benefit from including terms in your sales agreements or purchase orders that state how similar issues will be handled.

Review of a Purchase Order

This is a purchase order issued by a seller.

PURCHASE ORDER TERMS AND CONDITIONS

1. **Parties.** In these purchase order terms and conditions the term "Seller" refers to Miff Company of Boston and the term "Buyer" refers to the company purchasing Seller's goods and services.

   [It's as common to see no reference to a definition of the parties to the purchase order as it is to see a provision like this, because these terms may be included on the reverse of an order form that contains the name of the seller and buyer. If these terms are not attached to a document that indicates the seller's name, the seller should be specifically identified in these terms so a court interpreting this agreement would be able to determine what company issued these terms and conditions.]

2. **Seller's Acceptance of Order.** Buyer may from time to time submit written orders for products to Seller. No offer shall bind Seller until Seller has accepted the order in writing. On Seller's acceptance of the order, the terms applicable to the order shall be these Purchase Order Terms and Conditions. The contract between Buyer and Seller becomes effective on the date of Seller's acknowledgement unless Buyer has notified Seller in writing that it objects to these Purchase Order Terms and Conditions before that time.

   [The goal of this provision is to prevent the terms of the UCC from binding the seller to an order the seller does not want to fulfill because the terms are not beneficial. The UCC states that the seller accepts an order (thus creating a contract) when the goods are shipped. This provision causes the contract to be created much sooner, which is an advantage to the seller. Once the contract is created, the buyer will be in default if they back out of the order.]

3. **Buyer's Acceptance of Goods.** Buyer is deemed to have accepted the goods where Buyer fails to notify Seller in writing within five (5) days of delivery of the goods to Buyer of its rejection.
   [The UCC allows a reasonable time for the buyer to accept the goods. The short time frame here means that the five days will likely pass before the buyer even realizes the goods have been delivered. This prevents returns.) Notification of rejection to Seller must include reasonable detail concerning the reasons for rejection. Buyer may return a properly rejected product for credit, replacement, or refund at Seller's option. Goods not properly rejected will be deemed accepted. *(Under the UCC the buyer might be able to collect damages for rejected goods. The UCC allows the seller to limit remedies as the seller here has done.]*
4. **Orders.** Seller may ship up to ten (10) percent less than the quantity specified in any order from Buyer to Seller and such shipped quantity will fully satisfy Seller's obligations to deliver goods under the applicable order to Buyer.
   [Many buyers' purchase orders state that the order must be fulfilled exactly or the shipment will be deemed to be nonconforming as if the entirely wrong item had been sent. Because it's easy when dealing in large volumes of goods to receive a case of something that is short a small amount of product, this term is commonly found in sellers' purchase orders.]
   Orders may not be cancelled once accepted by Seller.
   [This is not a commercial term addressed by the UCC and is a smart business provision to have because it assures the seller that a sale will be completed.]
   When Buyer fails to accept delivery of any order, Buyer shall reimburse Seller for reasonable storage and insurance costs for the order until the order has been delivered to Buyer. Seller's invoice for storage and insurance costs shall be paid according to the payment provision of these Purchase Order Terms and Conditions. Buyer may not reschedule a shipping date or other time for performance without Seller's written permission.
   [This is also not a commercial term covered by the UCC, but in industries where orders are refused when buyers start experiencing the effects of an economic downturn, it provides some protection for the seller.]

Performance dates represent Seller's best estimates and Seller shall not be liable for failing to meet such dates. If Seller is more than thirty (30) days late in meeting a performance date, Buyer's exclusive remedy is to cancel the applicable order.
[The "time is of the essence" clause in many buyers' purchase orders is seeking to create a contract in which every date must be exactly met or the contract is breached. This clause is the seller's answer to that provision. It also limits remedies for missed delivery dates to canceling the order, negating the buyer's right under the UCC to damages.]

5. **Change in Terms.** Seller may increase the price, change the transportation terms, terms of payment, or minimum requirement per shipment at any time by notice mailed to Buyer thirty (30) days prior to the effective date thereof.
[The UCC has no provision regarding changes to terms of the contract or what effect changes have on orders already placed. It's a good business practice to retain the right to make changes to sales terms to account for your company's changing business needs.] Seller's price increases shall occur no more often than once every one hundred eighty (180) days. Buyer's failure to object to the change in regard to any order that is scheduled to be shipped after the effective date of the notice or placement of an order after receipt of the notice shall be deemed acceptance. Seller shall advise Buyer within fifteen (15) days from receipt of Buyer's written objection, if any, whether Seller will continue to supply at the terms and conditions in effect prior to the announced increase or change in regards to orders placed before the notice of change, or if the contract will be renegotiated at option of Seller.
[If the change in your company's purchase order terms will become effective after a buyer has placed an order but before it is shipped, your purchase order should indicate what effect the changes will have on the existing order. This provision provides the seller the right to renegotiate with the buyer if the buyer objects to the new terms. In reality the seller has this right anyway, but stating this might keep the buyer from simply seeking a new source of these products.]
The price hereunder may be decreased at any time by Seller.
[This provision contains some buyer-friendly terms presumably designed to make it more likely the buyer will accept these terms without objection. Heavily one-sided terms may encourage buyers to seek their products elsewhere.]

6. **Payment.** Buyer shall pay Seller net cash without set-off thirty (30) days from date of Seller's invoice.

   [Under the UCC, payment is due by buyer at the time and place the goods are delivered to the buyer. This is a surprise for most buyers, who expect a longer time to pay. If your company's purchase order is silent on payment, payment is due on delivery. If your company includes credit terms such as this provision does (payment to be made in 30 days), the UCC presumes that the time period starts from when the goods are shipped. However this provision negates that UCC presumption by stating that the credit period begins on the date of the seller's invoice. The UCC provides for a contract by contract right of set-off, so if your company does not want to be subject to this there must be specific reference to negate the right of set-off. A set-off is a deduction of amounts one company owes another before the other party is paid.]

   Buyer agrees to pay late charges of 1 1/2 percent per day on any unpaid balance more than thirty (30) days overdue and to reimburse Seller for all costs and expenses, including attorneys' fees, incurred in collecting any overdue amounts.

   [The UCC is silent on assessment of past-due charges or collection costs, so it's good practice to include them in sales terms if your company desires to have the right to assess them. The late charges here are unlikely to be enforceable because the annual interest rate equates to over 500 percent annually. Late charges or interest on past due amounts must be reasonable. Some states have usury laws that preclude charging interest over a certain amount. Your company should determine these limits in your state.]

7. **Failure to Pay.** Seller may alter payment terms, defer shipments, or terminate this agreement if Buyer fails to pay any invoice in accordance with the terms of this contract.

   [Under the UCC, if the buyer fails to pay, the seller can withhold or discontinue its own performance. The seller can also refuse to deliver the goods unless the buyer pays in cash if the buyer becomes insolvent (unable to pay its debts when due). This provision expands on what is provided under the UCC.]

   Seller may require cash payments, satisfactory security for future deliveries, or other adequate assurances of performance if Buyer's financial responsibility becomes unsatisfactory to Seller.

[The UCC already provides for this, so it's technically not necessary to be included here. The advantage to including a provision in your company's sales agreement that is already a part of the UCC is that if the buyer's purchase order contains a different term on the same issue, this provision and the different term will cancel each other out. Then the contract reverts to the UCC's treatment of the matter. By including the UCC provision, your company is almost assured of having the matter treated as the UCC provides.]

8. **Risk of Loss.** Risk of loss in all goods sold hereunder shall pass to Buyer on Seller's delivery to carrier at the shipping point.
   [Under the UCC all contracts are presumed to be shipment contracts in which title passes to the buyer at the point the goods are delivered to the shipper. However, risk of loss does not always pass with title. When the contract does not state when risk of loss passes from seller to buyer, under the UCC in shipment contracts this risk is presumed to pass on delivery to the carrier. Here both title and risk of loss would pass at the same time. This provision may seem unnecessary, because the UCC would have the same effect as this contract provision. However, in the next section the contract allows for the seller's transportation of the goods to the buyer, and in this case it might be presumed that a destination contract exists as to those goods. In a destination contract under the UCC, the risk of loss passes to the buyer on delivery to the buyer. This contract negates this UCC presumption if the following provision creates a destination contract.]
9. **Transportation of Goods.** If Seller has agreed to pay for transporting the goods as stated in an individual written order, Seller reserves the right to select the means of transportation. If Buyer requires a means of transportation other than that selected by Seller, any extra cost incurred by reason of using such other means shall be paid by Buyer. *(It's not clear in this provision if a destination contract is created. The prior provision allocates risk of loss and this provision allocates the costs of shipment. The allocation of risk in the prior provision would negate any implications of this being a destination contract.)*
10. **Assistance with Goods.** At Buyer's request, Seller may furnish technical assistance and information regarding the goods. Seller shall have no liability arising from such technical assistance and information or from the results of Buyer's use or nonuse

thereof. Buyer assumes all responsibility for its use or nonuse of such technical assistance and information.

[Under the UCC a statement by the seller concerning the product could be deemed to be the statement of an expert—(the seller—to a layperson—the buyer—that creates a warranty composed of whatever the statement consists of. This provision appears to be negating this potential warranty. The UCC requires disclaimers of warranties to be conspicuous, called to the buyer's attention, and in clear language. This is generally taken to mean that a warranty disclaimer is set in larger type than the surrounding contract. Because this provision is not in larger type or all capitals, it might not have the intended effect.]

11. **Seller's Right to Meet Competitive Offer.** If Buyer receives a written offer from a third-party seller unaffiliated with Buyer to supply goods of like quality, for a like use, and deliverable in like quantities as those supplied under this agreement at a delivered cost less than the delivered cost of Seller, Seller may, after receiving detailed written notice from Buyer of such competitive offer, within fifteen (15) days of receipt of Buyer's notice either amend this contract by meeting the competitive offer, or cancel this contract.

    [This appears to be an attempt to keep business that might otherwise go to a competitor. The UCC does not have provisions addressing this situation, but there is no reason not to include provisions like this if there are business reasons for doing so.]

12. **Warranty.** Seller warrants to Buyer that as of the date of shipment by Seller the goods shall conform to Seller's standard specifications for such products or to such other specifications as may have been expressly agreed to in the individual order issued by Buyer and agreed to by Seller and the goods shall be delivered free from any lawful security interest, lien, or other encumbrance. SELLER DISCLAIMS ALL OTHER EXPRESS OR IMPLIED WARRANTIES INCLUDING BUT NOT LIMITED TO THE WARRANTIES OF MERCHANTABILITY AND FITNESS FOR A PARTICULAR USE.

    [This warranty does not apply to any product that has been misused, neglected, or modified including improper installation, repair, or accident. In the warranty in this agreement, the seller has disclaimed the warranty of infringement, which is part of the warranty of title, and the warranties of merchantability, fitness for particular purpose, and course of dealings. The seller is warranting that the goods meet its specifications

or the specific buyer specifications and that the goods have no liens on them. This disclaimer meets the UCC requirement that the disclaimer be conspicuous, because it is set apart from the surrounding text by capital letters.]

13. **Patent Infringement.** If suit is brought against Buyer alleging that the manufacture or sale of any of the goods paid for by Buyer and bought from Seller, with the exception of goods made to Buyer's specifications, infringes any U.S. patent, Seller will defend Buyer and pay any awards against Buyer for such infringement, provided Buyer gives Seller prompt written notice and permits Seller to defend or settle such suit in its sole discretion.

    [In the prior provision the seller disclaimed the implied warranty that these goods do not infringe a third-party patent. In this provision the seller has agreed to defend any patent lawsuit if the buyer provides prompt written notice of the lawsuit and the buyer allows the seller to defend and settle the lawsuit. The seller may have undertaken this duty to induce the buyer to agree to defend any patent lawsuit brought as a result of the seller manufacturing to the buyer's specifications, which is what the second part of the paragraph requires. Notice that in the provision applicable to the buyer, the seller has not given the buyer the right to settle the suit, probably because settling could include agreeing to an action that hurts the seller but benefits the buyer.]

    If Seller is sued on the basis that Seller's manufacture or sale of goods made to Buyer's specifications infringes a U.S. patent, Buyer will defend Seller and pay any awards against Seller provided Seller gives Buyer prompt written notice and permits Buyer to defend said suit. Buyer assumes all responsibility for use of any goods either alone or in combination with any other products or in the operation of any process, and for the use of any design, trademark, trade name, or part thereof appearing on the goods at Buyer's request.

14. **LIMIT ON LIABILITY.** IN NO EVENT SHALL SELLER BE LIABLE FOR ANY INCIDENTAL OR CONSEQUENTIAL DAMAGES. SELLER'S LIABILITY AND BUYER'S EXCLUSIVE REMEDY FOR ANY CAUSE OF ACTION ARISING IN CONNECTION WITH THIS CONTRACT OR THE SALE OR USE OF THE GOODS, WHETHER BASED ON NEGLIGENCE, STRICT LIABILITY, BREACH OF WARRANTY, BREACH OF CONTRACT, OR EQUITABLE PRINCIPLES, IS EXPRESSLY LIMITED TO, AT SELLER'S OPTION, REPLACEMENT OF, OR REPAYMENT OF THE PURCHASE PRICE FOR THAT PORTION OF THE GOODS WITH RESPECT TO WHICH

DAMAGES ARE CLAIMED. ALL CLAIMS OF ANY KIND ARISING IN CONNECTION WITH THIS CONTRACT OR THE SALE OR USE OF THE GOODS SHALL BE DEEMED WAIVED UNLESS MADE IN WRITING WITHIN SIXTY (60) DAYS FROM THE DATE OF SELLER'S DELIVERY, OR THE DATE FIXED FOR DELIVERY IN THE EVENT OF NONDELIVERY.

[The UCC allows for limitation of remedies and damages, but provides that these are additional to those provided for in the UCC unless the contract states that the remedies are exclusive. Because this provision does state this, the seller has elected to limit the buyer to replacement of the goods or repayment of their purchase price for any claim under the contract—even claims unrelated to the products. These remedies are further limited to those where a notice of a claim is made to the seller in writing within 60 days of the delivery date.]

15. **Force Majeure.** In the event of breakage of equipment, terrorism, accident, war, fire, flood, strike, labor trouble, riot, act of governmental authority, act of God, commercial impracticality, or contingencies beyond the reasonable control of Seller or in the event of inability to obtain, on terms deemed by the Seller to be practicable, any raw material (including energy source) used in connection with the goods ordered hereunder, quantities so affected shall be eliminated from the contract without liability, but the contract shall otherwise remain unaffected.

    [The UCC excuses performance where something has occurred that the parties assumed would not occur when they entered into the contract. The contract term here broadens the UCC provision and eliminates the UCC requirement that the seller inform the buyer if any of these occurrences prevents its performance.]

16. **No Waiver.** Seller's failure to exercise on any one occasion any rights under this contract or applicable law shall not waive Seller's right to exercise the same right on another occasion.

    [The UCC does not discuss the effect of a seller waiving a right on subsequent enforcement of that right. When a company ignores a contract breach it may mean they can never enforce that part of the contract again. By including this provision, the seller's right to enforce a provision it chooses to waive on one occasion is retained.]

17. **Buyer's Receipt of Seller's Information.** Buyer acknowledges that it will receive or has received and is familiar with Seller's product labels, literature, and Material Safety Data Sheets regarding the goods and agrees to forward such information to its

customers and to those of its employees who handle, process, sell, or use the goods that are the subject of this information.

[This provision effectively transfers responsibility for proper use and storage of seller's products to buyer, perhaps providing a defense in the event buyer's employees or customers are hurt due to failure to heed the instructions and warnings presumably on seller's labels and other product information.]

18. **Entire Agreement.** The terms and conditions contained in this document supersede all prior oral or written negotiations and agreements between Buyer and Seller and any inconsistent course of dealing or trade practice that may previously have existed. These terms and conditions set forth the complete statement of the contract between Buyer and Seller and, except as otherwise stated here, they may be modified or amended only by a written agreement signed by both parties.

[Every agreement should have a provision similar to this—commonly called an "integration provision". This means that only this contract and the other documents specifically referenced in this provision comprise the agreement the parties have reached concerning the matters discussed in this contract. The trouble with this provision is that it does not reference the written document from the seller accepting an order, which presumably contains important parts of the agreement like price, delivery date, and what was ordered. By the terms of this provision, that written document cannot be considered a part of this contract. That makes this contract of not much use in governing the transaction between the buyer and the seller. This provision of the contract needs to expressly state that the terms and conditions in this document plus any written document indicating the quantity, specifications, price, and delivery destination of an order for goods between seller and buyer constitute the entire agreement between the parties.]

Seller's offer to sell the goods that are the subject of this document has been expressly conditioned on Buyer's assent to the terms and conditions set forth herein.

[Making your company's offer to sell the goods expressly conditional on the buyer's assent to these terms means that if the buyer does something that indicates it does not assent, like send a conflicting purchase order, there is no contract for the sale of goods to this buyer.]

19. **Governing Law/Venue.** This contract shall be governed by and construed in accordance with the Uniform Commercial Code in effect in the state of New Mexico except as the provisions of such code is modified by this contract.
    [This provision defines the contract as what is contained in this written agreement plus what is in the New Mexico UCC statutes. If the buyer is in another state, under the terms of this agreement that state's UCC provisions would not apply to this transaction.]
    Buyer agrees that any litigation regarding the validity, interpretation, performance, or breach of this contract, or in connection with the sale or use of the goods, shall be brought only in the state or federal courts sitting in New Mexico subject to New Mexico law without regard to its conflict of law principles, and Buyer consents to the jurisdiction of such courts for purposes of any such litigation.
    [The importance of including a governing law and venue provision depends on the likelihood of litigation over the agreement, and if there is litigation, that a state court will favor one company over the other. The venue for a lawsuit is also chosen to save the company choosing the location time and money.]
20. **Assignment.** Seller may assign this contract to any of its subsidiaries or affiliates; otherwise the rights and duties of this contract are not assignable or transferable by either party without the other's written consent.
    [Contracts are presumed assignable unless the contract states otherwise. This provision negates the right to assign except if the seller transfers the contract to another company that shares a common ownership with it.]

The appendix contains line by line analysis of a different seller's purchase order along with a checklist for reviewing agreements for the sale of goods. In situations where your company is the buyer of goods it should use the checklist from Chapter 10 to protect its interests, because sellers have very different interests than buyers.

PART FOUR

Exterminators and Stuffed Alligators

Buying Services and Products

CHAPTER 9

Contracts to Buy Services

A consultant delivers a custom software program to your business and it doesn't work right. The consultant is obligated to expend whatever time is necessary, at no cost to your company, to fix the program. A worker for the janitorial company that cleans your office trips over the mop bucket provided by the janitorial company and breaks his ankle. The worker sues your company for negligence. The janitorial company pays all the legal costs for this lawsuit and settles the claim with its employee, resulting in no costs to your company. The company that provides payroll services for your business is burglarized and personal information concerning your employees is stolen. Several of your employees have their bank accounts looted. The payroll company promptly repays the losses experienced by your employees. Your company achieves these positive outcomes because it incorporated the bulletproof terms and six secrets in the contracts it signed with these service providers.

In This Chapter

- Winning reasons for applying contract secrets to contracts to buy services
- Turning a contract to buy services to your advantage
- Using the service provider's proposal as a statement of work
- Review of an agreement to provide bookkeeping and payroll services

Winning Reasons for Applying Contract Secrets to Contracts to Buy Services

In the first scenario, the statement of work in the contract with the software programmer was highly detailed indicating each specific task that your company expected the software to perform when it was delivered. The statement of work also required that the software program perform to the reasonable satisfaction of your company. Having specific detailed requirements for the software program written into the contract along with a standard that the program must meet (reasonable satisfaction of the buyer) means that the service provider must correct the program at its expense if it is delivered and does not perform as promised. Otherwise the programmer has breached the contract and could be forced by a court to fix the program as well as pay your company for any damages that resulted.

In the second scenario where a janitorial company employee is injured, the service agreement contained an indemnification provision where the janitorial company agreed to indemnify your company for any claim by the janitorial company's employees related to injuries occurring or resulting from providing services to your company. As discussed in Chapter 2, promising to provide indemnification means that one party agrees to compensate the other party if a claim is made arising from an event described in the indemnification provision. In this case the service company agreed to compensate your company for claims against it by the service company's employees. When the jan-

itorial employee was hurt and filed a claim against your company, the service company was contractually obligated to step in and pay or defend the claim.

The third illustration, where payroll records are stolen, is resolved to the benefit of your company also because of the indemnification provision. In this case the provision requires the payroll company to indemnify your company as well as your company's employees, officers, and directors for any loss that occurs resulting from something the payroll company does that causes harm to your company and its employees, officers, or directors. Because the payroll company did not safeguard the payroll records and losses occurred as a result, the payroll company must pay for the resulting losses.

As these examples illustrate, including bulletproof terms and applying the six secrets can assure that your company gets what it pays for on time and within budget without losing time or money to disasters arising from having the service company do work for your company. If the contracts governing the three scenarios had not included these principles and techniques, it's likely your company would be stuck with a software program it could not use, would have lost thousands of dollars defending itself from the janitorial employee's injury claim, and would have faced costly payments to its employees to make good on their losses from the payroll company's negligence.

Turning a Contract to Buy Services to Your Advantage

To achieve an advantageous contract, maintain focus on what your company wants the contract to achieve. Then make sure those goals are specifically stated in the contract as tasks with deadlines and cost limits. Every service agreement should state a minimum acceptable level of performance, a final date on which the work must be completed, even if it a long time away, and a maximum not to exceed cost. It can't hurt your company's bargaining position and can greatly help if an issue arises.

When reviewing a contract for a client I was once told the timeframe for completing a security audit wasn't important to specify as it could be done "anytime" and the work only comprised about 40 hours of the contractor's time. The client thought that because the project was so small, it wasn't necessary to specify a due date. During the following year, the security auditor became busy and chose to complete contracts with specific due dates before this project, because it had no due date. Sixteen months later the project had not been started. My client was left in a weak bargaining position because the contract contained no deadline for performance. A simple sentence stating the work had to be completed within a year would have prevented this situation.

Consider the following issues and questions when reviewing a contract to buy services, modifying a service agreement form, or drafting your own contract:

- What is to be done, accomplished, built, written, provided?
- What expectations does your company have about how this will be accomplished—such as that the contractor will be at your company's site between the hours of 10:00 a.m. and 2:00 p.m. every day, that five interviews will occur, that the contractor will observe the operations of each of your 20 chicken farms for at least three days each, that the contractor will not contact your customers when they review your advertising effectiveness?
- What evidence will there be that the services were completed or accomplished? A report? A storage shed? A software program? A verbally presented system for treating disease in agricultural animals?
- What is the due date or deadline for completion of the services?
- Are there deadlines or due dates for any interim steps that your company expects to occur between the contract start date and the final product or result?
- How do you expect the final product to look? If it's a shed, how big is it according to dimensions? What is it made of? What color is it painted? Is it just the shell of a shed or is it finished inside with electricity and natural gas installed? Do you expect the area surrounding the shed to be returned to the condition it was before construction? Will the building debris be hauled away? Will it have to meet certain construction standards? If the final product is a report, what sections will it have? What subjects will it cover? Will a solution to a problem be included? Will that solution include details concerning implementation

such as costs and staffing? Will the report include details about what was done to reach the conclusion that was reached? How many copies of the report will the contractor provide? How long should the report be? If the final product is that the contractor will lead five training sessions on contract analysis, how long do you expect the sessions to be? Will handouts be provided? Will your company make handout copies or is the contractor expected to provide them? How long will the handouts be? Where will the training session be held? Will your company decide where and when the sessions are held or will the contractor? What subjects do you expect the training sessions to cover? You should include as much specificity concerning the services your company expects to receive as you can. Include the staff that will manage the contractor or that will be utilizing the final product in this process. There is no such thing as too much detail in this section of the contract.

In the section on payment consider the following:

- Will payment occur after deliverables are received by your company?
- Is receipt of a deliverable enough or do you want to condition payment on receipt and your company's approval or acceptance of the deliverable?
- Will payment be immediate (the same day) or do you need to provide that payment will be within a month or some other time after receipt and/or approval of deliverables or invoices?
- Is the time for payment calculated from the date of the invoice? The date your company approves the invoice? The date the deliverables are approved?
- How will payment be made—cash, check, wire transfer?
- Will payment be made in United States dollars? Euros?
- If payment is made after submission of invoices, what kind of detail does your company expect on the invoices?
- When are invoices to be submitted? Does your company require that they be submitted once a month on a certain date? Do you want to limit them to not more than once per week or per month?

- What about expenses—are those to be invoiced and paid on the same schedule as for performance of services? Should original receipts accompany an invoice for expenses? Must expenses be preapproved? Should the contract state dollar limits for certain expenses like hotel or airfare costs?
- If your company pays an up-front payment or otherwise does not link payment to receipt of a deliverable (so that it's possible that your company has paid the contractor and not yet received all the work your company paid for), does this contract need to provide a procedure for the contractor to pay back the advance fee if the contract is terminated?
- If your company terminates the contract before the services are completed, what is expected to be provided to your company such as work in progress? Be specific according to the services being contracted for.
- If payment is per hour, what is the maximum number of hours your company is willing to pay the contractor for the services? If payment is for completion of a project, what is the maximum your company is willing to pay for the project? State these maximums as a not-to-exceed figure. Otherwise the contractor can bill your company for almost anything and your company may be obligated to pay.

In the section on term or length of the contract, consider the following:

- Is there an effective date in the contract? Sometimes your company will want to sign the contract, binding the contractor to perform the work, but you will not want the contractor to begin until a later date. In that case the contract can be made effective on the date it is signed while specifying that the start date for performance of the services is a later date. The start date for the services should be stated in the "Term" section of the contract. For example, if the effective date of the contract is August 1, 2010 and the services are to start later, it could be stated as follows:

  Term: From October 15, 2010 through December 15, 2010.

- If your company wanted the services to begin from the effective date you could state that as follows:

Term: From the Effective Date [capitalized because you defined it elsewhere in the agreement] through December 15, 2010.

- Sometimes the expiration date for the contract cannot be known with certainty at the time the contract is written. In that case you can tie the expiration to the occurrence of some event and include a later drop-dead date. For example, if the contractor is retained to assist your company with 10 presentations to customers that have not yet been scheduled, the term could be drafted as follows:

  Term: From the Effective Date through completion of the Services (*assuming you have defined the Services as assistance with 10 presentations to your customers)* or December 15, 2010, whichever occurs first.

This means that the services must be performed starting on the effective date of the contract until the 10 presentations are completed, but if they have not been completed by December 15, 2010, the contract ends automatically. Your company will want to have the automatic end date to prevent the contractor from dragging performance of the services out longer than your company wants. Of course this only works if your company has tied payment to performance, because there will be no incentive to complete the work if payment has already been received.

The section of the contract that defines what services are to be performed should be written with language that makes performance of the required tasks mandatory. Words should be used that are absolute unless your company intends to let the service provider decide whether to perform the task. Use words like "shall" and "will" as opposed to "can" and "may" such as:

- "Contractor shall complete the report by May 1."

  rather than

- "Contractor can complete the report by May 1."
- "The report will include detailed costs for each recommendation"

rather than

- "The report may include detailed costs for each recommendation."

Using the Service Provider's Proposal As a Statement of Work

Service providers often offer written proposals that describe what the service provider can do if your company hires it. Often companies use this proposal as the statement of the service provider's duties in the contract they sign with the service provider. The trouble with that is that proposals are usually written to contain lots of possibilities but few commitments to complete specific tasks. After all they are designed to inform a customer of what could be done, not what will be done. If the contract goes awry there is little to hold the contractor to because the proposal didn't really promise anything and the contract contains no other statement of work for the service provider.

Proposals can be rewritten to be a good description of the services to be provided. Statements about what could be done need to be reworded to state what will be done and when it will be completed. If the contract has to be enforced by a court or arbitrator, what will be enforced is only what the service provider promised to do. Wording needs to reflect concrete, measurable promises.

Here is a short proposal to conduct an environmental audit:

> Following is a proposal for a safety audit of all of your company's sites in the United States. The purpose is to conduct an audit, described below, of the facilities and people in order to meet regulatory agency requirements that pertain to environmental health and safety. In addition we will look at programs that will cover you for issues relating to permitting of all facilities and processes.
>
> **ENVIRONMENTAL AUDIT:**
>
> - Compliance with Clean Air Act. (EPA)
> - Compliance with Clean Water Act. Ground water. (EPA)
> - RCRA Compliance.
> - Dry-well inspections based on local requirements.
> - Phase I and II inspection review if applicable.
> - Indoor air quality monitoring.
> - Exhaust, scrubbed, and fume hood certification.

This proposal doesn't really promise to do anything—it just describes what could be done. If it were attached to a contract as a description of the service provider's duties there would be little to enforce if the service provider failed to perform its expected duties. Below is a revision of this proposal making the service provider's duties more likely to be enforceable as part of a contract.

Contractor's Duties: Contractor will conduct a safety audit of Company's United States facilities, identifying regulatory agency requirements that pertain to environmental health and safety. Contractor will design all necessary programs that will cover Company for issues relating to permitting of all facilities and processes.
[Remember that if you have defined words, like "company" in the main agreement, you must continue to capitalize them here to indicate they are defined elsewhere.]

Contractor will assess Company for compliance with the following:

- Clean Air Act. (EPA)
- Clean Water Act. Ground water. (EPA)
- RCRA
- Local requirements for dry-well inspections
- Phase I and II inspection requirements
- Indoor air quality monitoring
- Exhaust, scrubbed, and fume hood certification

This description of tasks needs to be supplemented with deadlines for completion as well as a detailed description of what the final product is expected to look like and include.

Review of an Agreement to Provide Bookkeeping and Payroll Services

The following contract is for performance of bookkeeping and payroll services. It is annotated with comments in italics.

SERVICE AGREEMENT

This agreement ("Agreement") is effective ________________ between Service Company ("Company") and Moff Inc., ("Moff") for one year. *[Every contract must have a statement naming the parties bound by the contract, the date the contract is effective and how long the contract binds the parties [the term]. This sentence takes care of each of these requirements. Often these provisions are stated in separate paragraphs although there is no reason to do so if one sentence will accomplish the same result.)* For good and valuable consideration, the receipt and sufficiency of which are hereby acknowledged, the parties agree as follows: *(All contracts must have what the law calls "consideration," which just means that each party must pay something for the bargain that they receive in the contract. It may seem like only one party in a contract is receiving consideration where, like here, one party pays the other party to accomplish a set of tasks. However, the law sees this situation as both parties receiving consideration, because one party receives money and the other receives the benefit of the services. The prior sentence in this contract seeks to address any concerns a court reviewing this contract might have concerning whether or not the contractual requirement for consideration was met by stating that the parties have agreed that consideration exists. If the parties have agreed, a court will usually not question the agreement.]*

1. **Services.** Company shall provide the following services to Moff:
   - Routine bookkeeping including maintenance of Moff's financial records, reconciliation of Moff's accounts with financial institutions, and production of monthly financial reports.
   - Preparation of biweekly payroll including remittance of payroll taxes to governmental authorities in a timely manner.

   [It's always best to be as detailed as possible in the statement of services to be provided so that there are few, if any, unmet expectations on either side. If services are stated in general terms such as simply "monthly bookkeeping," the law will imply the services to include what is reasonable within that profession. If there is something specific your company wants to have done by the service provider, it must be specifically included the contract. If it is not, the service provider is not contractually obligated to perform that task.]

Company will provide these services in a timely, professional manner consistent with the standards for bookkeeping and payroll professionals.

[Service contracts should include a description of the standards that must be met for the services to be acceptable to the hiring company. At a minimum these should be the standards required of someone in the profession that the service provider is in. The standards should also include either the specific timing requirements for the services to be provided or a statement that the services should be provided in a timely manner. Leaving out a reference to timing means that the service company can perform the services within a reasonable time. Because what the service provider deems reasonable and what your company deems reasonable can differ greatly, if your company has expectations concerning when the services are to be completed they should be stated in the contract.]

2. **Performance of Services.** Services shall be performed at Moff's offices on Mondays and Wednesdays between 10:00 a.m. and 4:00 p.m. unless Moff agrees to a different schedule.

   [It's important for both parties to know the acceptable parameters for where and when the services can be performed. If your company had not specified that the services in this contract were required to be performed at its offices, the service provider could perform the monthly bookkeeping and payroll duties anywhere it likes. This may have been fine with your company, but if it were not and this sentence had not been included there would be little that your company could do to contractually make the service provider perform the services at your offices.]

3. **Payment.** Moff shall pay Company _________ dollars ($______) per calendar month for performance of the services.

   [This contract structures payment as a flat fee. An alternative would be to pay for completion of individual tasks or by the hour.]

   Payment shall be made on the last day of the calendar month, or the next business day if the payment day is a weekend or holiday, for services provided during the calendar month in which that payment was made or would have been made if not for the payment date falling on a weekend or holiday.

   [This means that payment is made at the end of the month for services provided during that month. It's more common to see payment made in advance in service contracts because the service provider will have to meet its payroll and other costs while providing

the services. Where payment is not made in advance, it's common to see a requirement that payment be made weekly for services rendered over the prior week, or to require payment of a deposit or retainer to cover instances where the hiring company fails to make timely payments. These payment arrangements limit the money the service provider must pay out before they receive payment. In this case, because your company is drafting the contract, it can structure the payment provision in whatever manner benefits it, as this contract does. Here your company receives the services for a month before paying for them.]

4. **Renewal.** This Agreement shall automatically renew under the terms specified herein for a one (1) year period on the expiration of the current term unless either party notifies the other in writing at least thirty (30) days prior to the expiration of the current term that this Agreement shall not be renewed.
   [I counsel companies to avoid agreeing to contracts that automatically renew. As the purchaser of services, the main reason your company would want to have an automatic renewal provision is to gain some assurance that the price of these services will not be changed or if they are, that it will be more difficult than if the contract expired after a set period. Having a contract in place usually provides a disincentive to seek modification of the terms of the original agreement. One reason to avoid automatic renewals is that they typically allow termination only within a small window immediately prior to the automatic renewal date and, unless you have someone tightly monitoring these dates, it will be easy to miss the opportunity to terminate the contract. Your company should weigh the advantage in having this service provider bound to a contract versus the difficulty your company will have terminating this contract.]
5. **Independent Contractor Status.** The parties intend this Agreement to create an independent contractor relationship. Neither Company nor its employees or agents are to be considered agents or employees of Moff for any purpose, including that of federal and state taxation, federal, state, and local employment laws, or employee benefits. The parties agree that this Agreement shall not entitle Company or its employees to workers' compensation benefits, unemployment compensation benefits, or any other benefits or protections that accrue from an employment relationship with Moff.
   [This section is included in this agreement in the event your company has to defend its

classification of the service company as an independent contractor, rather than an employee, for tax purposes. Even though the service provider may be a separate company from your company, it's possible for tax purposes they could be considered an employee. A discussion of this distinction is outside the scope of this book, but help can be found in IRS Publications 15-A, 17, and 505, as well as through many business associations and reference books. The fact that there is written evidence that the two companies agreed that an independent contractor relationship existed will be valuable if, for example, a terminated employee of the service company files a claim against your company's unemployment insurance stating they were your company's employee.]

6. **Insurance.** On execution of this Agreement and thereafter during the entire term of this Agreement, without limiting any liabilities or any other obligations of Company, Company shall purchase and maintain, at its sole cost and expense, the minimum insurance coverage at least as broad and with limits of liability not less than those stated below.

Commercial General Liability—Occurrence Form

General Aggregate	$2,000,000
Products—Completed Operations Aggregate	$1,000,000
Personal Injury	$1,000,000
Each Occurrence	$1,000,000
Fire Damage	$50,000
Medical Expense (Any One Person)	$250,000

Worker's Compensation and Employer's Liability insurance as required by the State of Nan Workers' Compensation statutes, as follows:

Worker's Compensation (Coverage A):	Statutory benefits
Employers Liability	$500,000 each accident
	$500,000 each employee/disease
	$1,000,000 policy limit/disease.

Automobile Liability—Any Auto or Owned, Hired, and Non-Owned Vehicles	
Combined Single Limit Per Accident	
For Bodily Injury and Property Damage	$1,000,000

The insurance requirements herein are minimum requirements for this Agreement and in no way limit the indemnity covenants contained in this Agreement. Neither party warrants or represents that this coverage will be sufficient to provide coverage for any specific accident or injury.

[Your company should consult its insurance agent to determine what insurance coverage is recommended for the possible liabilities arising from this specific contract. In some instances you will find that including or omitting certain language in the contract or failure to require certain coverage by the other party will void or reduce the insurance coverage your company has. Most insurance companies have booklets or handouts that they provide their commercial clients—usually only if requested—that outline the insurance coverage and contract language your company must require in your contracts to maintain your company's insurance coverage.]

Each insurance policy required by the insurance provisions of this Agreement shall provide the required coverage and shall not be suspended, voided, canceled, reduced in coverage or in limits except after thirty (30) days prior written notice has been given to Moff under the Notice provisions of this Agreement or where the coverage is replaced with equal or greater coverage by an insurer meeting the requirements of this contract and where there is no lapse in insurance coverage between the two insurers.

[Once insurance coverage has been required in a contract, make sure the contract language requires the coverage to be in force at the time the contract starts and to remain in force throughout the term of the contract.]

Insurance is to be placed with insurers duly licensed in the State of Nan and with a Best's rating of no less than A-.

[This means that the insurer must be financially strong enough to actually be able to pay out the policy limits if there was a claim and that the insurer is authorized to conduct business in the state where the coverage is provided. Financial rating standards tend to vary over time, so it's wise to consult insurance industry associations and your insurance provider for recommended criteria.]

7. **Compliance with Laws.** All services rendered by Company and its employees pursuant to this Agreement shall conform with and be in full compliance with all applicable laws, rules, ordinances, and regulations adopted or required by any federal, state, or local government.

[If the service company violates any laws, you or your company could be prosecuted as well as the service company. This could come about because by requesting that the service company perform the work, your company could be alleged to have either known or recklessly disregarded that a law would be violated. If there is a provision in your company's agreement with the service company that all laws must be complied with, it will provide your company valuable evidence that your company did not condone what the service company did. It also sends a strong message to the service company that your company expects the work to be performed in compliance with laws and regulations.]

Service Company shall maintain all necessary permits and licenses required during the term of this agreement.

[Your company should require the service company to have the licenses required by law to perform its work. If they do not and an injury occurs during performance of this contract as a result of something the service company does, your company could be dragged into any resulting litigation because it could be seen as negligent in retaining an unlicensed company. If the service company fails to obtain or maintain any required permit or license, your company could terminate this contract or seek damages for the breach. If maintaining licenses and permits were not required in the contract ,it would be much more difficult to terminate the contract due to the service provider's failure to have them.]

Service Company shall be entirely and solely responsible for the payment of employee and employer payroll taxes, contributions, and/or assessments, whether pertaining to federal, state, or local requirements, workers' compensation insurance, or other insurance, for its employees providing the services specified in this Agreement.

[Stating this obligation of the service company in this contract further emphasizes that the service company is the employer of any staff performing services under this agreement, not your company.]

8. **Confidentiality.** Company expressly agrees that Moff's non-public information in any form, which may include but is not limited to its policies and procedures, manuals, protocols, financial information, marketing plans, or contracts (collectively "Confidential Information") shall be maintained in strictest confidence. No Confidential Information shall be copied, removed from Moff's facilities, or otherwise disclosed to anyone.

[This is a very simple confidentiality provision that may discourage the service company

from copying or sharing your company's private information with third parties. The issue for both parties is that it is unclear what "non-public" information is. The service company probably won't know what to protect, and consequently your company may not be protecting the information it wants kept confidential. Unless a document is marked as non-public or confidential it would be difficult to enforce this provision against the service company. If your company has information it is maintaining as confidential information that the service provider may have access to, a separate confidentiality agreement should be executed between the parties to protect it. Note that if this is done, the integration provision ("This agreement is the entire agreement . . . ") in both the confidentiality agreement and this agreement must be changed to reference the separate confidentiality agreement.]

9. **Assignment/Sub-Contracting.** Company shall not assign its rights or delegate its duties under this Agreement.
[Without this provision, the service company is free to hire subcontractors, delegate performance of some or all of its tasks to others, or sell its business and assign this contract to the new company. This provision prevents that. Without a prohibition on assignment, contracts are presumed to be assignable.]
10. **Indemnification.** Company shall indemnify and hold harmless Moff, its parent, subsidiaries, affiliates, successors, assigns, employees, agents, or subcontractors from and against any and all suits, claims, losses, forfeitures, demands, fees, costs, expenses, obligations, or proceedings of any kind or nature, including reasonable attorney's fees that party may hereafter incur, become responsible for, or pay out.
[Indemnification means that the party who provides the indemnification agrees to defend any claim and pay any damages resulting from the occurrence of an event described in the indemnification provision The first part of this provision names a comprehensive set of people and companies related to Moff that might be sued or have a claim filed against them as a result of an act or omission of the service company. The next part of the provision seeks to be comprehensive in the kinds of claims the service company is agreeing to be responsible for. If the provision was limited to "lawsuits," then the service provider would only be agreeing to cover Moff for an actual lawsuit filed in a court of law. Instances where someone claims they were injured and is negotiating to settle the claim before filing a lawsuit—because then it would become public,

which the company might not want—would not be covered. Most injured parties attempt to receive compensation for their injuries prior to filing a lawsuit, and it's frequently smarter, if there is clear liability, to settle a claim this way. For that reason, being comprehensive in the kinds of matters the service company is responsible for is advisable. The next part of the provision states that the service company must cover not only actual payments made by Moff related to lawsuits and claims but also those Moff is responsible for but may not yet have paid. Under this part of the provision Moff could seek payment from the service company and then use this payment to pay the claim, instead of having to front their own money. From your company's perspective this is a great indemnification provision, because the service company is agreeing to cover any claims and lawsuits filed against Moff. The provision does not require that these claims be related to the contract or limit the service company's responsibility to claims and lawsuits filed against Moff arising from something the service company did or did not do. If your company is the one charged with indemnifying the other company, you would want this provision to continue with a list of situations that your company was agreeing to indemnify the other party in. These are typically one or more of the following: breach of contract, negligence, patent infringement, harmful environmental impact, and a lien or encumbrance.]

11. **Survival.** All provisions that logically ought to survive termination of this Agreement shall survive.

    [If this agreement ends, every provision in it is no longer effective. There are some provisions your company will want to continue to be effective such as Indemnification, Limitation of Liability, and Governing Law and Forum. In some cases there may be others like Publicity. The Survival provision allows provisions that logically are intended to govern events related to the agreement but that could occur after the agreement ends to continue to govern those events. An example would be where one party is sued concerning a service provided by the agreement, but the lawsuit is filed a year after the agreement ends. In that case, the Survival provision would allow the Indemnity and Limitation of Liability provisions to be enforced between the parties.]

12. **Termination on Insolvency.** To the extent permitted by law, this Agreement shall terminate on the initiation by or against Company of insolvency, receivership, or bankruptcy proceedings or any other proceedings for the settlement of Company's debts, on

Company making an assignment for the benefit of creditors, or on Company's dissolution or cessation of business. In the event of termination of this Agreement pursuant to this paragraph Moff shall be liable only for amounts owed as of the date of termination. *[If the service company is declared insolvent or files for bankruptcy it is possible that as part of the legal process involved, this contract could be taken over by another company, who would be considered to have replaced the insolvent or bankrupt company. Even though this contract may prohibit assignments, bankruptcy or creditor's rights laws may allow what is essentially an assignment of the contract to another company without your company's consent. This paragraph may avoid that outcome, although whether this provision is enforceable depends on state and federal law. This provision also provides that the contract terminates if the service provider is no longer a going concern. If the other party folds up shop but never declares bankruptcy, this contract technically continues until its expiration date. Including termination on insolvency avoids having a contract hanging out there that provides no benefits for your company.]*

13. **Notices.** Any notice shall be in writing and shall be delivered as follows with the notice date deemed by personal delivery, when delivered personally, by overnight courier, on written verification of receipt, or by certified or registered mail, return receipt requested, three (3) days after mailing. Notice shall be sent to Company at 1234 Work Street, Moxy, Nan 12345 and to Moff at 5678 Toil Street, Moxy, Nan 12345 or to such address as either party later designates according to the provisions of this paragraph.
[It's important to have a section stating how legal notices will be made to each other. If one party alleges the other party breached this agreement, you might not want official legal notice of this claim to be made through a telephone call to your purchasing agent. Contracts typically require one party to provide notice to the other party in the event one party thinks the contract was breached, where termination of the contract is desired, and in other instances specific to each contract. If your company forgets to state in the agreement that notice must be written, this clause would automatically require any mention of "notice" to require such notice to be written. Often legal notice is associated with a corresponding time period that must expire before the party giving the notice can take some action. An example would be where one party must provide a notice of non-payment and then allow 15 days for the other party to make the payment. In these cases there is frequently a dispute about when the time period began.

This clause might prevent many of these disputes, because it sets the start of any time period initiated by a notice to be on a date and time that can be easily verified or calculated. Including the address where notices must be sent is good practice to assure they are received where your company can best react to them. It's also wise to keep a list of all contracts that have these provisions so that if your company changes its address where it would like notices to be received, it can notify the other party to each contract—note that such a change of address would be a notice that would need to be delivered according to this paragraph. I recommend deleting a provision that states that notices will be made by fax as I have rarely found that faxes can be counted on to be delivered promptly or even to the correct person.]

14. **Governing Law and Forum; Legal Fees.** The laws of the United States of America and the State of Nan shall govern this Agreement. Each of the Parties irrevocably consents to the exclusive personal jurisdiction of the federal and state courts located in Nan for any matter arising out of or relating to this Agreement, except that in actions seeking to enforce any order or judgment, such personal jurisdiction shall be nonexclusive. If any dispute arises between the Parties with respect to this Agreement, which leads to a proceeding to resolve such dispute, the prevailing Party shall be entitled to receive reasonable attorneys fees, expert witness fees, and out-of-pocket costs incurred in connection with such proceeding in addition to any other relief to which such prevailing Party may be entitled.

    [The provision specifies where lawsuits arising from the agreement can be filed and what law applies. Note that often these paragraphs state where a lawsuit can be filed OR what state law applies, but not both. These are two separate issues. Each party will want to file a lawsuit in the state they do the most business in. That's usually because their lawyers are familiar with those courts, their employees will not have to travel to participate in the lawsuit, and it is generally thought that courts favor local "residents." This provision can be used as a bargaining chip in the overall contract negotiations. I generally prefer better business terms (price, delivery date, product specifications, etc.) over the right to sue in my state. I have found that many corporate legal departments are divorced from the business aspects of a deal and will insist on a forum selection clause (the legal term for this provision) naming their company's home state, even if their business people must give in on other key business terms. When their business people are

told they must obtain this provision, they will give in on business terms to get the contract past their legal department, because they can control the business terms but cannot control their legal department. Use this to your advantage when you believe the likelihood of a lawsuit is remote. The governing law issue concerns what law will apply to the case. Sometimes you see paragraphs that provide that lawsuits be brought in one state but applying the law of another state. In cases where lawsuits may be brought in federal court, the state law that will be applied to interpret the contract is important. Again, I would assess its applicability as a bargaining chip. This paragraph also contains a clause requiring the non-prevailing party in a lawsuit to pay the prevailing party's attorney's fees incurred in the dispute. Some states have laws that provide a right to recovery of legal fees from the non-prevailing party in a contract dispute. In the states where there is no statute allowing recovery of the prevailing party's legal fees, this contract provision would allow the recovery of attorney's fees and court costs. Having this provision in contracts is commonly thought to discourage the filing of a frivolous lawsuit or one not well grounded in evidence supporting the party filing it, because if the party initiating the lawsuit does not prevail they risk paying the other party's legal fees.]

15. **Severability.** If any provision of this Agreement is held by a court of competent jurisdiction to be illegal, invalid, or unenforceable, that provision shall be deemed amended to achieve as nearly as possible the same economic effect as the original provision, and the legality, validity, and enforceability of the remaining provisions of this Agreement shall not be affected or impaired thereby.
    [This is a common paragraph in contracts. Over the life of a contract, laws can be passed making some term in the contract illegal. To avoid the possible result that the entire contract would then become unenforceable, these provisions are included so that it is clear that the offending provision can be unenforceable without causing the entire contract to be. In reality, whether one provision can be removed from a contract and the rest be enforced is a matter of state law, and it's possible this provision has no effect in your state. However, including it is not likely to hurt your company.]
16. **Waiver.** No term or provision hereof will be considered waived and no breach of contract excused unless the waiver or consent is in writing signed by Moff. The waiver or consent to a breach shall not operate or be construed as a waiver of, consent to, or excuse of any other or subsequent breach by Company. By accepting late or otherwise

inadequate performance of any of Company's obligations, Moff shall not waive its rights to require timely performance or performance that strictly complies with this Agreement in the future.

[Where a contract breach occurs and the non-breaching party elects not to enforce the contract provision in that one instance, the non-breaching party may be deemed to have forever waived their right to enforce that provision of the contract in the future. By including this provision, if your company, for example, accepts deficient performance of the service once without claiming a breach of the contract, it could later claim breach of contract if the same deficient service were provided again.]

17. **Limit of Liability.** IN NO EVENT SHALL EITHER PARTY BE LIABLE IN CONTRACT, TORT, OR OTHERWISE FOR INCIDENTAL OR CONSEQUENTIAL DAMAGES OF ANY KIND, INCLUDING, WITHOUT LIMITATION, PUNITIVE OR ECONOMIC DAMAGES OR LOST PROFITS, REGARDLESS OF WHETHER THAT PARTY SHALL BE ADVISED, SHALL HAVE OTHER REASON TO KNOW, OR IN FACT SHALL KNOW OF THE POSSIBILITY.

    [I often have found that if an agreement contains an indemnification provision, it does not have a limitation of liability provision or vice versa. The two provisions are different and should both be included in an agreement. The limit of liability provision prevents the named party from being responsible for consequential damages. It can also limit liability for damages to a certain dollar amount. Make sure the limit on liability is for all types of legal claims, not just contracts. The remainder of this sentence excludes each party from liability for consequential damages, which are damages that arise indirectly from the harm that occurred. Consequential damages can be huge and include lost profits and the value of lost opportunities. These provisions must be conspicuous in the agreement to be enforceable, which is why they are usually set in capital letters.]

18. **Successors and Assigns.** This Agreement is intended to bind any and all of the parties' successors, heirs, and assigns.

    [If the ownership of your company changes, this contract may not be enforceable by the company's new owners unless you include a provision like this one that states that successors and assigns are bound by and receive the benefits of this agreement.]

19. **Entire Agreement.** This Agreement constitutes the entire agreement with respect to the subject matter herein and supersedes all prior or contemporaneous oral or written agreements concerning such services.

[Every agreement should have a provision similar to this—commonly called an "integration provision." This provision means that this written agreement is the only agreement that can be used by a court or arbitrator to determine what the parties agreed to. No other written documents or verbal agreements can be used as evidence of the agreement. Be certain that this provision lists every document that is part of your agreement such as the confidentiality agreement suggested in paragraph 8. Otherwise the additional agreements may be unenforceable as part of your company's agreement with the service company because of this paragraph.]

IN WITNESS WHEREOF, the Parties have executed this Agreement as of the date first written above.

Service Company Company

By: ______________________ By: ______________________

Name: ____________________ Name: ____________________

Title: _____________________ Title: _____________________

The Appendix to this book contains an analysis of two additional contracts to buy services, including an agreement to provide janitorial services and an independent contractor agreement. The janitorial contract is typical of what your company might draft as a result of receiving a proposal from a service provider that it wishes to accept. The agreement in the Appendix incorporates the proposal while adding legal terms and clarifying issues that your company requires. Independent contractor agreements are very useful agreements because they can be modified to apply to almost any service. The appendix also contains the checklists for these types of agreements.

The next chapter reviews contracts to buy products. These contracts are very different from service contracts, because state statutes called the Uniform Commercial Code create an automatic contract whenever goods and products are bought and sold. Contracts to buy products must focus on modifying this automatic contract rather than documenting what the parties have agreed to. It's not as hard as it sounds and there's a checklist to save you from random alligators, so plunge in.

CHAPTER 10

Contracts to Buy Products

Mark needs large quantities of pet shampoo, conditioner, disinfectant, and other supplies for his dog grooming business, which he orders through one distributor. The whole transaction is easy. Mark calls the distributor when he needs products, the distributor ships the items out accompanied by an invoice, and Mark's company pays the invoice within the month after delivery. The last order contained shampoo Mark's company did not order. When Mark contacted the distributor two weeks after he received the shampoo he was told the shampoo he received was a substitution for the shampoo he ordered, which was out of stock. Mark objected to the substitution and asked that the distributor arrange for return shipping at its expense for the substituted shampoo. The distributor informed Mark that it was too late to reject the shampoo. Mark argued that two weeks shouldn't be too late to return something he didn't order, but the distributor insisted that Mark's company had no legal right to return the goods.

In This Chapter

- Even if you don't sign a contract to buy goods, the law provides one
- How to modify the UCC to protect your company from alligators
- What if both parties send their purchase orders to each other?
- Defer to the seller's purchase order if you want to lose a limb or two
- Review of a buyer's purchase order

Even If You Don't Sign a Contract to Buy Goods, the Law Provides One

When your company buys goods but doesn't bother with a contract, one exists anyway. The Uniform Commercial Code (UCC) is a set of laws governing transactions in goods, which have been passed into law by all the states. Each state modified the UCC slightly to fit the needs of the particular state. For that reason, if your business involves buying goods you should review the UCC as it has been enacted in your state. State law is usually available on the Internet. The discussion in this chapter addresses the UCC in general and may not provide you with knowledge concerning a unique aspect of the UCC enacted in your state that might affect your transactions.

The major UCC terms are presented and discussed in Chapter 8. When drafting your company's purchase orders as the buyer of goods, review the UCC terms and decide which ones your company wants to eliminate or modify. You can accomplish that with a purchase order or a sales agreement—two types of contracts used to document the purchase or sale of goods.

Mark was forced to keep shampoo he didn't want because, under the UCC, a buyer has 10 days from delivery to reject an order. Because Mark waited two weeks to reject the goods, the distributor was correct when stating that Mark's company had no legal right to return the goods. Mark's company could have prevented this outcome by either placing the order or confirming the verbal order with the distributor using its own purchase order that contained terms modifying the UCC to allow Mark's company more time to inspect and reject an order.

How to Modify the UCC to Protect Your Company from Alligators

The UCC provides the commercial terms for a transaction involving the purchase of goods. It does not provide the essential legal terms that are needed to protect your company from serious risks. Only a few of the bulletproof terms described in Chapter 2 are included in the UCC. To protect your company, you need purchase orders or sales agreements that add some or all of the bulletproof terms from Chapter 2 included in the contract between your company and the seller.

Purchase orders are written documents that summarize an order for goods. They are often short and almost never signed. They can be sent by either by a seller, to document an order, or a buyer, to place an order. They state what is being purchased, for how much, when payment is expected, and how the goods will be delivered.

Smart buyers include bulletproof terms in their purchase orders. These contract terms become part of the contract for the purchase of goods if the seller does not object to them or, where the seller sends their own purchase order, where the seller's purchase order terms do not conflict with your company's. Bulletproof terms are commonly placed on the reverse of the purchase order. As long as the front of the purchase order specifically states that the terms on the reverse are incorporated into the agreement to purchase the goods and that the seller (when it is the buyer's purchase order) is agreeing to the terms when it completes the sale, the terms on the reverse of the purchase order are enforceable.

Sales agreements are signed contracts covering the sale of goods. They are common for ongoing transactions between the same buyer and seller or for large dollar purchases. Because they take time to negotiate and draft, they are often not used for small transactions or one-time purchases. Sales agreements look like typical contracts and are often lengthy documents with detailed terms covering warranties, delivery, taxes, and other details not found in purchase orders.

What If Both Parties Send Their Purchase Orders to Each Other?

If your company sends a purchase order to the seller documenting your company's order for products and the seller sends its purchase order to your company confirming the order, what happens? There are now two contracts covering the same deal and it's likely the two contracts conflict on some, or maybe all, points.

A contract is an agreement between two parties. It's obvious at this point that the parties are not in agreement. If the parties see the conflict and don't complete the transaction, there is simply no deal to document. If the parties complete the transaction, despite the conflicting agreements, the issue is murkier. Usually the contract is determined to be composed of the terms in each purchase order that do not conflict, and where the terms do conflict, the terms of the UCC where the UCC provides terms. If two terms conflict and there is no replacement term provided by the UCC, the two terms cancel each other out and there is no term on that point.

Although it sounds too confusing to be worthwhile, it is still wise to have purchase orders to document what your company buys. In many instances the other company won't have purchase orders or sales agreements and your contract terms will prevail. In many other instances where the seller sends its purchase order, the document will be so poorly drafted that it will have little impact on the resulting contract. In the remaining cases, your company is better off even if it only successfully incorporates one or two contract terms protecting it into the contract.

Defer to the Seller's Purchase Order If You Want to Lose a Limb or Two

By now you should be acutely aware that contracts are written to benefit whoever writes them. If your company defers to the seller's purchase order you are agreeing to very lopsided business terms. For example, here is a term from a seller's purchase order.

> **RETURNS**—With Seller's prior approval, goods may be returned for credit against unpaid invoices. The amount of the credit will be reduced by a restocking fee equal to 10% of the price of the returned goods.

Here is a similar term from a buyer's purchase order:

> **RETURNS**—Buyer may return the goods or any part thereof at Seller's expense within 30 days of delivery for a full refund or replacement at Buyer's sole election. Where Buyer elects a refund, such refund shall be made within 5 days of Buyer's delivery of returned goods to Seller.

The two terms clearly benefit the party that drafted them. This illustrates why your company should be the one drafting the contract terms documenting the transactions it enters into. Deferring to the other party's contract or purchase order voluntarily gives all the power to the other party.

Review of a Buyer's Purchase Order

Here is a typical buyer's purchase order for semi-custom electronic items. In this agreement your company, the buyer, is referred to as the Company.

> **PURCHASE ORDER TERMS AND CONDITIONS**
>
> *[A purchase order may have a definitions section or may have definitions following a defined term in the agreement. A word that is defined must be capitalized and any capitalized word, other than a proper name or those starting a sentence, must be defined. If there is no definition then do not capitalize the word.]*

1. **Definitions.** "Agreement" means these purchase order terms and conditions. "Authorized Buyer" means the individual employee designated in writing by Company for the purpose of providing the authorizations referenced in this Agreement.
[Authorized Buyer is an important term to consider including in an agreement of this type. Consider whether your company wants anyone to be able to change this order, or the specifications for this product, or whether your company wants to designate only certain staff to have this responsibility. If the purchase order does not specify, then anyone from your company may change this order at any time and the company will be bound by the change.]
"Change Order" means a written order to change a purchase order (PO) in any one or more of the following ways: (a) drawings, designs, and Specifications,
[Note that by capitalizing "Specifications" it indicates that there is a formal definition somewhere in the agreement.]
(b) method of packing and shipment, (c) place and time of delivery, (d) materials, methods, and manner of production and final product, (e) quantities, and (f) any other parameter Company specifies.
[Your company should always provide for the ability to change its order. If it does not, your company may be bound by the initial order and specification even if your company's needs have changed.]
"Company" means the company issuing this purchase order. "Confidential Information" means all Specifications, drawings, designs, inventions, improvements, developments, discoveries, and technical data supplied by Company to Seller and derivatives therefrom.
[It's important to safeguard any confidential information your company is providing to the other company. Even the fact that you are ordering the item may be something your company does not want your competitors to know. Consider what information you would like to keep secret that your company will be sharing with the seller as part of this agreement and make sure it is specifically designated as confidential information in the agreement. Be sure to include in the definition anything derived from your company's confidential information. Something developed from your company's confidential information may not be considered your company's otherwise.]
"Custom Products" means materials, supplies, items, equipment, work, or services Seller does not manufacture or supply for other customers.

[In this agreement the buyer is purchasing stock products as well as custom products. Stock products are defined under "products" below.]

"Delivery Date" means that certain date contained in the Purchase Order or any revised PO on which the Products shall be delivered to the location identified in the PO.

[Remember that under the UCC, specification of the delivery date means that delivery may occur within a short window around that date. This agreement makes the delivery date firm.]

"Hazardous Materials" means goods, chemicals, contaminants, substances, pollutants, or other materials that are defined as hazardous by relevant local, state, national, or international law, regulations, and standards. "Parties or Party" means both or either of Company or Seller as the context indicates. "Products" means products indicated by Company part numbers and incorporated herein by this reference, and which adhere to the mutually agreed on specifications ("Specifications") attached to the PO and incorporated herein by this reference.

[Notice how this secondary document has been correctly referenced in this definition so that it legally becomes part of this contract.]

"Purchase Order or PO" means an order issued by Company from time to time in electronic or written form, and any documented revisions thereto on Company's form labeled "purchase order," as well as any additional documents, including but not limited to Specifications, that may be referenced in or attached to the purchase order by Company. For the avoidance of doubt, Purchase Order or PO does not include the seller's purchase order or terms and conditions. "Seller" means the Party to whom this purchase order is directed.

[Make sure the definition of PO incorporates additional documents that you have supplied the seller that are critical to the order. These could include product specifications, trademark drawings, color samples, or designs. If these are not referenced as part of this agreement then the other party is not legally bound to comply with them under this contract.]

2. **Order Acceptance.** THE FIRST TO OCCUR OF ANY OF THE FOLLOWING EVENTS WILL CONSTITUTE SELLER'S ACCEPTANCE OF A PO: (a) written acceptance, (b) the expiration of five (5) days from receipt of a PO by Seller unless Seller rejects the PO in writing, stating in detail the reasons for such rejection, or (c) shipment in whole or in part

of any Products. Any acceptance of this PO is limited to acceptance of the express terms of the offer contained herein. Any proposal for additional or different terms or any attempt by Seller to vary in any degree any of the terms of this offer in Seller's acceptance is hereby objected to and rejected, but such proposal shall not operate as a rejection of this offer unless such variances are in the terms of the description, quantity, price, or delivery schedule of the goods but shall be deemed a material alteration thereof, and this offer shall be deemed accepted by Seller without said additional or different terms. If this PO shall be deemed an acceptance of a prior offer by Seller, such acceptance is limited to the express terms contained herein.

[This is a critical section of the agreement for both parties. It states when this agreement actually becomes a binding contract. The remainder of the paragraph is drafted to overcome a seller's purchase order if one is sent. It states that if there are conflicting purchase orders, the effect will be that a contract is formed on the terms in the buyer's purchase order. Whether your company's terms actually control will depend on state law, but this provision should throw more weight towards your company in the decision.]

3. **Price.** Seller will deliver the Products ordered at the price(s) stated in the PO. If the PO is placed on an open-price basis, then the price to Company, in the absence of subsequent written agreement, will not be higher than Seller's lowest prevailing price in effect on the date of the PO.

   [There should be a section in the PO stating how the price for the product is to be determined. Under the UCC an open price term means the price will be the market price at delivery.]

4. **Taxes.** Company will not be liable for any federal, state, excise, sales, or use taxes unless itemized on the PO and billed as a separate item. No sales/use tax will be added when an exemption is indicated on the face of the PO.

   [If a section describing who pays sales tax is not included in the PO, the Seller could add these later. This section clarifies the expectations concerning payment of taxes.]

5. **Specifications.** The Authorized Buyer or an officer of the Company are the only individuals who may authorize amendments to Specifications on behalf of Company. Amendments shall be mutually agreed to in writing to be effective.

   [It's important to define how amendments become effective. If there is no formal process either party can allege that the other authorized changes.]

This includes but is not limited to any change or modification that can impact performance, functionality, quality, reliability, safety, cleanliness, maintainability, serviceability, configuration, interface software and characteristics, interchangeability, replaceability, substitutability of parts, subassemblies and software, including embedded controllers, raw materials, piece part and subassembly vendors used, Products, and subassembly manufacture flow, or manufacturing site.

[This is a business-specific provision that should comprehensively describe what your company considers to be changes that would affect the product.]

The Products will be manufactured and will perform to all Specifications.

[The UCC requires the products to conform in all respects to the contract, so this is just a restatement of what the UCC requires. The value in doing this is that if the seller issues a purchase order with a different provision concerning conformance with specifications, the conflict between the seller's provision and this provision would mean that the terms of the UCC would prevail. It appears that in any event, this provision, restating the UCC, will govern the agreement.]

Any testing and calibration records, and certifications set forth in the specifications shall accompany the Product at delivery.

6. **Changes.** The Authorized Buyer may at any time issue a Change Order. If the change is a cancellation, paragraph 13 shall govern.

   [Sellers might not like this provision because it would allow your company to submit a change order a day before the product ships.]

   On receipt of a Change Order, Seller shall take all reasonable steps to minimize costs, if any, attributable to the Change Order. If a Change Order causes an increase or decrease in the cost or time required to perform the PO, Seller shall immediately inform Company. On the prior written agreement of the Parties, an equitable adjustment in price will be made based exclusively on the actual variable cost of the change, except that no claim for carrying costs shall be allowed. The PO will be modified to reflect any agreed-on equitable adjustment. Nothing contained in the foregoing will excuse Seller from diligently proceeding with performance under the PO after any cost of change has been authorized by Company.

   [This last statement binds the Seller to meet the delivery date in the original PO even if a change to the product is made a day prior to shipment.]

7. **Shipping and Delivery.** Products shall be delivered per routing instructions unless otherwise specified in the PO. If the Products are drop-shipped, Seller must provide proof of delivery by fax to the Authorized Buyer within twenty-four (24) hours of the drop shipment. All shipments shall be packaged in a manner that follows good commercial practice, with adequate protection from exposure to weather, acceptable by common carriers for shipment at the lowest rate, and adequate to ensure safe arrival. *[I have found that sellers and buyers frequently leave details concerning the manner in which a product is packaged for shipment out of contracts. In a dispute where one party alleges that damage occurred during shipment due to improper packaging by the seller, the law implies that what is expected is reasonable packaging where no specifics are included in the contract. As you can imagine, what is "reasonable" can be hotly contested. If you want certain packaging you should very specifically include it in the agreement.]*

   Seller shall mark all containers with necessary lifting, handling, unpacking, and shipping information, PO number, date of shipment, and the names of the Parties herein. A packing slip containing the same information, as well as the part number and quantity of the contents, shall be included inside the container. Time is of the essence to Company. *[The "time is of the essence" provision is a legal term of art that means that any timeframes included in the contract are absolute. If they are not met, the contract is breached. If an agreement does not include the "time is of the essence" language then a court may rule that if one party misses a deadline in an "immaterial" way (perhaps a few days or longer depending on the context) the contract is not breached, but the party whose deadline was not met may collect damages, if any, due to the missed deadline. Including this clause works both ways unless it is qualified here as applying to only one party. If you want to increase the likelihood that your company's deadlines are met, including this clause may encourage this. I recommend that whether your company is the buyer or seller you take special notice of contracts with "time is of the essence" clauses, and in a situation where your company has too many deadlines and not enough product, you make sure it is the contracts with this clause that receive product first. As the buyer, if your company needs to cancel a contract, it can monitor contracts with this clause for opportunities to negotiate with sellers who have breached the contract due to failing to meet a deadline. Your company may be able to arrange for canceling the contract in return for waiving the other party's breach of contract due to failing to meet the "time is of the essence" clause.]*

If a Product is delivered more than seven (7) days in advance of the Delivery Date, Seller shall reimburse Company for the actual commercially reasonable cost incurred by Company to store and insure the Product at a commercial storage facility.

[Providing for various events that may occur that would cause inconvenience or extra costs to your company is what a contract is for. In this contract, requiring the seller to pay storage and insurance costs for shipments received in advance of delivery dates is an example.]

Seller shall reimburse Company for all costs incurred pursuant to this paragraph, in United States Dollars, within thirty (30) days of receipt of an invoice from Company.

[Specifications concerning what currency payment must be made in are frequently left out of contracts because each party assumes a certain currency will be used, but it is never stated. If you don't want to be surprised by being paid in a currency you don't usually deal in, be specific. If you provide for payment in a currency other than United States dollars, include a provision on how the exchange rate with U.S. dollars will be determined, unless all your company's invoices are in the stated currency.]

If Seller fails to meet the delivery schedules specified in the PO, Seller agrees to pay for any additional shipping charges resulting from Company's request for express and partial shipments. If the PO does not contain a delivery schedule for all the Products, the Authorized Buyer may make subsequent written instructions with reasonable regard to then-current circumstances affecting Seller's ability to deliver. Such instructions will constitute the original delivery date in the unspecified portion of the PO.

[These are all very business-specific purchasing terms not provided for in the UCC but that may save this buyer significant costs.]

8. **Acceptance and Inspection.** All Products may be inspected and tested at reasonable times and places during and after manufacture and will be subject to final inspection and acceptance after delivery. Payment will not constitute final acceptance. Company may reject any Products that contain defective material or workmanship, do not meet Specifications, or otherwise do not conform to the PO. Company's inspection and acceptance does not relieve the Seller from liability for latent defects.

   [The UCC provides that the buyer is deemed to have accepted the goods where it has

had time to inspect them and failed to reject them within a reasonable time or does something to assert ownership over the goods. Payment might be considered asserting ownership. This provision negates that UCC provision. This provision probably does not effect that UCC provision. The UCC does not address latent defects, so that section of this agreement may allow acceptance to be conditional.]

On rejection of Products Company may, at its sole option (a) return the Products at Seller's risk and expense for prompt issuance of a credit for the amount of previous payments, if any, (b) return the Products at Seller's risk and expense for prompt replacement with conforming Products, (c) halt the Products for prompt correction by Seller at Company's facility, or (d) accept the Products subject to an equitable adjustment in price. All corrective work will be performed at Seller's expense. If Company elects to return nonconforming Products, Seller shall issue a return material authorization ("RMA") within forty eight (48) hours of Company's request. If no RMA is received within forty-eight (48) hours, Company may return the Products without Seller authorization. If Seller fails to promptly refund prior payments or replace or correct rejected Products with conforming Products, Company may at its sole option (a) replace or correct the rejected Products and Seller will be liable for all of Company's costs therefore, or (b) cancel the PO for cause under Paragraph 13.

[Under the UCC the seller has the right to fix whatever problem there is with the products. This provision removes that right and instead provides many buyer-friendly remedies.]

9. **Invoices.** Invoices must reference the PO number, part number, product description, quantities, PO line item number, Seller's packing slip number, unit and extended price. Individual invoices must be issued for each shipment applying against the PO. Delay in receiving an invoice, invoicing for Products shipped to arrive other than on the Delivery Date, or invoices rendered with errors and omissions will be just cause for Company to withhold payment without losing discount privileges or incurring penalties. The date of scheduled delivery, actual delivery, or of the invoice, whichever is later, shall be the date from which any discount is calculated.

   [This provision allows your company to take the maximum time to pay while retaining discounts offered by the seller. The remainder of this section contains business-specific terms that are the type of details that should be considered in your company's PO.]

10. **Warranties.**

New Products. Seller warrants that all new Products will (a) be free from defects in design except to the degree such goods are manufactured to Company's design, (b) conform to applicable Specifications, drawings, samples, or other written requirements, (c) be free from defects in materials and workmanship, (d) be merchantable and fit for such particular purposes and uses as specified by Company or otherwise known to Seller, (e) be free of liens and encumbrances, and (f) be free of defects in title and not infringe any patent, copyright, mask work, and other intellectual property rights of any third party for a period of three (3) years or for the manufacturer's warranty, whichever is longer, from the date that Company ships to its customer Company's product, whether that product is a spare part produced by Seller or a product that incorporates Seller's Products.

[This is a very broad and comprehensive warranty, which could last for many years longer than the three years that are stated. That's because if the product is not shipped to your company's customer for three years, the warranty would not begin until that shipment three years from now. The seller might have a warranty obligation for six years under this scenario. The UCC automatically provides for several new product warranties, all for four years. The provision here offers both express and implied warranties.]

Repaired Products. Seller warrants Products repaired by Seller to be free from defects in materials and workmanship for a period of ninety (90) days or for the manufacturer's warranty, whichever is longer, from the date the repaired Product is placed back into production, or for the duration of any existing new product warranty, whichever is longer.

[The UCC does not apply to services like repairs, so if your company desires to have a warranty on repairs it must include it in its purchase orders or sales contracts.]

Refurbished Products. Products refurbished (used products restored to like-new condition) by Seller are warranted by Seller to be free from defects in materials and workmanship for a period of six (6) months or for the manufacturer's warranty, whichever is longer, from the date the refurbished product is placed into production. At Company's option, Seller shall at Seller's expense, promptly repair, replace, or refund the purchase price and shipping cost of all Products that do not meet the warranties specified herein, or Company shall correct such Products and charge Seller with the cost of such correction.

[Usually the seller has the option to decide what remedy to provide if the goods do not conform to the warranty. Here the buyer is retaining that right.]

In the event of breach of warranty, Company will be entitled to avail itself cumulatively of all remedies provided in law or in equity.

[The UCC also provides that all remedies are cumulative, but if this is a provision your company wants to have, it's wise to include it so that in any conflict between this and the seller's purchase order, the UCC provision will prevail.]

Seller will make timely responses to Company's notification of breach of warranty and will respond with the understanding in all instances that time is of the essence to Company.

[The "time is of the essence" language means that all deadlines must be exactly met. The provision here applies only to the seller's deadlines. If the sentence simply stated "time is of the essence" it would apply to both the seller and the company.]

11. **Corrective Action.** In the event the Products are defective or nonconforming, or there are other material issues regarding the Product's quality, delivery, or other matters, on notice by Company, Seller must conduct root cause analysis in a timely manner and promptly provide a detailed corrective action plan to meet Specifications. Where a corrective action plan is required, Company may perform inspection, testing, and evaluation of the Products at Seller's facility by giving two (2) days prior notice to Seller.

[A "corrective action" clause is not often found in purchase orders although it is very useful if a problem arises with a product. If something goes wrong it's better to have set out ahead of time how you would like it handled, because negotiating at the time a problem occurs is never as good as when neither party is aggrieved.]

If a Product is returned for non-warranty service, Seller shall perform an evaluation of the Product at no cost to Company and provide Company with a report and cost estimate concerning the repair issues. Company is liable for the cost to repair a Product not under warranty only where Company has provided written authorization to perform the repair.

[Most sellers charge a fee to evaluate a product to determine the repair costs. This provision requires the evaluation to be completed at no cost. It also would prevent the seller from repairing the returned product without first obtaining authorization from your company. That might prevent a situation where the product was repaired at great

cost without your company's prior knowledge of the costs, but your company needs the product back and is forced to pay the repair costs to get the product returned.]

12. **Credit Hold.** Seller shall provide thirty (30) days advance written notice to Company prior to placing Company on credit hold, stating the issues and steps to be taken to resolve the issues that Company may take so that no credit hold is placed at the expiration of thirty (30) days.

    [If you are not familiar with this term, a "credit hold" is when a party accepts orders only on advance payment from a company that they believe may not pay if a product is shipped on credit. Credit holds are usually determined at the time an order is placed. They can be very disruptive to the buyer.]

13. **Cancellation without Cause.** Company may cancel any PO in whole or in part on written notice to Seller.

    [This provision could greatly benefit a buyer because it would allow your company to cancel at any time without liability.]

    Seller will thereon immediately stop work on the PO, or the canceled portion thereof, and notify any subcontractor to do likewise. Company's sole and exclusive liability and Seller's sole and exclusive remedy for such cancellation of Custom Products shall be: (a) ninety (90%) percent of the cost of Custom Products scheduled for delivery within seven (7) days of receipt of notice of cancellation, (b) eighty (80%) percent of the cost of Custom Products scheduled for delivery within eight (8) to fourteen (14) days of receipt of notice of cancellation, (c) seventy (70%) percent of the cost of Custom Products scheduled for delivery within fifteen (15) to twenty-one (21) days of receipt of notice of cancellation, (d) sixty (60%) percent of the cost of Custom Products scheduled for delivery within twenty-two (22) to thirty (30) days of receipt of notice of cancellation, and (e) no liability for Custom Products scheduled for delivery after thirty-one (31) days of receipt of notice of cancellation. If the terminated PO or portion thereof is not for Custom Products, Company's sole and exclusive liability and Seller's sole and exclusive remedy for such cancellation is payment of the agreed price for Products delivered or performed and accepted prior to cancellation. Seller's cancellation claim must be submitted to the authorized buyer in writing not later than thirty (30) days from the date the cancellation notice is received.

[The effect of this sentence is that even if the seller has a claim for a cancelled order under the terms of the contract, if the claim is not submitted in 30 days, the claim is lost. My experience is that it takes longer than this for a seller to even realize they can make such a claim. It's wise to specifically outline the payments that will be owed if an order is cancelled so that there can be few, if any, disputes later.]

Seller shall refund any amounts paid as pre-payments or otherwise for Products that have not been received and accepted by Company, as well as any amounts paid that exceed the cancellation costs.

14. **Cancellation for Cause.** Company may at any time on ten (10) days written notice cancel the PO in whole or in part if Seller (a) becomes insolvent, makes an assignment for the benefit of creditors, ceases operation, or has a receiver appointed, or (b) fails to perform, performs unsatisfactorily, or fails to make progress so as to endanger performance of any of its obligations under the PO and such failure is not corrected to Company's satisfaction within ten (10) days after receipt of written notice. If one or more POs or a portion of a PO is canceled for cause, Seller shall refund any payments made by Company for the PO or canceled portions of a PO. Company will return any Products it has received from Seller under canceled portions of the PO. Seller will diligently continue to perform any uncancelled portion of a PO.

    [If the seller becomes insolvent or closes down, the contract needs to provide some manner for the contract to be terminated, as this does. It's also important that your company contractually provide for a method of terminating an order if it appears the seller cannot perform or actually breaches the agreement. The difference between this provision and the cancellation without cause provision is that this provision does not provide any payments to the seller for the cancelled order. This provision does not include the right to cancel if the seller declares bankruptcy, because under bankruptcy law, a clause giving the buyer the right to terminate the contract if the seller goes bankrupt is likely to be unenforceable.]

15. **Assignment.** Seller may not assign any rights (including the right to receive monies due) or obligations under a PO without Company's prior written consent. Any purported assignment without such consent will be void. Company may assign its rights under a PO to any parent company, subsidiary, or affiliate on written notice and without additional consideration.

[If the seller is dissolved and its equipment and employees transferred to another company, your company would have to provide its consent to have the new company perform the contract. Your company could transfer this order to a related company at its choice.]

The Parties intend this Agreement to bind any and all of the Parties' successors, heirs, and assigns.

[Without this provision, if this purchase order is transferred to another company with your company's consent, the successor business could argue that this agreement is no longer effective and a new one needs to be negotiated.]

16. **Risk of Loss.** Title and risk of loss or damage to Products delivered in compliance with a PO will pass to Company on delivery to the F.O.B. point. All shipments will be F.O.B. destination unless expressly stated otherwise on the face of the PO.

    [Under the UCC all contracts are presumed to be shipment contracts where risk of loss passes to the buyer on delivery to the carrier. This provision provides that risk of loss passes to your company on delivery of the product to its destination.]

17. **Patents.** Seller shall defend any claim, suit, or proceeding that may be brought against Company or Company's customers for alleged patent infringement related to Products provided under any PO (provided that such claim, suit, or proceeding is not solely based on Company's design), as well as for any alleged unfair competition resulting from similarity in design, trademark, or appearance of Products provided under any PO. Seller will indemnify Company and Company's customers against any and all expenses, losses, liability, royalties, profits, and damages, including court costs and attorneys fees, resulting from any such claim, suit, or proceeding, including any settlement thereof.

    [This provision makes the seller liable for a broad range of intellectual property based claims.]

    If delivered Products, or any part thereof, are held to constitute an infringement and the use of such Products, or any part thereof, is enjoined, Seller will at its own expense (a) procure for Company the right to continue using the good or any part thereof, (b) replace the same with noninfringing Products, or parts thereof, or (c) modify the Products so that they become noninfringing. In the event of the impossibility of the foregoing options, Seller will promptly refund the purchase price of the Products.

[These are common remedies for a seller to provide a buyer where the seller's product is alleged to infringe a patent. It is equally common to find a complete disclaimer in a seller's purchase order for liability for patent infringement by a seller's product because procuring the rights provided in this section could be very costly for the seller.]

18. **Confidential Information.** Confidential Information is and remains the property of Company. Seller shall use the same care to protect Confidential Information as used to protect Seller's confidential information, but not less than reasonable care. Seller shall limit use of Confidential Information to the performance of Company's PO, and disclosure Confidential Information only to employees who have a need to know such information to perform their duties under this agreement. On Company's request, Seller will promptly return or certify the destruction, at Company's sole determination, of Confidential Information and copies thereof.
    [This is a very simple confidentiality provision. If your company wants better protection a separate confidentiality agreement should be executed between the parties.]
19. **Implied License.** Nothing in this Agreement shall be deemed to have granted a license or other property right to any Confidential Information or Custom Products.
    [A license is a legal term for, among other things, a right granted to another party by the owner of the confidential information to use that information. Licenses are usually written documents but can also arise by implication, such as when the owner of the confidential information requests that a manufacturer produce a product that can only be made if the confidential information is disclosed to the manufacturer. Even though the owner may not have granted a formal license to the manufacturer, the law implies that the owner gave the manufacturer a limited license to use the information by asking that the manufacturer produce the product. This provision in the agreement makes it clear that no licenses can be implied; only formally granted. This provision is often included in agreements so no inadvertent licenses are granted.]
20. **Indemnification.** Seller shall indemnify, defend, and hold harmless Company, as well as its officers, employees, and consultants, from and against any claim, loss, damage, cost, charges, attorneys fees, legal costs, liens, death, personal injury, accidents, or property damage that relate to or arise from Seller's obligations, duties, or rights under this purchase order, breach of the terms of sale existing between the parties, and any Custom Product or Product provided to Company.

[This provision requires the seller to defend your company and pay any claims or damages resulting from something the seller did or did not do under whatever terms are determined to govern over this sale or where the claim or damages result from seller's product.]

21. **LIMITATION OF LIABILITY.** IN NO EVENT SHALL COMPANY BE LIABLE IN CONTRACT, TORT, OR OTHERWISE FOR INCIDENTAL OR CONSEQUENTIAL DAMAGES OF ANY KIND, INCLUDING, WITHOUT LIMITATION, PUNITIVE OR ECONOMIC DAMAGES OR LOST PROFITS, REGARDLESS OF WHETHER COMPANY SHALL BE ADVISED, SHALL HAVE OTHER REASON TO KNOW, OR IN FACT SHALL KNOW OF THE POSSIBILITY. NOTWITHSTANDING ANYTHING TO THE CONTRARY IN THIS AGREEMENT, IN NO EVENT SHALL COMPANY'S LIABILITY ARISING FROM OR IN CONNECTION WITH THIS AGREEMENT OR ANY PURCHASE ORDERS EXCEED THE TOTAL PRICE SPECIFIED IN THE APPLICABLE PURCHASE ORDER OR AS OTHERWISE AGREED TO IN WRITING BY COMPANY, LESS ANY AMOUNTS ALREADY PAID TO SELLER UNDER THIS AGREEMENT.

    [This means that your company may be liable for damages that directly arise from your company's wrongful act, things like medical costs or property damage, but your company is not liable for indirect damages that occur because of the wrongful act, things like lost revenue, lost profits, and lost income. Indirect or consequential damages can be huge, so disclaiming them is a way of reducing risk in the contract. The last sentence limits the amount your company will pay in any damage claim to the amount your company is obligated to pay the seller under the purchase order. Because the limit of liability applies only to your company, the seller has potentially unlimited liability.]

22. **Compliance with Laws.** Seller will at all times comply with all applicable federal, state, and local laws, rules, ordinances, and regulations governing, including but not limited to, the manufacture, transportation, performance, and sale of the Custom Products and Products.

    [If the seller violates a law while performing its obligations to produce the products your company ordered, it's possible your company could be liable as an accessory or co-conspirator. Contractually obligating the seller to comply with all laws reduces that possibility.]

    If Seller has employees who will be performing work at Company, Seller must provide documentation verifying each employee has completed all safety training required by

OSHA. This would include an approved Basic Safety Awareness course and any additional job-specific training. All safety training of Seller's employees must be provided at Seller's cost.

[This is a good provision to include if the other party is going to have their employees at your location. If one of those employees were to be injured, it might limit your responsibility for the injury if your company has required the seller to provide safety training for its employees. Of course this assumes your company provides this training for its employees.]

23. **Hazardous Materials.** If Products provided in any PO include Hazardous Materials, Seller represents and warrants that Seller and any subcontractors understand the nature of and hazards associated with these materials. Prior to causing Hazardous Materials to be on Company's property, Seller shall obtain written approval from the Authorized Buyer. Seller will be fully responsible for and indemnify Company from any liability resulting from the actions of Seller or its subcontractors in connection with (a) providing such Hazardous Materials to Company, and (b) the use of such Hazardous Materials in performance under any PO.

    [This is a very important term if hazardous materials are a part of the transaction. If the Seller is providing hazardous materials, your company should require that they are appropriately labeled and packaged. If your company does not require this and your employee is injured as a result of the lack of labeling or safe packaging, your company could be found negligent. Technically the indemnification section of this agreement provides the same indemnification in this paragraph. Reiterating it here emphasizes the obligations to the seller.]

24. **Notice.** All notices under this Agreement shall be in writing and shall be hand-delivered, sent by an international common courier, or registered or certified U.S. mail, return receipt requested, postage prepaid, addressed to the last known address of the Party to be noticed.

    [It's important to have a section stating how legal notices will be made to each party. If one party alleges the other party breached this agreement, you might not want official legal notice of this claim to be made through a telephone call to your company's purchasing agent. In general notices should be in writing and mailed. I always delete a provision that states that notices will be made by fax as I have rarely found that faxes

can be counted on to be delivered promptly or even to the correct person. This provision fails to specify when notices will be deemed delivered. Most contracts state that a notice sent by mail will be deemed delivered after some number of days so that the other party cannot avoid the notice by refusing delivery. By leaving this out, the notice would be deemed delivered when actual delivery occurred.]

25. **Publicity.** Neither Party may make a public notice concerning the subject matter or existence of this Agreement without the prior written consent of the other Party.
[Publicity concerning the terms of or even the existence of this agreement may or may not be important to either party. Many publicly traded companies will want to issue a press release concerning a major sale of products. As the buyer your company may want to have the opportunity to review this release and edit it. That right would be provided under this provision. If there is no reference to or prohibition against publicity in a contract either party is free to publicize the existence or terms of the contract conditioned on not revealing anything that is designated as confidential.]

26. **Governing Law and Forum.** This Agreement shall be governed in all respects by the laws of the State of Nan and the United States of America. Each of the Parties irrevocably consents to the exclusive personal jurisdiction of the federal and state courts located in Nan, as applicable, for any matter arising out of or relating to this Agreement, except that in actions seeking to enforce any order or any judgment of such federal or state courts located in Nan, such personal jurisdiction shall be nonexclusive.
[This provision specifies where lawsuits arising from the agreement can be filed and what law applies. Note that often these paragraphs state where a lawsuit can be filed or what state law applies, but not both. They are two separate issues. Each party will want to file a lawsuit in the state they do the most business in. That's usually because their lawyers are familiar with those courts, their employees will not have to travel to participate in the lawsuit, and it is generally thought that courts favor local "residents."]

27. **Legal Fees.** Should legal action arise concerning this Agreement, the prevailing party shall be entitled to recover all reasonable attorneys fees and related costs, in addition to any other relief that may be awarded by any court or other tribunal.
[Some state law provides for the prevailing party in a contract lawsuit to recover its legal fees and costs from the non-prevailing party. If the state where a lawsuit occurs

does not have such a law, this contract provision would provide the same right. This provision is thought to discourage frivolous lawsuits, because the party filing one risks payment of the other party's legal costs if it is not the prevailing party in the lawsuit.]

28. **Severability.** If any provision of this Agreement is held by a court of law to be illegal, invalid, or unenforceable, that provision shall be deemed amended to achieve as nearly as possible the same economic effect as the original provision, and the legality, validity, and enforceability of the remaining provisions of this Agreement shall not be affected or impaired.

    [This is a common paragraph in contracts. It began to be included because over the life of a contract, laws could be passed making a provision of the contract illegal. To avoid the possible result that the entire contract would then become void, these provisions were included so that it was clear that the offending provision would be void but not the entire contract. In reality, whether one provision can be removed from a contract and the rest be enforceable is a matter of state law, and it's possible this provision has no effect in your company's state. However, it's not likely to hurt your company by its inclusion.]

29. **Waiver.** No term or provision hereof will be considered waived and no breach of this Agreement excused unless such waiver or consent is in writing. The waiver or consent to a breach of any provision of this Agreement shall not operate or be construed as a waiver of, consent to, or excuse of any other or subsequent breach.

    [This provision states that even if your company ignores a breach of contract once (and that would have to be in writing according to this provision), it doesn't mean your company has decided to ignore all future breaches. Without this provision, when a company ignores a contract breach it may mean it can never enforce that part of the contract again.]

30. **Force Majeure.** Neither party shall be held responsible for any delay or failure in performance of any part of this Agreement to the extent such delay or failure is caused by fire, flood, explosion, war, embargo, government requirement, civil or military authority, act of God, or other similar causes beyond its control and without the fault or negligence of the delayed or non-performing party.

    [This provision provides that if some catastrophe prevents either party from performing their part of the contract, it will not be considered a contract breach unless the catastrophe was the fault of the party who can no longer perform its part of the contract.]

Seller will notify Company in writing within ten (10) days after the beginning of any such cause that would affect Seller's performance.

[It is less common to see a requirement that either party notify the other of the occurrence of a catastrophe, but it is a provision that makes good business sense. Note that this notice requirement applies only to the seller, even though the provision relieving a party of performance applies to both parties.]

Notwithstanding, if delivery is delayed for a period exceeding thirty (30) days from the PO delivery date, Company will have the right, without any liability to Seller, to cancel the affected PO or part thereof.

[This is also not a common provision but, again, makes good business sense. The force majeure provision excuses performance until the catastrophe is over, but if your company is the party waiting, it will not want to be obligated to wait for months or years.]

31. **Headings.** The section and paragraph headings contained in this Agreement are for convenience only and shall not affect in any way the meaning or interpretation of this Agreement.

    [This provision allows the use of brief headings without being concerned that they will affect the interpretation of the agreement because they may not describe all the provisions in the paragraph. This provision is found less and less in contracts.]

32. **Survival.** All provisions that logically ought to survive termination of this Agreement shall survive.

    [If this agreement ends, every provision in it is no longer effective. There are some provisions your company will want to continue to be effective such as Indemnification, Limitation of Liability, and Governing Law and Forum. In some cases there may be others like Publicity. The Survival provision allows provisions that logically are intended to govern events related to the agreement but that could occur after the agreement ends to continue to govern those events. An example would be where one party is sued concerning a product governed by the agreement but the lawsuit is filed a year after the agreement ends. In that case, the Survival provision would allow the Indemnity and Limitation of Liability provisions to be enforced between the parties.]

32. **Entire Agreement.** With the exception of quantity, price, delivery date ,and product specifications, these terms and conditions supersede, terminate, and otherwise render

null and void any and all prior written or oral agreements or understandings between the Parties relating to the subject matter of this Agreement.
[This is a very important provision. It means that these purchase order terms and conditions plus quantity, price, delivery date, and product specifications for products constitutes the entire agreement that the parties have reached concerning their business deal and that no other written documents or verbal agreements can be used as evidence of the agreement if there is a dispute. This provision makes any verbal agreements unenforceable. If there are other written documents that your company wants to become part of the transaction or transactions that this agreement governs, you must specifically reference them in this paragraph or elsewhere in the agreement, as the definition of specifications does in this purchase order, or by the terms of this paragraph, they have no enforceability. In this case, this agreement governs purchases between the parties. These purchases are completed through orders that specify the product being purchased, the quantity of that product, product specifications like color or size, the delivery date, and the price. If this paragraph did not specifically reference those terms, they would not be enforceable against either party. However, your company would not want to simply state "With the exception of a purchase order issued by a party, these terms and conditions. ..." That's because the other party's purchase order could include their own purchase order terms and conditions. By referencing the purchase order your company may inadvertently incorporate those purchase order terms into this agreement. Unless the written document your company is referencing is something that has been signed by both parties and therefore cannot be changed easily, reference the specific terms, as this paragraph does, that your company wants incorporated into this agreement.]

The answer to the question "Are there alligators in that contract?" is "Yes, probably many". Try the quick review system with the next three contracts that cross your desk. Then you'll see how easy it is to turn a document full of risks and pitfalls into a career and business asset. After reading this book I am confident you will find most of the alligators and relocate them to a nice alligator retirement home. There may be some juvenile ones still lurking, but these don't usually take limbs off or cut careers in two. Happy hunting!

APPENDIX

Sample Agreements

Chapter 2: Sample Bulletproof Terms

Assignment/Subcontracting—Four Alternatives

Neither party shall have the right to assign or subcontract any part of its obligations under this agreement.

Neither party shall have the right to assign or subcontract any of its obligations or duties under this agreement without the prior written consent of the other party, which consent shall not be unreasonably withheld or delayed.

Neither party shall have the right to assign or subcontract any of its obligations or duties under this agreement, without the prior written consent of the other party, which consent shall be in the sole determination of the party with the right to consent.

Notwithstanding the foregoing, either party may, without the consent of the other party, assign the agreement to an affiliate or subsidiary or to any person that acquires all or substantially all of the assets of a party.

Attorney's Fees

The non-prevailing party in any dispute under this Agreement shall pay all costs and expenses, including expert witness fees and attorneys' fees, incurred by the prevailing party in resolving such dispute.

Choice of Law or Governing Law

This Agreement shall be governed by and construed in accordance with the internal laws of the State of XXX, U.S.A., without reference to any conflicts of law provisions.

Choice of Venue

Each party hereby submits to the exclusive jurisdiction of, and waives any venue or other objection against, any federal court sitting in the State of XXX, U.S.A., or any XXX state court in any legal proceeding arising out of or relating to this Contract. Each party agrees that all claims and matters may be heard and determined in any such court and each party waives any right to object to such filing on venue, forum non convenient, or similar grounds.

Compliance with Laws

Each party shall comply in all respects with all applicable legal requirements governing the duties, obligations, and business practices of that party and shall obtain any permits or licenses necessary for its operations. Neither party shall take any action in violation of any applicable legal requirement that could result in liability being imposed on the other party.

Conflicts

The terms of this Agreement shall control over any conflicting terms in any referenced agreement or document.

Cumulative Rights

Any specific rights or remedy provided in this contract will not be exclusive but will be cumulative of all other rights and remedies.

Force Majeure

Neither party shall be held responsible for any delay or failure in performance of any part of this Agreement to the extent such delay or failure is caused by fire, flood, explosion, war, embargo, government requirement, civil or military authority, act of God, or other similar causes beyond its control and without the fault or negligence of the delayed or non-performing party. The affected party will notify the other party in writing within ten (10) days after the beginning of any such cause that would affect its performance. Notwithstanding, if a party's performance is delayed for a period exceeding thirty (30) days from the date the other party receives notice under this paragraph, the non-affected party will have the right, without any liability to the other party, to terminate this agreement.

Indemnity

Each party shall indemnify, defend, and hold the other party harmless from and against any and all claims, actions, suits, demands, assessments, or judgments asserted and any and all losses, liabilities, damages, costs, and expenses (including, without limitation, attorneys' fees, accounting fees, and investigation costs to the extent permitted by law) alleged or incurred arising out of or relating to any operations, acts, or omissions of the indemnifying party or any of its employees, agents, and invitees in the exercise of the indemnifying party's rights or the performance or observance of the indemnifying party's obligations under this Agreement. Prompt notice must be given of any claim, and the party who is providing the indemnification will have control of any defense or settlement.

Insurance

Each party agrees to maintain insurance in commercially reasonable amounts covering claims of any kind or nature for damage to property or personal injury, including death, made by anyone, that may arise from activities performed or facilitated by this contract, whether these activities are performed by that company, its employees, agents, or anyone directly or indirectly engaged or employed by that party or its agents.

Integration Provision or Entire Agreement

This Agreement sets forth and constitutes the entire agreement and understanding of the parties with respect to the subject matter hereof. This Agreement supersedes any and all prior agreements, negotiations, correspondence, undertakings, promises, covenants, arrangements, communications, representations, and warranties, whether oral or written of any party to this Agreement.

Limit of Liability—Two Alternatives

IN NO EVENT SHALL EITHER PARTY BE LIABLE TO THE OTHER OR ANY THIRD PARTY IN CONTRACT, TORT, OR OTHERWISE FOR INCIDENTAL OR CONSEQUENTIAL DAMAGES OF ANY KIND, INCLUDING, WITHOUT LIMITATION, PUNITIVE OR ECONOMIC DAMAGES OR LOST PROFITS, REGARDLESS OF WHETHER EITHER PARTY SHALL BE ADVISED, SHALL HAVE OTHER REASON TO KNOW, OR IN FACT SHALL KNOW OF THE POSSIBILITY.

IN NO EVENT SHALL EITHER PARTY BE LIABLE FOR ANY INCIDENTAL OR CONSEQUENTIAL DAMAGES. SELLER'S LIABILITY AND BUYER'S EXCLUSIVE REMEDY FOR ANY CAUSE OF ACTION ARISING IN CONNECTION WITH THIS CONTRACT OR THE SALE OR USE OF THE GOODS, WHETHER BASED ON NEGLIGENCE, STRICT LIABILITY, BREACH OF WARRANTY, BREACH OF CONTRACT, OR EQUITABLE PRINCIPLES, IS EXPRESSLY LIMITED TO, AT SELLER'S OPTION, REPLACEMENT OF, OR REPAYMENT OF THE PURCHASE PRICE FOR THAT PORTION OF THE GOODS WITH RESPECT TO WHICH DAMAGES ARE CLAIMED. ALL CLAIMS OF ANY KIND ARISING IN CONNECTION WITH THIS CONTRACT OR THE SALE OR USE OF THE GOODS SHALL BE DEEMED WAIVED UNLESS MADE IN WRITING WITHIN SIXTY (60) DAYS FROM THE DATE OF SELLER'S DELIVERY, OR THE DATE FIXED FOR DELIVERY IN THE EVENT OF NONDELIVERY.

Notices

All notices shall be in writing and shall be delivered personally, by United States certified or registered mail, postage prepaid, return receipt requested, or by a recognized overnight delivery service. Any notice must be delivered to the parties at their respective addresses set forth below their signatures or to such other address as shall be specified in writing by either party according to the requirements of this section. The date that notice shall be deemed to have been made shall be the date of delivery, when delivered personally; on written verification of receipt if delivered by overnight delivery; or the date set forth on the return receipt if sent by certified or registered mail.

Relationship of the Parties

The relationship of the parties under this Agreement is that of an independent contractor and the company hiring the contractor. In all matters relating to this Agreement each party hereto shall be solely responsible for the acts of its employees and agents, and employees or agents of one party shall not be considered employees or agents of the other party. Except as otherwise provided herein, no party shall have any right, power, or authority to create any obligation, express or implied, on behalf of any other party. Nothing in this Agreement is intended to create or constitute a joint venture, partnership, agency, trust, or other association of any kind between the parties or persons referred to herein.

Severability

If any provision of this Agreement shall be declared by any court of competent jurisdiction to be illegal, void, or unenforceable, the other provisions shall not be affected but shall remain in full force and effect. If the non-solicitation or non-competition provisions are found to be unreasonable or invalid, these restrictions shall be enforced to the maximum extent valid and enforceable.

Successors and Assigns

This Agreement shall be binding on and inure to the benefit of the parties hereto and their respective heirs, legal or personal representatives, successors, and assigns.

Survival

All provisions that logically ought to survive termination of this Agreement shall survive.

Termination for Cause

If either party breaches any provision of this Agreement and if such breach is not cured within thirty (30) days after receiving written notice from the other party specifying such breach in reasonable detail, the non-breaching party shall have the right to terminate this Agreement by giving written notice thereof to the party in breach, which termination shall go into effect immediately on receipt.

Termination for Convenience

This Agreement may be terminated by either party on thirty (30) days advance written notice effective as of the expiration of the notice period.

Termination on Insolvency

Either party has the right to terminate this agreement where the other party becomes insolvent, fails to pay its bills when due, makes an assignment for the benefit of creditors, goes out of business, or ceases production.

Waiver

Failure of either party to insist on strict compliance with any of the terms, covenants, and conditions of this Agreement shall not be deemed a waiver of such terms, covenants, and conditions or of any similar right or power hereunder at any subsequent time.

Warranty Disclaimers

EXCEPT AS EXPRESSLY STATED IN THIS AGREEMENT, THE SELLER EXPRESSLY DISCLAIMS AND NEGATES ANY IMPLIED OR EXPRESS WARRANTY OF MERCHANTABILITY, ANY IMPLIED OR EXPRESS WARRANTY OF FITNESS FOR A PARTICULAR PURPOSE, AND ANY IMPLIED OR EXPRESS WARRANTY OF CONFORMITY TO MODELS OR SAMPLES OF MATERIALS.

Written Modification

> This Agreement may be amended or modified only by a writing executed by both parties.

Chapter Four: Checklist for Modifying or Extending an Existing Contract

- ❑ Document is numbered in title
- ❑ Clearly states it is an amendment, modification, or supplement
- ❑ Refers to name and date of original agreement
- ❑ Refers to parties of original agreement
- ❑ States parties have received good and valuable consideration for modification
- ❑ Effective date
- ❑ States term being deleted and states its replacement
- ❑ States term being modified and how it is modified
- ❑ Includes terms to be added
- ❑ Correct signature blocks and dates
- ❑ Agreement signed and initialed on all pages by both parties

Chapter 7

The following is an example of an agreement used in a repair business.

Service Evaluation and Repair Agreement

EQUIPMENT OWNER INFORMATION

NAME:____

ADDRESS:______________________________________

CITY: ________________ STATE: __________ ZIP: _____

HOME PHONE: __________ WORK PHONE: ______________

DESCRIPTION OF EQUIPMENT

MAKE: ______________________________ MODEL: ________________________________

SERIAL NUMBER: ______________________ COLOR: _______________________________

APPROX. AGE:_______________ PROBLEM: _____________________________________

____

____

DIAGNOSTIC FEE (Must be paid prior to service evaluation)

$_________________ Date Paid __________________

[This section should describe the equipment being left for repair so that anyone reading the contract could pick this equipment out among a group of similar equipment.]

AGREEMENT

1. **Terms**—The Diagnostic Fee must be paid when the item is checked in for service and is nonrefundable. When Company has completed its examination of the equipment, Company will contact the owner listed above to discuss the results of the examination. Owner may be presented with a Repair Price Quote. If a Repair Price Quote is provided, Owner must authorize the repair before Company will proceed to repair the Equipment. If the Repair is authorized the Diagnostic fee paid by Owner will be credited towards the Repair Price Quote.

   [The service agreement should describe, like all service contracts, what your company is contracting to do for the customer. It should also indicate payment conditions like this section does, where the nonrefundable nature of the diagnostic fee is stated, as well as the fact that the fee must be paid up front.]

2. **Repair Price Quotes**—The price quoted to repair the Equipment is good for five business days from the date the Owner is notified by phone of the Quote. On the expiration of the fifth business day the Quote will no longer be honored and the Equipment must be picked up by Owner within thirty (30) days. Company relies on the Owner to accurately describe all problems in order to properly determine the cost of repair. If the problem description proves to be inaccurate or incomplete, additional charges may apply. Company may not be able to repair your Equipment through no fault of Company's and you will be informed if this is the case.

   [Anytime your company quotes a price for something, the quote should carry an expi-

ration date. Legally the quote is an offer, and if there is no expiration date on the offer, it's possible the customer could accept the offer in a year when your costs have increased. If your company is relying on the customer to assist in the diagnosis and repair, it's important to state this so that if the repair is not successful due to an undisclosed issue, your company will not be deemed to have breached the warranty provided in the agreement.]

3. **Warranty**—Company's technicians will use generally recognized commercial practices and standards to resolve all reported issues.

   [This is the warranty this company is providing. It is not a promise that the equipment will work for any length of time, just that the issues that the customer identified above will be resolved. It's more common to see a warranty that the equipment will function for 60 or 90 days after repair.]

   Company will re-repair any repair not performed in accordance with the foregoing warranty, provided that Company receives notice from Owner within thirty (30) days after the Equipment is returned to Owner.

   [It's important to specifically state what your company will do if the equipment malfunctions while under warranty. If you do not elect a remedy, the customer may elect a remedy, which could be a refund, repair of the equipment at your company's expense, or payment of damages. Because the warranty offered here is not for a specific time period, the condition that the company receive notice of any malfunction within 30 days has the effect of being a thirty-day warranty.]

   If Company is unable within a reasonable time to re-repair the Equipment, Company will refund the Repair Price Quote paid by Owner.

   [Again it's important to elect your remedies if the attempt to repair the equipment fails. Otherwise the customer may elect a costlier remedy.]

   These warranties will not apply if Company determines that the re-repair is due to improper or inadequate maintenance or calibration or improper use or operation of the Equipment.

   [If a requirement is not included that the customer properly use the equipment, your company could be liable to repair the equipment even if the malfunction is due to something the customer did rather than any defect in your company's services.]

THE ABOVE WARRANTIES ARE EXCLUSIVE AND NO OTHER WARRANTY, WHETHER WRITTEN OR ORAL, IS EXPRESSED OR IMPLIED. COMPANY SPECIFICALLY DISCLAIMS THE IMPLIED WARRANTIES OF MERCHANTABILITY AND FITNESS FOR A PARTICULAR PURPOSE.

[Certain warranties may be implied by law, depending on the contract and the state where it is entered into. The law requires a disclaimer or limitation on implied warranties to be conspicuous in the contract. If the remedy in the contract is exclusive, this must also be conspicuous. This is generally deemed to mean that the limitation or disclaimer is set off from the rest of the contract through the use of all capital letters, bold or colored type, or some other device making it stand out. The effect of this provision is to limit the liability of your company to the customer to either repair of equipment that was not fixed or did not remain fixed for 30 days after its return to the customer or to refund the cost of the repair. The customer could elect no other remedy.]

4. **Abandonment**—Equipment not picked up by the Owner within *30 days* of the date the Diagnostic Fee is paid is considered abandoned without notice and becomes the sole property of Company, which may dispose of the Equipment in any manner it chooses without payment or notice to Owner.

   [State law usually sets out the number of days the owner of something may leave it at a business before it is considered abandoned. You can state the same time frame in your service agreement or vary it. Either way it's a good practice to inform the equipment's owner of the deadline for retrieving the equipment and that it will be abandoned without notice or payment for its value. If the contract does not state this, your company must store it for the owner until the limits set by state law.]

5. **Limitation of Liability**—COMPANY'S LIABILITY TO OWNER UNDER THIS AGREEMENT FOR DAMAGES OR LOSSES OF ANY KIND OR NATURE RESULTING FROM COMPANY'S BREACH OF THIS AGREEMENT OR NEGLIGENT CONDUCT SHALL BE LIMITED TO THE AMOUNT PAID TO COMPANY BY OWNER UNDER THIS AGREEMENT.

   [Your company can limit its liability to the owner for any claim the owner may have against your company. Without this limitation on liability, your company can be legally obligated for many types of damages as well as the equipment owner's legal costs. Liability limit provisions should also be conspicuous.]

6. **Complete Agreement**—This agreement constitutes the complete agreement between Company and Owner and supersedes all prior or contemporaneous agreements or representations, written or oral, concerning the subject matter of this agreement. This agreement may not be modified or amended except in writing signed by Company and Owner (no other act, document, usage, or custom shall be deemed to amend or modify this agreement).
[Every agreement should have a provision similar to this—commonly called an "integration provision". This means that only this contract comprises the agreement the parties have reached concerning the repair of this equipment. A provision like this makes it unlikely any verbal statements—"They said they would fix it for free." "The technician said there was a 90 day warranty."—would be enforceable to prove what the parties agreed to.]

ACCEPTANCE OF TERMS AND AUTHORIZATION FOR EVALUATION

My signature below indicates that I accept these terms and conditions and authorize Company to conduct any and all evaluations that it, in its sole discretion, determines are necessary to diagnose the condition of the equipment listed above.

Owner: ______________________________ Date: __________________________

[Repair agreements should always be signed as evidence that the customer agreed to the terms in the agreement. Otherwise it will be difficult to hold the customer to these terms.]

REPAIR PRICE QUOTE

Date of Quote: ______________________ Technician: _________________________

Who was contacted: _________________ How/At what number: ________________

Repair Authorized: __________________ Date Promised: _____________________

ACKNOWLEDGEMENT OF RETURN OF EQUIPMENT

I acknowledge that the Equipment referenced above has been returned to me:

Owner: __________________________ Date: ________________________

[Service agreements should document that the equipment was returned. If there is no written indication that the owner retrieved the equipment, your company is leaving itself open to a claim that it was not, even though it was.]

Service agreements should also anticipate possible claims or controversies against your company and seek to resolve them through the contract. Put some thought into this and draft provisions in your service agreements that head off the claims or controversies. Some possible claims here are for non-return of the equipment or that the equipment broke after being returned repaired. This contract has addressed these by including a limited warranty, a limitation on damages, a requirement that the equipment be properly maintained after return, and a requirement that the owner indicate that the equipment has been returned by signing for it. Each type of service will have differing claims or controversies that need to be addressed. For example, a pet-sitting business might need to address what the pet-sitter's responsibility is if the pet becomes ill and the pet owner's responsibility of the pet-sitter is injured on the pet owner's property. A facility manager for a defense contractor might need to address maintaining the company's security and safety procedures in a contract the manager enters into with an on-site repair contractor.

The following is an example of a service agreement where the services are construction.

CONSTRUCTION AGREEMENT

This Construction Agreement is made this 10th day of December 2009 by and between Fancy Construction LLC located at 12 Hope Street, Boston, MA (hereinafter called Contractor) and Mary Smith located at 20 Charity Street, Boston, MA (hereinafter called Owner).

[By linking a description with a specific word in the parens it is no longer necessary, after this point in the agreement, to use the official legal name of either party, because you have legally made the association between the shorthand terms "Contractor" and "Owner" and the specific description. This can also be accomplished by placing the shorthand term in quotes after the description.]

WITNESSETH *This legal term is unnecessary but is still found in many agreements.*

Owner and Contractor, for the considerations named below, agree as follows:

[Somewhere, usually at the start of the agreement, it's important to state that the parties are entering into an agreement, that there is consideration for the agreement, and that what has been agreed is written in the document. This sentence accomplishes that.]

CONSTRUCTION

Contractor shall furnish all labor and materials necessary to replace ten kitchen cabinets in the home at 20 Charity Street, Boston, MA (hereinafter referred to as Project). Owner warrants that she is the owner of this property and has the legal right to authorize this work.

[As in all contracts, your company must identify with specificity what service it is contracting to perform. In a construction contract that means identifying where the construction will occur, what labor and materials are being provided, and what is being constructed according to what specifications. If your company's service involves changing or repairing something, it's wise to obtain a statement from the person hiring your company that they promise they have the authority to authorize work on the thing being changed or repaired. Your company will need this if the true owner of the house or the equipment sues your company for making unauthorized changes to their stuff.]

PLANS

Contractor shall construct the Project in conformance with the attached Drawing, which describes specifications and costs.

[In all construction agreements there should be a separate document with detailed drawings and specifications of what is to be done. This also applies to landscape remodels, interior design, or anything else where your company is modifying or creating property. Services such as furniture refinishing or plumbing repair could be described in the body of the document.]

The Project will be completed in a workmanlike manner.

[This means that your company must perform up to the standards generally accepted in the industry in which your company operates.]

Contractor is not responsible for labor or materials other than those listed in the Drawing.

[This limits your company's responsibility to what is stated in the attachment. If some additional materials are needed your company could charge extra for them.]

Contractor reserves the right to make changes and/or substitutions to the specifications in the Drawing as may be necessary because of the unavailability of materials through Contractor's ordinary and usual sources of supply, provided the changes are of equal or better quality and there are no additional costs to Owner.

[If a provision allowing substitutions is not included, if the materials described in the attachment are not available, it could be a basis for the owner to claim the contract was

breached, either because the completion date is not met or your company failed to provide what it promised. Construction contracts should always include a provision indicating what effect inability to obtain required materials will have on the agreement, such as this provision does. They should also address the possibility that something will occur that will make a specific product much more expensive than the original contract contemplated. As the business performing this construction, your company should build into the contract contingencies for recovering unexpected price increases in materials or labor.]

TIME

Contractor shall begin the Project on January 5, 2010 and shall complete it by March 31, 2010.

[I have seen many contracts without start or end dates. Where there are none, the contractor could start the work anytime, perhaps a year later, and complete it whenever that happened to occur. However, having also served as the attorney for a state agency overseeing contractors, I know that the failure to start or complete a project in a timely manner is one of the chief sources of complaints by customers. From a customer-relations perspective I would always recommend including a start date and end date for the work, providing plenty of time to complete the project. I would not do what the drafter of this contract has done and contractually obligate itself to start this project exactly on January 5, 2010 though. Many occurrences could prevent starting on this exact date. It would be better to state "on or about January 5, 2010" to allow some leeway.]

This commitment is conditioned on access to the Project location between the hours of 7:00 a.m. and 4:00 p.m. Monday through Friday. Should access not be available for all or any portion of this time, the Project's completion date of March 31, 2010 may be extended or the Project cost may be increased.

[Consider thoroughly every contingency within the owner's control that could prevent your company from completing this work in a timely manner or with the quality your company promises. In remodeling, access to the site is critical. In other types of services other resources will be critical, like availability of the other party's staff for feedback or decisions, or access to the other party's financial records or computer system. Anything that the other party must provide for your company to complete its work should be required in the contract, along with a specific consequence if the required resource is not made available.]

OWNER'S RESPONSIBILITIES

Owner shall provide access to the Project location as described above. The actual Project site shall be cleared of all personal items, broom clean, and free of debris. When Contractor is working on the Project at the Project site, Owner shall cause there to be no people or animals within the boundaries of the area determined by Contractor other than those authorized by Contractor. Owner shall safeguard any Contractor materials necessary to be left at the project site prior to completion of the Project. Owner shall provide uninterrupted water and 220-volt electrical service to the Project site.

[This provision continues to detail the resources and cooperation this company requires to perform its work. It's wise to think about your company's needs completely and thoroughly If your company has failed to require something in the contract that the owner needs to provide, your company cannot complain that its performance was delayed or hampered by the other party's failure.]

PAYMENT

Owner shall pay contractor the sum of Five Thousand Dollars ($5,000) for completion of the Project. This amount shall be paid as follows: One Thousand Dollars ($1,000) on signing this agreement and Four Thousand Dollars ($4,000) within three days of Contractor's notice that the Project is completed.

[Payment provisions should always state what is owed, and when and how it is to be paid. Be careful that the triggers for payment be dates or events that are not subject to interpretation. If this provision had simply stated that the final payment was owed at the Project's completion there could be a dispute as to whether the project was complete or not. By stating that the project completion is to be determined by the contractor, there can be no dispute about when the final payment is due. The payment provision should also specify how payment should be made, such as by check or in cash.]

CONTRACTOR'S RIGHT TO TERMINATE

If Contractor's access to the Project site is restricted for any reason for a period of seven (7) days or more, through no fault of the Contractor, then Contractor on seven (7) days' written notice to Owner may terminate this contract and recover from Owner payment for all work completed, any loss sustained, and reasonable profit and damages.

[This is the only discussion of termination in this contract. The only basis for termination

belongs to the contractor, and only if access to the site is restricted. Your company may desire to terminate this contract for other reasons, such as the owner's breach of the contract or your company's belief that the owner will not be able to pay for this work when it is completed. If your company sees a notice of foreclosure on the door of the home when it arrives for work one day, there is probably cause to be concerned, but according to this contract's terms, that is no reason for terminating the contract. Review Chapter 2 for alternative termination provisions.]

INABILITY TO COMPLETE PROJECT

Contractor shall not be liable if it is unable to complete the Project or for any delays in completion of the Project if the inability or delay is due to governmental restrictions on the manufacture, sale, distribution, and/or use of materials required for the Project, inability to obtain materials because of strikes, lockouts, fires, floods, terrorism, earthquakes, or other acts of God, military operations and requirements, national emergencies, or other unforeseen acts outside Contractor's control, or failure of necessary utilities to the Project site.

[This is the equivalent of the "force majeure" section commonly found in contracts. It states that the service provider is not responsible for its inability to perform the work if the inability is due to occurrences beyond its control. Consider what could occur that would prevent your company's performance and list it here.]

OWNER'S INSURANCE REQUIREMENTS

Owner agrees to maintain insurance in commercially reasonable amounts calculated to cover any and all claims of any kind or nature by Contractor's employees, owners, agents, or subcontractors for damage to Contractor's property or personal injury due to actions or inactions of Owner and that arise from Contractor's performance of its duties under this agreement. Owner also agrees to maintain insurance in commercially reasonable amounts calculated to cover any and all claims of any kind or nature for damage to the Project not caused by Contractor.

[In the event that there is a fire or other catastrophe at the work site that destroys your company's work in progress or materials left at the site or where your company's employees are injured as a result of the negligence of the owner, requiring the owner to have insurance to cover such claims can provide a valuable back-up to the insurance your company should carry. Your company may be further protected by requiring the owner to pro-

vide a certificate from their insurance company indicating that your company is a "Named Insured" on the policy and that the policy is in force. A "Named Insured" is an individual or entity, other than the person or company that purchased the insurance, that is named on the policy as insured against all the risks that purchaser of the insurance is covered for.]

LEGAL TERMS

This agreement is binding on the heirs, executors, administrators, and successor in interest of the respective parties.

[It's especially important if your company is contracting with an individual that there is a contract term that binds the individual's heirs to this contract. Otherwise your company may not be able to enforce this contract against whoever inherits the home where this work is being done.]

If payment to Contractor is not made when due, Owner shall pay Contractor's reasonable attorneys fees, collection charges, and interest on all past due amounts at the rate of 18% per annum.

[Assessing late fees is a business decision, but failure to require them in the contract probably prevents your company from collecting them later. Some states have usury laws that preclude charging interest over a certain amount. Your company should determine these limits in your state. This provision is poorly drafted because it fails to link the attorneys fees that are owed to the collection of past due payments. The lack of clarity may make the entire provision unenforceable.]

Owner agrees that acceptance of payment after default shall not be deemed a waiver by Contractor of any action or right that may arise by reason of such default.

[This means that where the owner does not make a payment on time but pays later, the late payment would still provide a basis for a breach of contract action by the contractor. The contractor could still maintain a lawsuit to recover any damages resulting from the breach of contract even though the payment had been made eventually.]

This agreement including the attached Drawing contains the entire agreement between Contractor and Owner concerning the Project and nothing is binding on either of them that is not contained in this agreement.

[This means that no written documents other than this contract and the referenced drawing and no verbal agreements can be used as evidence of what the parties agreed to if

there is a dispute over what agreement is in effect.]

Any amendment or modification of this agreement must be in writing and signed by both parties to be binding.

[This is a very important provision to include. Otherwise, for example, the owner can claim your company agreed to a price reduction and it's possible a court would side with the owner. This provision makes clear that all agreements must be written and signed to be effective.]

FANCY CONSTRUCTION LLC

____________________________ ____________________________

Bob Builder, Managing Member Mary Smith

This next agreement has a counterpart in Chapter 9. In that chapter the agreement is drafted to benefit your company as the buyer of the services. Here it is drafted to benefit your company as the seller of the services.

SERVICE AGREEMENT

This agreement ("Agreement") is effective ________________ between Moff Inc. ("Moff") and Retail Store Inc. ("Company") for one year.

[Every contract must have a statement naming the parties bound by the contract, the date the contract is effective, and how long the contract binds the parties [the term]. This sentence takes care of each of these requirements.]

For good and valuable consideration, the receipt and sufficiency of which are hereby acknowledged, the parties agree as follows:

[All contracts must have what the law calls "consideration," which just means that each party must pay something for the bargain that they receive in the contract. It may seem like only one party in a contract is receiving consideration where, like here, one party pays the other to do something. However, the law sees this situation as both parties receiving consideration, because one party receives money and the other receives the benefit of the services. The prior sentence in this contract seeks to address any concerns a court reviewing this contract might have concerning whether or not the contractual requirement for consideration was met.]

1. **Services.** Moff shall provide the following services ("Services") on a non-exclusive basis to Company.

   [Service contracts should state whether the services are provided exclusively or non-exclusively to the company hiring the service provider. If there is no designation, it's assumed that the services are provided non-exclusively unless other provisions of the contract imply otherwise.]

   Routine bookkeeping including maintenance of Company's financial records, reconciliation of Company's accounts with financial institutions, and preparation of monthly financial reports

   Preparation of bi-weekly Company payroll including remittance of payroll taxes to governmental authorities in a timely manner

   [It's always best to be as detailed as possible in the statement of the services to be provided so that there are few if any unmet expectations on either side. If services are stated in general terms such as simply "monthly bookkeeping," the law will imply that to mean what is typical for that service in that profession.]

2. **Performance of Services.** Records necessary for Moff to perform its duties will be available to Moff on the schedule and in the manner set forth by Moff. Moff shall not be responsible for untimely or incomplete performance of Services due to Company's failure to provide, have available, or maintain complete and accurate records.

   [As the service provider, your company should make sure the contract lists the specific details of what resources your company requires from the company receiving the services in order to perform your company's contractual duties. In this contract your company has agreed to keep the buyer's financial records in order. If, for example, the other company throws away its bank statements as they arrive in the mail, doesn't record checks written, or spends cash and doesn't keep receipts for what is bought, the result will be that your company may not be able to perform its contract duties. It's important to contractually obligate the other company to do what is necessary so that your company can do its job and to disclaim liability if the other company fails to provide required cooperation and resources.]

3. **Payment.** Company shall pay Moff ________ dollars ($xxx) per calendar month for performance of the Services.

[This contract structures payment as a flat fee. An alternative would be to pay for performance by the hour or for individual tasks.]

Payment shall be made within five (5) days of the first calendar day of each month without set-off or deduction as payment for services to be performed over the calendar month in which payment is made.

[Because your company has to meet its payroll and expenses for performing this work over the calendar month, it's fair to request payment in advance or at least to obtain a deposit or retainer to assure that your company does not work for a month and not get paid.]

Failure to pay any payment when due shall result in immediate discontinuance of performance of Services.

[If the contract fails to state the consequence for non-payment, in order to avoid liability for breach of contract, your company will have to continue performing its duties under the contract even though it is not being paid. For this reason it's critical that your company contractually require that its duty to perform the services be contingent on the buyer's duty to make payment.]

Where payment is brought current prior to the 15th calendar day of the month, Moff may, at its sole discretion, resume performance of Services. Where the current payment owed has not been paid prior to the 16th day of any calendar month, this contract shall terminate.

[If there is an automatic termination provision, make sure it is not overly stringent. I have seen contracts that automatically terminate if payment is not made within five days of the due date. In those cases the contract could end over something as simple as a mail delay or an administrative error. Contracts that end over one party's non-performance tend to create ill will and are difficult to resurrect, even if the non-performance is something the other party could live with, like a six-day payment delay when only five is allowed. Automatic termination provisions should be written so that there is at least one chance to bring the payment current before the contract ends, although repeated instances of late payments may be treated differently.]

4. **Renewal.** This Agreement shall automatically renew under the terms specified herein for a one (1) year period on the expiration of the current term unless either party noti-

fies the other in writing at least thirty (30) days prior to the expiration of the current term that this Agreement shall not be renewed.

[As the service company, having a contract that automatically renews may provide some psychological advantage over the other company, because the other company may choose to continue with your company's services just because there is already a contract executed rather than go to the effort of initiating a contract with a new company. One reason to avoid automatic renewals is that they typically allow termination only within a small window immediately prior to the automatic renewal date and, unless your company has someone tightly monitoring these dates, it will be easy to miss the opportunity to terminate the contract. My experience is that business people do not like reviewing contracts and will not unless they have to. With a contract in place that renews forever, your company may retain this customer longer than it would have without the automatic renewal provision.]

5. **Indemnification.** Company shall indemnify, defend, and hold Moff harmless from and against any and all claims, actions, suits, demands, assessments, or judgments asserted and any and all losses, liabilities, damages, costs, and expenses (including, without limitation, reasonable attorneys' fees to the extent permitted by law, accounting fees, and investigation costs) alleged or incurred by third parties arising out of or relating to any operations, acts, or omissions of Company or any of its employees or agents in the exercise of Company's rights or the observance of Company's obligations under this Agreement.

   [The first part of this provision should name all the possible categories of people and related businesses that might be sued if your company is sued over the actions or inactions of the other company. Because this provision names just Moff, if Moff has a parent company or subsidiaries they would not gain the benefits of this indemnification provision. By naming the indemnified party as only Moff, it may leave the possibility open that Moff's owners, officers, employees, consultants, and subcontractors might be sued and not receive the benefit of this indemnification provision. Your company should redraft this to include categories of individuals that might be sued as well as other related companies. The next part of the provision lists the types of actions, claims, and damages that might be filed against your company that your company is seeking indemnification for. If the clause was limited to "lawsuits," then only an

actual lawsuit filed in a court of law would result in the other company covering your company's costs resulting from the damages caused by the other company. This part of the provision should include claims, damages, and payments as well as lawsuits. The final part of the clause defines the basis for the claim against your company that would trigger the other company's duty to defend your company or pay for damages. This provision states that the claims would have to be based on something the other company did or did not do as part of this contract.]

6. **Survival.** All provisions that logically ought to survive termination of this Agreement shall survive.
   [If this agreement ends, every provision in it is no longer effective. There are some provisions your company will want to continue to be effective such as the Indemnification provision. This provision allows provisions that logically are intended to govern events related to the agreement but that could occur after the agreement ends to continue to govern those events.]
7. **Termination on Insolvency.** To the extent permitted by law, this Agreement shall terminate on the initiation by or against Company of insolvency, receivership, or bankruptcy proceedings or any other proceedings for the settlement of Company's debts, on Company making an assignment for the benefit of creditors, or on Company's dissolution or cessation of business.
   [If the other company is declared insolvent or files for bankruptcy it is possible that your company would be bound to continue providing services even though your company might not get paid or might be forced to accept a lower payment. In bankruptcy court this provision might not be enforceable, but where it is, or in situations where there is no bankruptcy filing but the company is operating in a similarly distressed state, it would provide grounds to terminate this contract.]
8. **Notices.** Any notice shall be in writing and shall be delivered as follows with the notice date deemed by personal delivery, when delivered personally, by overnight courier, on written verification of receipt or by certified or registered mail, return receipt requested, three (3) days after mailing. Notice shall be sent to Company at 1234 Work Street, Klog, Tun 12345 and to Moff at 5678 Toil Street, Moxy, Nan 12345, or to such address as either party later designates according to the provisions of this paragraph.
   [It's important to have a section stating how legal notices will be made to each other.

If one party alleges the other party breached this agreement, your company might not want official legal notice of this claim to be made through a telephone call. Often legal notice is associated with a corresponding time period that must expire before the party giving the notice can take some action. This clause might prevent such disputes, because it sets the start of any time period initiated by a notice to be on a date and time that can be easily verified or calculated. Including the address where notices must be sent is good practice to assure they are received where your company can best react to them.]

9. **Governing Law and Forum; Legal Fees.** The laws of the United States of America and the State of Nan shall govern this Agreement. Each of the parties irrevocably consents to the exclusive personal jurisdiction of the federal and state courts located in Nan for any matter arising out of or relating to this Agreement, except that in actions seeking to enforce any order or judgment, such personal jurisdiction shall be nonexclusive. If any dispute arises between the parties with respect to this Agreement that leads to a proceeding to resolve such dispute, the prevailing party shall be entitled to receive reasonable attorneys' fees, expert witness fees, and out-of-pocket costs incurred in connection with such proceeding in addition to any other relief to which such prevailing party may be entitled.
   [This provision requires that the state law applied to interpretation of this contract is the law of the state where your company is located (Nan). It also provides that any lawsuit must be filed in the courts located in Nan. This paragraph also contains an attorneys fees clause. Some states have statutes providing for recovery of a prevailing party's attorneys fees and court costs in any contract dispute, but some do not. In the states where there is no statute addressing this issue this provision would have the same effect.]
10. **Severability.** If any provision of this Agreement is held by a court of competent jurisdiction to be illegal, invalid, or unenforceable, that provision shall be deemed amended to achieve as nearly as possible the same economic effect as the original provision, and the legality, validity, and enforceability of the remaining provisions of this Agreement shall not be affected or impaired thereby.
    [This is a common paragraph in contracts. It began to be included in contracts because over the life of a contract, laws could be passed making a provision of the contract

illegal. To avoid the possible result that the entire contract would then become void, these provisions were included so that it was clear that the offending provision would be void but not the entire contract.]

11. **Waiver.** By accepting late or otherwise inadequate performance of any of Company's obligations, Moff shall not waive its rights to require timely performance or performance that strictly complies with this Agreement in the future.

    [Where the other party breaches this agreement and your company elects to ignore the breach, your company may have waived its right to enforce that contract provision in the future. By including this provision, the parties are agreeing that even if your company waives late or inadequate performance once, it won't preclude later enforcement of the same provisions.]

12. **Limit of Liability.** IN NO EVENT SHALL MOFF BE LIABLE IN CONTRACT, TORT, OR OTHERWISE FOR INCIDENTAL OR CONSEQUENTIAL DAMAGES OF ANY KIND, INCLUDING, WITHOUT LIMITATION, ECONOMIC DAMAGE OR LOST PROFITS, REGARDLESS OF WHETHER MOFF SHALL BE ADVISED, SHALL HAVE OTHER REASON TO KNOW, OR IN FACT SHALL KNOW OF THE POSSIBILITY.

    [This provision should prevent your company from being liable for anything but direct damages. Direct damages would be damages arising directly from the event that your company is deemed to be liable for. Indirect or consequential damages are damages such as lost profits, lost revenue, and other types of damages that are consequences of the injury your company may have caused. Because consequential damages can be far larger than direct damages they are routinely disclaimed in contracts. In fact some insurance policies require them to be disclaimed for the insurance policy to be effective.]

13. **Successors and Assigns.** This Agreement is intended to bind any and all of the parties' successors, heirs, and assigns.

    [If the ownership of your company changes, this contract may not be enforceable by the company's new owners unless you include a provision similar to this one that states that successors and assigns are bound by and receive the benefits of this agreement. If the buyer is owned by an individual and that individual dies, this agreement may not be enforceable against the owner's estate unless your company includes a similar provision.]

14. **Entire Agreement.** This Agreement constitutes the entire agreement with respect to the subject matter herein and supersedes all prior or contemporaneous oral or written

agreements concerning such services.

[This means that only this contract may be used to determine what the agreement between the parties was. No oral agreements or other written agreements may be used as evidence of this agreement.]

IN WITNESS WHEREOF, the Parties have executed this Agreement as of the date first written above.

Moff Inc. Retail Store Inc.

By: ________________________ By: ________________________

Name: ______________________ Name: ________________________

Title: _______________________ Title: ________________________

Checklist for Service Agreements Where Your Company Is the Service Provider

- ❑ Correct legal name of parties
- ❑ Effective date of contract
- ❑ Date work starts, if different
- ❑ Definitions for capitalized terms
- ❑ Term of contract
- ❑ Detailed description of duties:
  - What is to be done
  - How is it to be accomplished
  - When is it to be done
  - What are final products or deliverables
  - What are the specifications for the final products or deliverables
  - Deadlines for deliverables and project milestones
  - What cooperation or assistance is required from the other party
  - Designate specific person from customer to be key contact or otherwise involved
  - What specific labor and materials are supplied by your company
  - Quality standards
- ❑ Payment terms
  - Will your company require a retainer or deposit

- Will it keep this as security or bill against it
- When is payment due and how is this calculated
- Is an invoice sent or amount due automatically
- If invoice what are the invoice intervals
- What is payment amount
- In what currency
- How is payment to be made—cash, check, electronic funds transfer, or other
- Late fees assessed and if so how
- Out-of-pocket expenses reimbursable, if so on what basis and when
- No right of set-off or deduction
- If a repair agreement, is there a deadline for the customer to pick up the repair
- What happens if not picked up

❑ If a repair agreement, does customer sign acceptance of the terms and conditions

- Does customer sign for repair quote
- Does customer sign for return of goods

❑ Return of confidential information on termination

❑ Destruction of confidential information on termination

❑ Confidential information

- How defined
- What are acceptable uses and disclosures
- Term of confidentiality obligations
- Duties towards confidential information
- Exceptions to duties of confidentiality

❑ No solicitation of employees

- Length of restriction

❑ Non-compete

- In what geographic area
- For how long
- In what markets

- ❑ Alternative dispute resolution
  - Negotiation
  - Mediation
  - Arbitration
  - Is alternative exclusive or required before litigation
  - Who pays for alternative
  - Who specifically is required to participate in alternative
  - Required qualifications of neutral party officiating over the alternative
  - What is the timeframe for alternative
  - Where does alternative dispute forum occur
  - What rules govern alternative dispute forum
  - If neutral party renders a decision is it binding
- ❑ Assignment/subcontracting permitted
  - Preclude partial or complete assignment but allow subcontracting
  - Preclude subcontracting but allow partial or complete assignment
  - Allowed with consent not to be withheld unreasonably
  - Allowed with consent at other party's sole discretion
  - Allowed if a party is sold
  - Allowed if a party is transferred to an affiliate or subsidiary
  - If subcontractors permitted will sub be required to maintain confidentiality of all confidential information
- ❑ Recovery of prevailing party's expenses in litigation
  - Attorneys' fees
  - Legal costs
  - Expert witness fees
  - Investigation costs
- ❑ Choice of law to interpret agreement
- ❑ Choice of venue for litigation
- ❑ Compliance with laws
- ❑ If required, specify material compliance with laws applicable to this contract
- ❑ Conflicting language between agreements is resolved in what manner
- ❑ Rights provided in contract are cumulative or exclusive

- ❑ Force Majeure—consider inclusion of fire, accident, acts of public enemy, terrorism, severe weather, acts of God, labor disruption, flood, failure of suppliers to deliver, difficulty obtaining supplies, epidemics, nuclear strike, government intervention, government or freight embargo, quarantine, difficulty obtaining transportation
  - Notice required if event occurs
  - Right to terminate if event lasts specified amount of time
- ❑ Indemnity
  - Who provides indemnification
  - To your company, officers, employees, consultants, directors, agents, parent company, subsidiary
  - For claims, liabilities, losses, damages, costs, charges, attorneys' fees, legal costs, liens, death, personal injury, accidents, property damage.
  - Arising out of actual or alleged negligence, gross negligence, breach of the contract, claims of liens, or encumbrances
- ❑ Integration (or Entire Agreement) provision
  - All documents making up the agreement referenced
  - Requirement to obtain and maintain insurance
  - Insurance certificates required to be produced
  - Your company a "named insured" if insurance requirement is on other party
  - Limitation on liability
  - Consequential damages—special, indirect, incidental, exemplary
  - Limitation on remedies and if so is word "exclusive" included
  - Limitation on amount of damages
  - Limitation on liability provision conspicuous
- ❑ Notice provision
  - Is address for notices included
  - Acceptable ways to make delivery specified
  - Time that the other party is deemed to have received the notice specified
- ❑ No joint venture, agency, partnership, trust, or association
- ❑ Relationship is that of independent contractor

- ❑ Severability—illegal or otherwise unenforceable provisions can be severed
- ❑ Successors and assigns—agreement binding on
- ❑ Survival—certain terms of the agreement survive termination or expiration
- ❑ Termination provision
    - How much notice is required before contract terminates
    - For cause
    - Is right to cure default provided
    - Any breach or material breach
    - For convenience
    - If elected by either party, does any party have a right to damages
    - Insolvency
    - Bankruptcy
    - Assignment for benefit of creditors
    - Receiver appointed
    - Initiates reorganization
    - Closes business
    - Stops operating
- ❑ Waiver—waiver of breach not agreement to waive all breaches
- ❑ No third-party beneficiaries
- ❑ Publicity
    - Allow with other party's written consent not to be unreasonably withheld
    - Allow for your company at its discretion
    - Prohibit entirely
    - Allow use of customer's name in advertisements
- ❑ Warranty
    - How long and for what
    - If disclaimed, express, implied, merchantability, fitness for purpose, title
    - Voided for improper use or operation, inadequate maintenance or calibration
    - If remedy limited is word "exclusive" clearly stated
    - If disclaimer or exclusive remedy is language conspicuous
- ❑ Written modification—all modifications in writing and signed

- ❑ Correct signature blocks
- ❑ Agreement signed and each page initialed by both parties

Chapter Eight

Here is a simple purchase order from a seller.

TERMS OF SALE

1. **ORDER ACCEPTANCE**—Acceptance of buyer's order is subject to credit approval.
   [Under the UCC order acceptance occurs anytime there is a definite acceptance. This statement in the purchase makes it clear a definite acceptance must include approval of credit.]
2. **PRICE**—Prices shall be those in effect at time of shipment.
   [The UCC implies a reasonable price at the time of delivery so this provision varies the UCC term.]
3. **SHIPPING**—Goods shall be shipped F.O.B. shipping point.
   [Older versions of the UCC defined risk of loss and transfer of title by using terms like F.O.B. (free on board). F.O.B. means the seller pays for transportation costs and bears the risk of loss to the F.O.B. point. In this provision the shipping point is left unclear so this could either be a shipping contract or a destination contract depending on the shipping point designated in the order.]
4. **PAYMENT**—Invoices are eligible for cash discount if paid by the 10th of the month following the invoice date. All invoices are due on the 15th of the month following the invoice date. Payments not made when due shall incur a monthly service charge of the lesser of 1 1/2 percent or the maximum permitted by law.
   [Under the UCC, payment is to be made at the time of delivery, so this provision varies that requirement. The UCC does not provide for payment of interest on past due amounts, so if your company desires to assess interest it must be included in the purchase order or sales contract. Some states have usury laws that preclude charging interest over a certain amount. Your company should determine these limits in your state.]
5. **TAXES**—Prices do not include sales or other taxes imposed on the sale of goods, which shall be separately invoiced unless Buyer provides Seller with an acceptable tax exemption certificate.

[Your company must assess sales tax unless it has a copy of the buyer's tax exemption. It's common for buyers to deduct the taxes assessed on an invoice, stating the sale is tax exempt, but fail to provide a copy of their tax exemption. This provision makes the provision of the certificate a contract requirement if the buyer desires not to pay sales tax.]

6. **RETURNS**—With Seller's prior approval, goods may be returned for credit against unpaid invoices. The amount of the credit will be reduced by a restocking fee equal to 10% of the price of the returned goods.
   [The UCC does not address return of goods that are not alleged to be defective. This company has made a business decision to consider returns on request and charge a restocking fee if the return is accepted.]
7. **DELIVERY**—Seller shall not be liable for any delay in delivery that is the result of acts not under Seller's control such as weather, strikes, and acts of God. Delivery dates are best estimates only.
   [Under the UCC's commercial impracticability exception, the seller would probably be excused for delivery delays like the ones enumerated here even if this provision was not in the purchase order. The UCC implies a duty of good faith in all contracts, so the seller might not be seen as acting in good faith if its best estimated delivery date was significantly different than the actual delivery date. This provision does make clear a delivery date is not a firm promise to deliver on that date.]
8. **WARRANTIES**—Seller warrants that all goods sold are free of any security interest. SELLER MAKES NO OTHER EXPRESS OR IMPLIED WARRANTIES, AND SPECIFICALLY MAKES NO IMPLIED WARRANTIES OF MERCHANTABILITY OR FITNESS FOR PURPOSE.
   [This seller is providing a limited warranty of title only and disclaiming all other warranties. This warranty is a limited warranty of title because the warranty of title provides an additional warranty that the seller here has disclaimed—the warranty that the product does not infringe a third-party intellectual property right.]
9. **LIMITATION OF LIABILITY**—Seller's liability shall be limited to either repair or replacement of the goods or refund of the purchase price, all at Seller's option, and in no case shall Seller be liable for incidental or consequential damage of any kind for any reason.
   [This limitation of liability is probably ineffective for at least two reasons. One is that it

is not conspicuous as required by the UCC. Another is that it does not contain the word "exclusive." The UCC provides that any remedy stated in an agreement is in addition to those in the UCC unless the parties expressly agree that the remedy is exclusive to all others.]

10. **WAIVER**—The failure of Seller to insist on the performance of any of the terms or conditions of this contract or to exercise any right hereunder shall not be a waiver of such terms, conditions, or rights in the future, nor shall it be deemed to be a waiver of any other term, condition, or right under this contract.

    [This provision is not unique to sales contracts and is intended to protect the seller's right to excuse contract performance in one instance while retaining the right to enforce that same contract provision later.]

11. **MODIFICATION OF TERMS AND CONDITIONS**—No terms and conditions other than those stated herein, and no modification of these terms or conditions, shall be binding on Seller without Seller's written consent.

    [This provision would act as a rejection of any terms in the buyer's purchase order that conflict with these terms. Under the UCC the resulting sales contract would be composed of terms the two forms agree on plus the terms of the UCC. If the buyer is not another business, and assuming the offer to sell these goods comes from the seller in the form of these purchase order terms and conditions, the seller's terms would prevail.]

Definitions for capitalized terms

- Acceptance of order by seller
- Acceptance governed by seller's purchase terms
- Orders must be in writing
- Acceptance shall be in writing

Rejection of goods

- Time limit for rejection of products
- Final acceptance presumed after some period
- Payment is final acceptance
- Rejection must be in writing detailing reasons
- Remedy for rejection is at exclusive election of seller
- Repair, replace, refund

Changes to order—process
- Order not cancelable
- Provision for additional charges if seller accepts changes
- Provision of additional time for delivery if seller accepts changes

Seller expressly objects to any conflicting terms in buyer's PO

Technical assistance—disclaim any warranty arising from

How are prices for goods determined

No "most favored nation" or "we promise you our lowest price" clause
- If necessary limit to orders on substantially similar terms for same volumes and substantially identical product
- Not applicable for promotional pricing
- Applies only for same period as for third party

Shipping
- Quantities may be up to 10 percent less and still be considered in compliance with order
- If delivery by seller rejected or delayed by buyer, buyer pays storage and insurance costs
- When does title pass
- Who designates carrier
- Packaging and labeling requirements

Risk of loss passes between parties at what point

Delivery date
- Seller's performance dates are estimates only
- Remedy for seller failing to meet date is order cancellation if more than 30 days past date
- Buyer may not reschedule delivery date without seller's written permission

Returns
- Return material authorization number required
- Return shipping paid by whom
- Other details of process

Warranty
- Free from defects in workmanship or materials

- Meets certain specifications
- Remedy limited to repair, replacement, or refund at seller's option
- If remedy limited is word "exclusive" clearly stated
- If disclaimer or exclusive remedy is language conspicuous
- Warranty period—period of time, period of use, period of performance
- Disclaimer of implied warranty of merchantability, fitness for purpose, title
- Disclaim liability for packaging and labeling, defects in material or workmanship
- Warranty voided for improper use or operation, modification, inadequate maintenance or calibration

Will buyer provide tooling or otherwise have its own property at seller

- Disclaim all responsibility for damage, destruction or return of tooling
- Buyer provides tooling at own expense

Publicity

- Allow with other party's written consent not to be unreasonably withheld
- Allow for your company at its discretion
- Prohibit entirely
- Allow use of customer's name in advertisements

Taxes—included in price or additional to price

Patent infringement warranty

- If required by buyer limit to indemnification for U.S. patents
- Require notice of claim, right to defend and settle
- Seller has right to procure for buyer right to use product
- Seller has right to modify product to become non-infringing
- Seller has right to refund price
- No buyer's right if product made to buyers specifications, product includes buyer's parts or parts designated by buyer, products modified after purchase, or seller's products combined with another seller's.

Payment terms

- When is payment due and how is this calculated
- Is an invoice sent or amount due automatically
- If invoice what are the invoice intervals
- In what currency

- How is payment to be made—cash, check, electronic funds transfer, or other
- Late fees assessed and if so how
- No right of set-off or deduction

Confidential information

- How defined
- What are acceptable uses and disclosures
- Term of confidentiality obligations
- Duties towards confidential information
- Exceptions to duties of confidentiality

Alternative dispute resolution

- Negotiation
- Mediation
- Arbitration
- If don't want any of these include provision specifically rejecting
- Is alternative exclusive or required before litigation
- Who pays for alternative
- Who specifically is required to participate in alternative
- Qualifications of neutral party officiating over the alternative
- What is the time frame for alternative
- Where does alternative dispute forum occur
- What rules govern alternative dispute forum
- If neutral party renders a decision is it binding

Assignment/subcontracting permitted

- Preclude partial or complete assignment but allow subcontracting
- Preclude subcontracting but allow partial or complete assignment
- Allowed with consent not to be withheld unreasonably
- Allowed with consent at other party's sole discretion
- Allowed if a party is sold
- Allowed if a party is transferred to an affiliate or subsidiary
- If subcontractors permitted will sub be required to maintain confidentiality of confidential information

Recovery of prevailing party's expenses in litigation

- Attorneys fees
- Legal costs
- Expert witness fees
- Investigation costs

Choice of law to interpret agreement

Choice of venue for litigation

Compliance with laws

- If buyer requires specify material compliance with laws applicable to this contract

Conflicting language between agreements is resolved in what manner

Rights provided in contract are cumulative or exclusive

Force Majeure—consider inclusion of fire, accident, acts of public enemy, terrorism, severe weather, acts of God, labor disruption, flood, failure of suppliers to deliver, difficulty obtaining supplies, epidemics, nuclear strike, government intervention, government or freight embargo, quarantine, difficulty obtaining transportation

- Notice required if event occurs
- Right to terminate if event lasts specified amount of time

Indemnity

- Which party is providing the indemnification
- To the other company, officers, employees, consultants, directors, agents, parent company, subsidiary
- Claims, liabilities, losses, damages, costs, charges, attorneys' fees, legal costs, liens, death, personal injury, accidents, property damage
- Arising out of actual or alleged defects in material and workmanship, negligence, gross negligence, breach of the contract, claims of liens, or encumbrances

Integration (or Entire Agreement) provision

- All documents making up the agreement referenced

Limitation on liability

- Consequential damages
- Limitation on remedies and if so is word "exclusive" included
- Limitation on amount of damages
- Limitation on liability provision conspicuous

Notice provision
- Are both parties' addresses included
- Acceptable delivery methods
- Time that the other party is deemed to have received the notice specified

No joint venture, agency, partnership, trust, or association

Severability—illegal or otherwise unenforceable provisions can be severed

Successors and assigns—agreement binding on

Survival—certain terms of the agreement may survive termination

Termination provision
- How much notice is required before contract terminates
- For cause
  - Is right to cure default provided
  - Any breach or material breach
- For convenience
  - If elected by either party, does any party have a right to damages
- Insolvency
  - Bankruptcy
  - Assignment for benefit of creditors
  - Receiver appointed
  - Initiates reorganization
  - Closes business
  - Stops operating

Waiver—waiver of breach not agreement to waive all breaches

Written modification—all modifications in writing and signed

If terms on back of a form, does the front call attention to the terms

Checklist for Sales Agreements Where Your Company Is the Seller

The checklist for purchase orders is applicable for sales agreements with the addition that a sales agreement needs:

❑ Correct legal name of parties

- ❑ Effective date of contract
- ❑ Term
- ❑ No third party beneficiaries
- ❑ Correct signature blocks
- ❑ Agreement signed and each page initialed by both parties

Chapter 9

The following service agreement is typical of what your company might draft as a result of receiving a proposal from a service provider that it wishes to accept. This agreement incorporates the proposal while adding legal terms and clarifying issues that your company requires.

AGREEMENT TO PROVIDE JANITORIAL SERVICE

Janitorial Company located at 25 Clean Street, Harmony, NM ("Janitor") and Moff, Inc., located at 12 Oak Street Harmony, NM ("Moff") hereby agree to enter into this contract on the terms and conditions set forth below effective as of ______________ and continuing for one year thereafter.

[Placing a word in quotes has the legal effect of indicating that the word in quotes is being used as shorthand for whatever description came immediately before the word in quotes. In this case the word "Moff" will be used in this agreement as shorthand for Moff, Inc. located at 12 Oak Street Harmony, NM. It is no longer necessary, after this point in the agreement, to use the official legal name of this company because you have legally made the association between the shorthand term Moff and the correct legal name.) In consideration of the premises and the obligations hereinafter set forth and for other good and valuable consideration, the receipt and sufficiency of which are hereby acknowledged, the parties agree as follows:

(All contracts must have what the law calls "consideration," which just means that each party must pay something for the bargain that they receive in the contract. It may seem like only one party in a contract is receiving consideration where, like here, one party pays the other to do something. However, the law sees this situation as both parties receiving consideration, because one party receives money and the other receives the benefit of the services. The prior sentence in this contract seeks to address any concerns a court reviewing this contract might have concerning whether or not the contractual requirement for consideration was met.]

1. **Services.** Moff accepts Janitor's proposal dated December 2, 2010 ("Proposal") to provide cleaning services at Moff's facilities as described in the proposal, and Janitor agrees to perform the services described in the Proposal as modified by the terms and conditions contained in this agreement.
[The legal effect of this provision is to create a contract composed of the referenced proposal and the provisions below. If something in the proposal conflicts with one of the provisions below, the provision below would take precedence because this paragraph states that the proposal is modified by what is below.]
2. **Access Requirements.** Janitor shall assign to Moff only Janitor employees that have completed, to Moff's satisfaction, Moff's standard safety training program. Moff has the right to refuse access to its facilities to Janitor employees who have not completed such training and shall not be obligated in any manner to Janitor by such refusal.
[This contract is drafted from the viewpoint of Moff, and this provision demonstrates how Moff's interests are being protected and perhaps Janitor's could be better protected. One can guess that the facilities being cleaned contain equipment or materials that could be safety hazards. If this is so, it's to both parties' advantage to have Janitor's employees complete a safety training program presumably designed by Moff to protect workers against specific hazards in Moff's facilities. What could better protect Janitor's interests is a requirement that the safety training be offered at times and locations convenient for Janitor employees, that sufficient training sessions be scheduled to accommodate turnover so that Janitor can get new employees on the job quickly, and that Moff's right to determine completion of the safety training to its satisfaction be exercised in a reasonable manner. It would be even better to actually have a schedule for the safety training in the contract, such as a provision that Moff offer a training class from 3:00 p.m. to 5:00 p.m. on a Monday within two weeks of any request by Janitor.]
3. **Cost.** Moff shall pay Janitor for actual time that Janitor employees work at Moff at the rate of XXX ($XX) per hour, pro-rated for any partial hour worked, not to exceed two hundred (200) hours per week.
[This seems to cover all the bases of a good provision describing costs, because it states the maximum that can be billed in a specific time period, the rate for a specific time period, and on what basis the fee is earned (actual time worked). One unclear

point is whether attendance at the training program required above is to be considered time worked at Moff.]

4. **Payment Schedule.** Janitor shall bill Moff every four (4) weeks from the Effective Date for actual time worked at Moff during the previous four (4) week period. Moff shall not be obligated to pay any payment due at a time when Janitor is in breach of this Agreement until the breach is remedied to the satisfaction of Moff.
   [This provision limits how often Janitor can bill Moff and relieves Moff of the obligation to make payments if there is a contract breach. It also fails to require Moff to pay the bill sent by Janitor. To protect Janitor's interests, this provision should include a requirement that payment be made within a specified time after the bill date, perhaps that any payment received after the specified amount of time bear interest until paid in full, that the contract can be terminated if payment is not made within a certain time frame, and that Moff's right to determine if a breach has been remedied to its satisfaction must be exercised in a reasonable manner. Note that if the provision above contained the caveat that Moff's right to determine if a breach is remedied to its satisfaction is "in its sole determination," this would give Moff the right to determine the breach was not remedied for almost any reason, and therefore to terminate the contract. For example, Janitor might have failed to clean one office on its weekly cleaning, resulting in Moff withholding all payments then due. Janitor could immediately clean that office, making a special trip to do so, and Moff could still determine, in Moff's sole determination, that the breach was not remedied and the contract should terminate. If your company is Moff it probably won't change this provision because it provides flexibility for Moff.]
5. **Renewal.** This Agreement shall automatically renew under the terms specified herein for a one (1) year period on the expiration of the current term unless either party notifies the other in writing at least thirty (30) days prior to the expiration of the current term that this Agreement shall not be renewed.
   [I counsel companies to avoid agreeing to contracts that automatically renew, because it's rare for the company receiving the product or service to monitor the contract dates closely enough to send a notice of non-renewal within the short window usually contained in automatically renewing agreements. However, this agreement also contains a cancellation for convenience provision, which means that the contract may be termi-

nated at any time during the term of the contract. In that case, the automatic renewal does not tie either company to anything they cannot easily get out of.]

6. **Cancellation for Convenience.** Either party may terminate this Agreement by sending written notice to the other party thirty (30) days prior to the date on which the Agreement shall terminate.
[Cancellation for convenience provisions provide maximum flexibility for both parties. There are many reasons why a contract may need to be terminated other than non-performance by either party. A company owner may experience an illness and decide to close the business. One company may be sold to a new owner who desires to use another contractor or who does not have any contract for these services. Having this clause provides a simple manner for terminating the contract by either party. This clause should include a provision that any duties or obligations that accrued prior to the termination of the contract shall survive the contract's termination. This means that if payments need to be made for services received prior to the contract's end, they would still have to be made, or that tasks Moff had paid for that had yet to be done would still have to be done. Cancellation for convenience clauses should also contain detailed procedures for how cancellation will be communicated to the other party and what time period must expire before the termination is effective. If either party requires anything returned to it at the time the contract terminates, this should be stated here. This might include all the work product the contractor has produced up through the date of termination. Assume this type of provision will be exercised by the other party half-way through the contract and determine what your company would require from the contractor at that point. Then state these requirements here.]
7. **Presence of Hazardous Materials.** Janitor acknowledges that Moff stores and uses hazardous materials throughout Moff's facilities. Janitor assumes the risk of harm to its employees, their property, or the property of Janitor resulting from contact with hazardous materials while Janitor's employees or property are on Moff's premises.
[This is another provision that protects your company, in this case, Moff more than Janitor. The fact that Moff is disclosing this hazard is a smart legal move, because it greatly lessens the possibility that Moff will be responsible for injuries to Janitor and its employees due to a hazard it has not been warned of. If your company is Janitor, the requirement that Janitor assume all liability for potential injuries that may result is not to

Janitor's advantage. If Moff negligently causes some of these materials to harm one of Janitor's employees, because Janitor has assumed the risk of this occurring, Moff might not be responsible. In your company's viewpoint this lack of liability would be a good thing, but if your company were Janitor it would want this provision to be redrafted to provide that it assumed the risk of injury except where Moff acts negligently.]

8. **Compliance with Laws.** All services rendered by Janitor and its employees pursuant to this Agreement shall conform with and be in full compliance with all applicable laws, rules, ordinances, and regulations adopted or required by any federal, state, or local government.
   [This seems like an innocuous sentence, but it is not. Any failure to comply with all laws all the time might be a breach of this agreement. Your company could use this provision as a basis to terminate this contract when it wanted out for business reasons and found an infraction it could leverage against Janitor under this provision. This is fine if your company is the one asking the other party to agree to this provision, but if your company is the one having to comply, then a less onerous provision should be negotiated, like the following: "Each party will at all times comply with all applicable <u>*material*</u> *laws, rules, ordinances, and regulations." The inclusion of the word "material" limits the applicability to serious infractions of the law that have a direct effect on the contract. Also notice that this provision is written to apply only to Janitor. Because the contract has already revealed safety issues as well as the presence of hazardous materials at the site Janitor is cleaning, it's probably advisable on Janitor's part to require Moff to also comply with all laws and regulations.]* Janitor shall be entirely and solely responsible for the payment of employee and employer payroll taxes, contributions, and/or assessments, whether pertaining to federal, state, or local requirements, workers' compensation insurance, or other insurance for Janitor and all of its employees providing the services specified in this Agreement.
   [As the employer, Janitor should be doing everything stated in this provision anyway. Restating these requirements in the contract emphasizes the requirements to Janitor and provides the basis for a cause of action for breach of contract if Janitor does not perform any of these duties. If this provision were not included and Janitor failed to pay workers' compensation insurance premiums, Moff would have no basis for taking any action against Janitor, but because it is included, Moff could use the non-payment as the basis of a breach of contract lawsuit.]

9. **Insurance.** Janitor agrees to maintain insurance in commercially reasonable amounts calculated to protect Moff and Janitor from any and all claims of any kind or nature for worker's compensation, as required by the state where this contract is performed, and for damage to property or personal injury, including death, arising from acts or omissions of Janitor in performing its duties under this agreement, whether the acts or omissions are those of Janitor, its employees, or agents, or anyone directly or indirectly engaged or employed by Janitor or its agents.
   [It's important that the service company maintain insurance calculated to reasonably cover claims that might arise from performance under this contract. If the company fails to have insurance and is found to have few assets in the event a claim is filed related to damages incurred during performance of this contract, it is more likely that the claim will then be filed against Moff as the company that caused the work to be done. If the injured party can obtain compensation from Janitor through insurance, it's less likely that they would file a claim against Moff. If Janitor fails to maintain the insurance required in this section, it would be a basis for a breach of contract action and would allow Moff to potentially receive damages and/ or terminate the contract. Further protection could be obtained by requiring Janitor to provide a certificate from their insurance company indicating that Moff is a "Named Insured" on the policy and that the policy is in force. A "Named Insured" is an individual or entity, other than the company that purchased the insurance that is named on the policy, as insured against all the risks that the company purchasing the contract is insured for.]
10. **Independent Contractor Status.** The parties intend this Agreement to create an independent contractor relationship. Neither Janitor nor its employees or agents are to be considered agents or employees of Moff for any purpose, including that of federal and state taxation, federal, state, and local employment laws, or employee benefits. Janitor, not Moff, shall furnish all labor, tools, equipment, vehicles, licenses, and registrations necessary to perform the services.
    [This section is included in this agreement in the event that Moff has to defend its classification of Janitor as an independent contractor. The fact that there is written evidence that the two companies agreed that an independent contractor relationship existed will be valuable if the relationship is questioned by tax or other authorities.]
11. **Assignment/Sub-Contracting.** Janitor shall not assign its rights, delegate its duties,

or subcontract any part of its obligations under this Agreement without prior written consent of Moff.

[In the absence of this provision, Janitor is free to hire subcontractors, delegate performance of some or all of its tasks to others, or sell its business and assign this contract to the new company. This may be a concern because, although Moff has reviewed the skills, experience, and reputation of Janitor, Moff will have no opportunity to assess the new company if the contract is delegated, subcontracted, or assigned without its consent. This provision allows Moff to review the new company's skills and experience and decide if consenting to assignment, delegation, or subcontracting is in Moff's best interest. Note that the law implies that Moff's consent will be reasonable under the circumstances unless other wording is included in the contract requiring another standard. If, for example, Janitor is sold to Moff's president's worst enemy and Moff simply does not want to do business with that company, that would probably not be a reasonable reason for withholding consent to assignment of this contract to the new company. By including the caveat that the decision to consent is in Moff's sole determination, Moff's reasons for withholding consent can be based on any reason it chooses.]

12. **Conflicts between Agreements.** The terms of this Agreement shall control over any conflicting terms in the Proposal or any referenced agreement or document.

[Any time a contract is created that is composed of more than one document, there is the possibility that a provision in one document will conflict with a provision in the other document. For that reason there should be a provision in at least one of the documents stating how such conflicts should be resolved. This is most often accomplished by stating that one of the documents takes precedence over the other. If there are more than two documents, then list the order in which they should be used to decide the conflict.]

13. **Indemnification.**

[Indemnification means that the party who provides the indemnification agrees to defend any claim or lawsuit and pay all the costs of doing so related to any event listed in the indemnification provision. Frequently a company's insurance provider will require certain language be included in the indemnification section of all contracts a company enters into in order not to void the company's insurance coverage. It's wise

to check on this so that your company does not find out after the fact that it has no insurance coverage because the contract failed to include required language.]

Janitor shall indemnify, defend, and hold Moff, its parent company, subsidiaries, officers, and employees harmless from and against any and all claims, actions, suits, demands, assessments, or judgments asserted and any and all losses, liabilities, damages, costs, and expenses (including, without limitation, reasonable attorneys' fees to the extent permitted by law, accounting fees, and investigation costs) alleged or incurred by third parties arising out of or relating to any operations, acts, or omissions of Janitor or any of its employees or agents in the exercise of Janitor's rights or the performance or observance of Janitor's obligations under this Agreement.

[The first part of this provision names individuals and businesses that might be sued based on the actions or inactions of Janitor. The next part of the provision lists types of actions the indemnifying party is responsible for. This provision covers not only lawsuits but claims and other types of actions for damages that Moff might face as a result of something Janitor does. The final part of the clause should define the types of things the claim against Moff would have to be based on for Moff to be able to seek indemnification from Janitor. This provision states that the claims would have to be based on something Janitor did or did not do as part of this contract.]

14. **Survival.** All provisions that logically ought to survive termination of this Agreement shall survive.

    [If this agreement ends, every provision in it is no longer effective. There are some provisions you will want to continue to be effective, such as the Indemnification provision. This provision allows provisions that logically are intended to govern events related to the agreement but that could occur after the agreement ends to continue to govern those events.]

15. **Severability.** If any provision of this Agreement, or the application thereof to any person or circumstance, shall be held invalid or unenforceable by any court of competent jurisdiction, the remainder of this Agreement or the application of such provisions to persons or circumstances, other than those as to which it is held invalid or unenforceable, shall not be affected thereby.

    [Where the law changes, making a term in a contract unenforceable or even illegal,

the entire contract may be void because it contains the now illegal or unenforceable term. This provision allows a court to simply delete the term, leaving the rest of the contract to stand as it is. Whether a court will do that is a matter of state law, but it's wise to have this sentence in case the state law that applies to the contract allows striking the offending provision while leaving the remaining contract enforceable.]

16. **Entire Agreement.** This Agreement, consisting of the Proposal and this document, constitutes the entire agreement with respect to the subject matter herein and supersedes all prior or contemporaneous oral or written agreements concerning such services. *[A provision like this means that any verbal agreements—"They said they wouldn't enforce that provision." "The e-mail he sent me said the company would pay extra for that."—and any other written agreements not listed here are not admissible as evidence in any dispute over the meaning of this agreement or to prove what the parties had intended their agreement to be comprised of. Only the written agreements listed here are evidence of what the parties agreed.]*

IN WITNESS WHEREOF, the parties have executed this Agreement as of the date first written above.

Janitor Company Moff Inc.

a Delaware corporation a Nan corporation

By: ______________________	By: ___________________________
Name: ____________________	Name: _________________________
Its: ______________________	Its: ___________________________

It's common to see signature blocks that include reference to the state that the company is incorporated in. This is usually done so that if it is necessary to file a lawsuit and the nature of the lawsuit is such that the lawsuit must be filed in the home state of the corporation, it will be easy to determine where that is.

The janitorial agreement omits many bulletproof terms. Can you name some? Use the checklist as a cheat sheet.

Line-by-Line Review of Independent Contractor Agreement

Independent contractor agreements are useful agreements because they can be modified to apply to almost any service. The body of the agreement should contain the basic legal terms governing the relationship, while an attachment or supplement is drafted that specifies the services being provided, the payment to be made, and the time frame for delivery of the service. This agreement follows this format.

CONTRACTOR AGREEMENT

This independent contractor agreement ("Contract")

[Placing a word in quotes and capitalizing it has the legal effect of indicating that the capitalized word is designated as shorthand for whatever description came immediately before the word in quotes. In this case the word "Contract" will be used in this agreement as shorthand to refer to the entire independent contractor agreement.]

is effective on May 1, 2008 ("Effective Date")

[Your company should make a point of deciding when you want a contract to start. It should be effective as of the date one or both parties begin taking actions described in the contract. If the contractor starts work before the contract's effective date your company is at risk for all the reasons it would be if there was no contract at all.]

by and between Moff Inc. with its main office at 12 Oak Street, Harmony, NM ("Customer").

[Include correct mailing addresses for each party so that if a legal notice must be sent, the correct address is readily available.]

and Miff Company LLC with its main office at 25 Maple Street, Harmony, NM ("Contractor"). Moff desires to retain the services of Contractor and Contractor desires to provide its services according to the terms in this Contract.

[Contracts must be bargains where each party agrees to do something they do not otherwise have to do. This sentence is stating the legal bargain being struck in this contract.]

The parties acknowledge that the relationship between them is an independent contractor relationship and not an employment relationship and that these services shall be provided on a short-term or occasional basis.

[The clear statement that the relationship between your company and the worker is not an

employment relationship can be used as evidence if there is ever a question about the relationship of the parties.]

In consideration of the mutual promises set forth in this Contract, the parties agree as follows:

[Consideration is another legal requirement for a contract, and this statement is seeking to satisfy the legal requirement for consideration by stating that both parties acknowledge that there is consideration for this agreement.]

A. SERVICES TO BE PERFORMED

The services to be performed by Contractor under this Contract ("Services") are described in Attachment One. The Services are hereby incorporated into and made a part of this Contract.

[Because this is a form agreement, designed to be used over and over with as few simple changes as possible, the document containing the main changes is an attachment that can be redrafted without making changes to the main agreement.]

B. CONTRACTOR'S DUTIES

Contractor is solely responsible for its acts and omissions as well as any and all legal requirements, including but not limited to workers' compensation insurance, federal and state unemployment taxes, federal and state tax withholding, and reporting requirements, unemployment compensation insurance, and compliance with all federal, state, and local employment laws.

[This is a statement that reiterates the responsibilities of the contractor for the typical duties of an employer. This is more evidence of the independent contractor relationship.]

C. TERM OF CONTRACT

Unless this contract is terminated earlier as allowed in section D, this Contract shall be effective for the length of time stated in Attachment One or one (1) year from the Effective Date, whichever is earlier.

[The attachment will contain the key requirements for what services are performed, how they will be paid for, and when they will be provided. If whoever drafts that document forgets to include a final completion date for the services, this provision makes the agreement automatically end in a year. Otherwise you could have contracts with no end dates or end dates that neither party can determine with any accuracy.]

D. TERMINATION

(1) Moff may terminate this contract effective on the date contained in a written notice of termination provided to Contractor. In no case may the termination date be less than thirty (30) days from the date of the notice.

[There always needs to be a provision for terminating a contract before either party has completed their duties. The provision can provide for termination on the basis of a contract breach or simply for convenience. A termination for convenience means that there does not need to be any reason to terminate and therefore the contract can be terminated at any time. A termination provision allowing only for termination on a contract breach is harder to exercise because it requires a wrongful act or omission by the other party and it can also lead to controversy concerning whether the other party actually did breach the contract. Termination provisions can be mutual or provide that only one party can exercise the right to terminate. Because your company is drafting this contract it can provide that only it has the right to terminate. In that way the contractor must perform his or her duties unless your company decides they are no longer wanted or needed. Your company should consider what it would expect if the contract was terminated before its completion. Would you want the contractor to provide everything completed to that point? Would your company need, for example, copies of building permits, interview notes, or software code written or obtained by the contractor? State these requirements on the attachment, because it is the part of the agreement that is unique to this contractor.]

(2) Within thirty (30) days of the termination of this Contract each party shall return to the other party any and all Confidential Information, as defined below, or other property or information belonging to the other party.

[This is a good provision to have in a form even if your company does not provide anything to the contractor that it desires to have back. There will be instances where your company does provide information that it wants returned, and if it is not forthcoming, this provision would allow your company to sue for breach of contract to have it returned. As a breach of contract lawsuit, because this contract contains a provision for reimbursement of legal fees if one party has to sue to enforce the contract, your company could recover its legal fees. A lawsuit to recover this information that was not a breach of contract lawsuit might not result in recovery of legal fees unless a state law provides for their recovery.]

E. PAYMENT TO CONTRACTOR

Contractor will be paid for the Services as described in Attachment One. Moff will reimburse Contractor for out-of-pocket expenses incurred in performance of the Services if these expenses have been approved by Moff in writing in advance. To obtain reimbursement of these expenses Contractor must submit an invoice to Moff that indicates each expense in detail accompanied by actual receipts for the expenses.

[The attachment will describe payment terms, because different services will require different payment arrangements. However, if out-of-pocket expenses are reimbursed to the contractor, there should be a blanket provision that they be approved by your company in advance and that your company obtains the receipts. I have seen contractors claim expenses greater than the cost of their services, and there is always the rare contractor who decides to travel to your city first class and stay at the suite in the highest price hotel in town when your company assumed they would fly coach and stay in the hotel closest to your office. If your company wants to pay for first-class travel there is nothing wrong with that, but your company should have the final decision on these costs if it is paying. This provision, while making your company's expectations clear, allows your company to reject any expenses submitted for reimbursement that were not approved in advance.]

F. INDEPENDENT CONTRACTOR RELATIONSHIP

The parties intend this Contract to create an independent contractor relationship. Contractor is not to be considered an agent or employee of Moff for any purpose. Moff does not require Contractor to provide services exclusively to Moff. Contractor shall complete the Services according to its own methods of work, which are not controlled by Moff. Contractor shall not have the right to enter into any agreement that binds Moff, to transact any business in the name of Moff, or to make any promises or statements on behalf of Moff. The parties agree that this Contract shall not entitle Contractor to workers' compensation benefits, unemployment compensation benefits, or any other benefits or protections that might result from an employment relationship with Moff.

[This section clarifies further that the parties are contracting, not entering into an employment relationship. It also serves a valuable purpose in making clear to the contractor that it will not be entitled to the protections of an employee such as unemployment insurance. This may come as a surprise to some contractors.]

G. WARRANTY

[A warranty is a promise that what is being sold is as represented or will be as promised.]

Contractor warrants that (1) he or she has the proper skill, training, and background to be able to perform the Services in a competent and professional manner, (2) Moff will have clear title to all products, materials, or deliverables developed under this Contract, and (3) for a period of one (1) year from the time Contractor completes the Services, Contractor will, at no charge to Moff, correct any defects in the products, materials, or deliverables developed under this Contract.

[This warranty has the effect of promising that the contractor has the same skill as the average worker in the field in which they work, that deliverables provided will not have, for example, liens on them for unpaid bills or claims that they violate someone's copyright or patent, and that the contractor will fix any problems with the deliverables for one year from the time the contractor finishes the project. Pay careful attention to when a warranty begins. Your company will want it to begin when it starts using whatever the contractor is providing to you. If a warranty begins on delivery of the software code to your company but your company does not begin using the code for six months, the one-year warranty in this provision will really only be useful for six months.]

H. INDEMNITY

[Indemnification means that the party who provides the indemnification agrees to defend any claim or lawsuit and pay all the costs of doing so for any damages that arise from the three causes listed in the indemnification provision. Your company's insurance provider may require certain language be included in the indemnification section of all contracts in order not to void your company's insurance coverage. It's wise to check on this so that your company does not find out after the fact that it has no insurance coverage because the contract failed to include required language.]

Contractor shall indemnify and hold harmless Moff, and its officers, directors, employees, and agents, from and against any and all suits, claims, losses, forfeitures, demands, fees, costs, expenses, obligations, or proceedings of any kind or nature, including reasonable attorneys fees that Moff may hereafter incur, become responsible for, or pay out as a result of death or personal injury to any person, destruction or damage to any property, contamination of or adverse effects on the environment, or violation of governmental law, regulation, or orders, arising out of or connected with contractor's breach of any term or provision of this Contract, any negligent act or omission or willful misconduct of the Contractor in the course of performing this Contract, or a claim of lien or encumbrances made by third parties.

[If this clause was limited to "lawsuits" then only an actual suit filed in a court of law would be covered. Instances where someone claims they were injured and is negotiating not to file a lawsuit would not be covered. Most injured parties attempt to receive compensation for their injuries prior to filing a lawsuit and it's frequently smarter, if there is clear liability, to settle a claim this way. For that reason, being comprehensive in the kinds of matters the contractor is responsible for is advisable. This provision states that the contractor must indemnify for not only actual payments but those your company is responsible for but may not have paid yet. Your company could seek payment from the contractor and then use this reimbursement to pay any damages due, instead of having to front the money. If there are potential damages your company may incur as a result of this contract that are not included in this clause, be sure to include them in the part of the sentence that indicates what damages are covered by the indemnification.]

I. INSURANCE REQUIREMENTS

Contractor agrees to maintain insurance in commercially reasonable amounts calculated to protect Contractor and Moff from any and all claims of any kind or nature for damage to property or personal injury, including death, made by anyone, that may arise from Contractor's activities performed or facilitated by this Contract.

[If the contractor injures someone while performing the duties in this contract and the injured person sues your company as a result of the contractor's actions, your company will seek indemnification from the contractor for defending the lawsuit and paying any damages. In that case will the contractor have the funds to pay these costs? If your company has required the contractor to maintain insurance to cover these damages, it's likely your company will obtain the benefits of the indemnification provision rather than depending on the contractor's assets. Your company can further protect itself by requiring the contractor to provide a certificate from their insurance company indicating that your company is a "Named Insured" on the contractor's policy and that the policy is in force during the entire term of this contract. A "Named Insured" is an individual or entity, other than

the person or company purchasing the insurance that is named on the policy, as insured against all the risks that the purchaser of the insurance is insured for.]

J. COMPLIANCE WITH LAWS AND REGULATIONS

Contractor shall comply with all applicable laws, rules, ordinances, and regulations adopted or required by any federal, state, or local government.

[If the contractor violates any laws, your company could be prosecuted as well as the contractor. By requesting that the contractor perform the work, your company could be alleged to have either known or recklessly disregarded that a law would be violated. If there is a provision in your company's agreement with the contractor that all laws must be complied with, it will assist your company in defending prosecution for a law the contractor broke. It also sends a strong message to the contractor that your company expects the work to be performed in compliance with all laws and regulations.]

K. PROTECTING CONFIDENTIAL INFORMATION

(1)

[This is a very important section of the agreement that you should put thought and detail into. Think about what is unique to your company. Is it a special customer service system? A certain assessment technique you use to hire staff? A list of sources for your products that you took years to develop? Formulas? Computer programs you developed? Designs? Pricing systems? Inventory management? Think about what makes your business different from others. Another way to look at this is to examine why your customers do business with your company rather than your competitors. It's likely that many of those reasons either are or arise from what is legally called confidential information.]

"Confidential Information" means all information and material disclosed by Moff to Contractor or obtained by Contractor through observation of Moff's property or facilities that is either marked or described as, identified in writing as, or provided under circumstances indicating it is confidential or proprietary.

[The definition in the prior sentence should apply to everything you consider to be confidential to your company. Put some thought into this and make sure it does. Note that the prior sentence applies only to information that is disclosed by Moff to the contractor. It does not safeguard anything the contractor discloses. This provision states that information is confidential if it is provided under circumstances that indicate it's confidential.

These circumstances might be statements that the process being observed or the information being reviewed is secret or proprietary, signs on doors or walls stating this, or execution of facility access agreements that state that what the visitor might observe while visiting is confidential and proprietary. Your company should have these safeguards to protect its confidential information. It's better to draft this section to state with as much detail as possible what your company is protecting, whether it is marked confidential or not.]

Confidential Information includes, without limitation, any trade secret, know-how, idea, invention, process, technique, algorithm, program, hardware, device, design, schematic, drawing, formula, data, plan, strategy and forecast of, and technical, engineering, manufacturing, product, marketing, servicing, financial, personnel, and other information and materials of Moff and its employees, consultants, investors, affiliates, licensors, suppliers, vendors, customers, clients, and other persons and entities.

[The prior sentence defines the types of information your company is protecting. I would not advise just copying this sentence for your agreement. The sentence should be directly applicable to your business and be comprehensive. You can always change it as you develop new lines of business.]

For the avoidance of doubt, Confidential Information includes all analyses, compilations, forecasts, data studies, notes, translations, memoranda, or other documents or materials prepared by or for Moff, its employees, representatives, or contractors, if any, containing, based on, generated or derived from, in whole or in part, any Confidential Information.

[This is a key sentence in this section and should be included in your agreements. If your company does not include a similar sentence then anything based on or developed from your company's confidential information may not be protected as confidential information even though it contains confidential information. Because what is developed is not your exact information, it's arguable that it does not meet the definition of confidential information above.]

(2)

[This subsection details what the contractor's duties are when dealing with your company's confidential information. Put some thought into this to be sure to include any specific duties that apply to your business.]

Contractor shall hold all Confidential Information in strict confidence and shall not disclose any Confidential Information to any third party. Contractor shall not use any Confidential Information for the benefit of itself or any third party or for any purpose other than to perform the Services.

[Up to this point your company has made clear that certain information that belongs to your company is secret and that it cannot be disclosed to others. However, you have not prevented the contractor from using your company's confidential information for its own benefit. This sentence requires the contractor to limit its use of the information to performing its duties under the contract.]

Contractor shall take the same degree of care that it uses to protect its own confidential and proprietary information but in no event less than reasonable care and avoid the unauthorized use, disclosure, publication, or dissemination of the Confidential Information.

[This sentence requires the contractor to protect the information once it is in their hands. Some contractors will not be familiar with handling confidential information and will not have systems in place to protect such information. In those cases it's important to have a statement that requires the contractor to use reasonable care in protecting your confidential information. Legally this requires the contractor to do what a reasonable person would do when safeguarding any valuable property like cash or jewels. The word "avoid" in this sentence implies less of a duty than simply stating that the contractor shall not allow unauthorized use. Perhaps this company meant to obligate the contractor to a lesser duty of care or perhaps this is an inadvertent error.]

Contractor shall not make any copies of the Confidential Information except to the extent reasonably necessary to carry out performance of Services, or unless otherwise approved in writing in advance by Moff.

[Making copies of confidential information is problematic. Copies may not be marked as confidential and those receiving the copies may not be aware of your company's ownership or that the information is secret. The more copies of your company's information there are, the more likely the information will become publicly known. This sentence places a duty on the contractor to limit copies.]

Any copies made shall be identified as the property of Moff and marked "confidential," "proprietary," or with a similar legend.

[This further limits the likelihood of disclosure of your company's information through

release of copies, because even copies made for performance of the contract must be marked as confidential and that they belong to your company.)

These obligations shall survive and continue for five (5) years from the date of termination or expiration of this Contract.

[Your company would not want the duties placed on the contractor in this section to end if this contract were terminated tomorrow due to a breach of contract. The duty to maintain the confidentiality of this information may last as little or as long as is necessary to protect the information. The time frame should be realistic for your industry and information.]

(3) The obligations of this Contract, including the restrictions on disclosure and use, shall not apply with respect to any Confidential Information if it (a) is or becomes publicly known through no act or omission of Contractor; (b) was rightfully known by Contractor without having violated any duty of confidentiality to anyone before it was received from Moff, as evidenced by written records; (c) becomes known to Contractor without violating any duty of confidentiality from a source other than Moff that does not owe a duty of confidentiality to Moff with respect to the Confidential Information; or (d) is independently developed by Contractor without the use of, reference, or access to the Confidential Information, as evidenced by written records.

[This provision is included to be fair to the contractor. Under the terms of this agreement, if information meets the definition of confidential information at the time of disclosure, even if your company later makes it public, the contractor would still have all the duties of confidentiality towards that information that it had at the time the information was originally disclosed. This section releases the contractor from its duties towards information that was confidential but that became public through no fault of the contractor or became known to the contractor without disclosure from your company.]

Contractor may use or disclose Confidential Information if approved in writing by Moff or Contractor is legally required to disclose the Confidential Information, but only if Contractor gives Moff reasonable advance notice that it must legally disclose the Confidential Information and cooperates with Moff if Moff seeks to challenge or restrict the legal requirement.

[It is common to see a provision that states that information can be disclosed if required by a court order but only if the order is challenged and that challenge is denied, resulting in a

legal duty to disclose. This provision seems to be more reasonable in that it allows the contractor to respond to a valid subpoena when it is presented as long as the contractor informs your company that it was compelled to disclose the information. Avoid agreeing to a provision that requires your company to challenge a subpoena requesting the other party's information. Legal challenges are costly and it's not even your information.]

Either party may disclose this Contract in connection with enforcing this Contract.

[This is not a common provision but it should be. If your company has agreed that the existence and/or terms and conditions of this agreement are confidential information, there should be an exception to maintaining this confidentiality for instances where your company must disclose the existence of the contract or the terms in order to enforce it, such as to a collection agency.]

L. OWNERSHIP OF INTELLECTUAL PROPERTY

(1) Contractor desires to act as an independent contractor for Moff in a role where Contractor may create or contribute to Confidential Information.

[Be careful that you have described Confidential Information as only that which belongs to Moff. If your company has made the prior section mutual at the request of the contractor (each party is exchanging confidential information with the other), it's likely the definition of Confidential Information includes both party's secrets. The present provision states that any invention arising from Confidential Information belongs to your company. If the definition of Confidential Information includes the other party's secrets, then this provision is stating that your company owns any invention created from the other party's information. The overreaching aspects of this might mean this section of the contract is unenforceable. In that case, your company might not own an invention created from your company's confidential information.]

In return for the compensation and other benefits Contractor receives from Moff and in consideration for being given access to Moff's Confidential Information, Contractor agrees that any and all inventions, discoveries, improvements, trade secrets, source, object and executables codes for computer programs, libraries and test and debug programs, algorithms and concepts for such codes and other works of authorship, whether or not patentable, copyrightable, or subject to other forms of protection, conceived, created, authored, or first made by Contractor in the course of performing Services, or in the course of providing advice or performing other services to Moff ("Creations") shall be the sole and exclusive property of Moff.

[This is a long sentence but all of it is potentially necessary. You might be tempted to remove parts of the sentence that describe what may be created (inventions, discoveries, improvements, trade secrets, source, object and executables codes for computer programs, libraries and test and debug programs, algorithms and concepts for such codes) if you think that there is no chance that a particular item will be created. For example if your company is a medical device manufacturer and is contracting for an analysis of competitive products and services, you might think that there is no possibility that the contractor would create "source, object and executables codes for computer programs, libraries and test and debug programs". But what if the contractor takes all the information they collect and creates a computer program to analyze it in order to present a report to your company? Although your company has not asked for the creation of such software, your company in fact has paid for its development in order to produce the product your company requested—the analysis and report. Although if the reference to computer programs was removed from this sentence it most likely would have no effect on the ownership of the program, because the remainder of the sentence states that all things conceived, created, authored or first made while performing the services belongs to your company, including it makes the comprehensiveness of your company's ownership clear to the contractor.

Your company's agreements should have a provision that what is created in performance of the contract as well as what is created while working with your company or at your company's request, even if not pursuant to the contract, is owned by your company. It is common, once a contractor and a company begin working together, for the contractor to perform other services that are not included in the contract and for which no additional contract is ever executed. It is common for contractors to be asked for or to offer business advice about matters not covered under this or any other contract. In those cases having the provision included above—in the course of performing Services, or in the course of providing advice or performing other services to Moff—makes it clear that anything created for Moff belongs to Moff.

It's important that the final clause state that the creations "shall be the sole and exclusive property of Moff" not just "shall be the property of Moff." The law generally provides that where two inventors contribute to a creation, each party has a separate ownership interest in half the creation. The sentence should make clear that the contractor is bargaining away this legal right and that anything created is owned by Moff alone.]

(2) Contractor waives all moral rights and shall assign, cause to be assigned ,and does hereby assign to Moff, its successors, assigns, and nominees, sole and exclusive right, title, and interest in and to the Creations including but not limited to copyrights, inventions, patent applications, or patents.

[Technically the contractor owns what is created at the time it is created. In order to transfer legal ownership to your company the ownership in the invention must be assigned. This sentence deals with this legal technicality. If your company is sold and desires to include ownership of anything invented as an asset in the sale, there must be a provision in your company agreements providing that the rights in the agreement can pass to the successor of your company. Your company probably also wants to be able to sell the right to this invention and that sale would again be done through an assignment. This provision allows transfer of your company's rights in the contractor's invention to others.]

Moff shall retain any and all rights to prepare patent applications and obtain patent protection, copyright registrations, and/or seek other forms of protection on Creations.

[It's possible for the contractor to complete these filings and assign the resulting patents, copyrights, or other intellectual property registrations to your company, but it's a better idea for your company to control this process by registering the invention and requiring the contractor to cooperate in the process. One reason for your company to maintain control over the patent process is because how the claims in a patent are described has a great effect on the ultimate issuance of the patent and the description is controlled by the party filing the patent.]

Contractor agrees to assist Moff, at Moff's expense, so that Moff obtains, perfects, defends, and enforces its rights in and to Creations in any country, including disclosure to Moff of all pertinent information and data Moff may reasonably request and execution of applications, assignments, and other instruments to apply for and obtain copyright protection and letters patent.

[Make sure your company does not limit your rights to register inventions to the United States or another country. Registration is accomplished country by country, so if your com-

pany intends to obtain ownership throughout the world, state that.]

(3) Contractor grants Moff a non-exclusive, royalty-free, perpetual, worldwide, transferable license to use, make, or have made derivative works to everything provided by Contractor as part of the Services that may contain work that is copyrighted, patented, or is otherwise owned or controlled by Contractor. Moff or Moff's customers may make copies or adaptations for Moff's or Moff's customers' use, including, but not limited to, archival and backup purposes.

[If the contractor, for example, develops a software program for your company that is based on a template that the contractor developed prior to contracting with your company, the contractor owns that template. Under the terms of this agreement, the final product, a refinement of that template, is owned by your company. The ownership of the software you have gained through this agreement gives your company the right to use this product but probably doesn't give your company the right to sell it, further modify it, copy it, or allow others to use it, because it is based on the template owned by the contractor. The legal mechanism that allows your company to use, make, or have made creations derived from creations the contractor owns is called a license. This section provides such a license.]

M. MISCELLANEOUS PROVISIONS

(1) This Contract constitutes the entire agreement between the parties concerning this subject matter and supersedes all other representations, negotiations, conditions, communications, and agreements, whether oral or written, between the parties relating to the same subject matter except where the other agreement is specifically incorporated into this Contract. This agreement contains the entire agreement of the parties with respect to this subject matter.

[The effect of this statement is that a court would be very unlikely to use any other written document or testimony of a verbal agreement to determine what the agreement between the parties was if there is a dispute over this agreement. The only evidence of the agreement would be this document. If there are other agreements your company has entered into as part of this agreement (perhaps a more detailed confidentiality agreement) they must be referenced here in order to be effective because this provision negates all other written agreements not specifically referenced.]

(2) If the terms of Attachment One conflict with this Contract, this Contract prevails.

[Anytime your company references another document into an agreement you should specify how any conflicts between the other documents and this agreement will be decided.]

(3) Subject to the written consent described below, this Contract shall be binding on the parties and their heirs, legal representatives, successors, and assigns.

[If your company is sold or the contractor dies this contract may not be enforceable by the new owner of your company or against the contractor's estate. This may be a concern because the new owner of your company may suddenly find itself without the services provided here, or your company may want information the contractor had but find that the contractor's estate has no duty to provide it.]

(4) Contractor shall not assign its rights or delegate its duties under this Contract without prior written consent of Moff.

[This provision prevents the contractor from hiring or allowing anyone else to perform its duties under this agreement without your company's consent. It also prevents the contractor from assigning its rights, such as the right to payment, to someone else.]

(5) Any specific rights or remedy provided in this Contract is not exclusive but is cumulative of all other rights and remedies.

[This sentence allows your company to enforce all the rights and remedies in the contract, not just one. For example, if the contractor signs an agreement on your company's behalf (a violation of paragraph F) this sentence would allow your company to both terminate the contract as provided in section D and sue the contractor for damages for violating paragraph F.]

If any one or more of the provisions of this Contract are held to be invalid, illegal, or unenforceable by a court or arbitrator of competent jurisdiction, the validity, legality, and enforceability of the remaining provisions shall not be affected or impaired.

[Where the law changes making a provision in a contract unenforceable or even illegal, the entire contract may be void because it contains the now illegal or unenforceable provision. This sentence may allow a court to simply delete the provision, leaving the rest of the contract to remain enforceable. Whether a court will strike a void provision is a matter of state law but it's wise to have this sentence in case your state allows such action.]

(6) IN NO EVENT SHALL MOFF BE LIABLE TO CONTRACTOR OR ANY THIRD PARTY IN CON-

TRACT, TORT, OR OTHERWISE FOR INCIDENTAL OR CONSEQUENTIAL DAMAGES OF ANY KIND, INCLUDING, WITHOUT LIMITATION, PUNITIVE OR ECONOMIC DAMAGES OR LOST PROFITS, REGARDLESS OF WHETHER MOFF SHALL BE ADVISED, SHALL HAVE REASON TO KNOW, OR IN FACT SHALL KNOW OF THE POSSIBILITY.

[The limit of liability provision precludes your company from responsibility for consequential damages—things like lost profits and lost revenue. Consequential damages can be huge and are usually not damages your company is contemplating if the agreement is breached.]

(7) Any and all disputes arising out of or relating to this Contract shall be subject to good faith negotiations between the parties before legal proceedings.

[This sentence would allow your company to ask a court to dismiss a lawsuit filed by the contractor if good faith negotiations had not occurred prior to filing the lawsuit. "Good faith" usually means that both parties participate in the negotiations, that those participating have the authority to come to an agreement on the issue, and that a reasonable amount of time is spent negotiating before a lawsuit is filed. Lawsuits are expensive, time-consuming, and distracting from a company's business. Requiring that the parties to a dispute talk before filing one is good business. However, in a serious dispute I have found that one or both parties will no longer desire to speak to each other. Having a contract provision that requires speaking to each other in a negotiation often bridges this hurdle and allows a resolution short of court.) This Contract shall be governed by and construed in accordance with the laws of the state of Nan, without reference to its conflict of laws provisions. *(If this sentence is taken out and a lawsuit is filed, the court will apply the law of the state where the lawsuit was filed. If it is important to your company that the law of the state your company is located in is applied in a lawsuit, your company can include this provision in agreements.]*

Each party hereby submits to the exclusive jurisdiction of, and waives any venue or other objection against, any federal court sitting in the State of Nan, U.S.A., or any Nan state court in any legal proceeding arising out of or relating to this Contract, and each party agrees that all claims and matters may be heard and determined in any such court.

[This sentence means that all lawsuits over the contract must be filed in courts located in the specified state. The location of a lawsuit can affect the costs involved—more or less

expensive attorneys, travel costs—and is commonly thought to influence outcomes of a case—courts may favor the "hometown" company.]

If any party seeks to enforce its rights under this Contract by legal proceedings or otherwise, the non-prevailing party shall pay all reasonable costs and expenses of the prevailing party.

[Some states provide for recovery of the prevailing party's attorneys fees and other costs in a contract lawsuit but some do not. In states where there is no statute governing recovery of the prevailing party's legal fees, this contract provision would allow the recovery. Having this provision in contracts is commonly thought to discourage the filing of a frivolous lawsuit or one not well-grounded in evidence supporting the party filing it, because the filing party risks paying the other party's fees and costs.]

(8) No breach of this Contract can be waived except in writing. Waiver of any breach shall not be deemed to be a waiver of any other breach of the same or any other provision of this Contract.

[This section prevents anything but a written waiver from waiving a breach of contract. It also allows waiver of one breach of the contract while retaining your company's right to enforce the same provision in the future.]

(9) No amendment, modification, or waiver of any provision of this Contract shall be effective unless in writing and signed by both parties.

[This is a very important provision to include. Otherwise, for example, one person can say that payment for the services was agreed to be double what the contract states and it's possible the new fee could be enforced.]

"Moff" "Contractor"

[By placing the names here in quotes you are indicating that these are shorthand for the official names, which are included elsewhere. If your company intends to use this as a form agreement to be used over and over for many different services you will want to limit changes that have to be made. By using the quotes here you have made it unnecessary to actually type in the official legal names of the contractor and your company. It would only have to be done where the words in these quotes are defined (in the preamble before section 1].

By: ______________________ By: ______________________
Name: ______________________ Name: ______________________
Title: ______________________ Title: ______________________
Date: ______________________ Date: ______________________

ATTACHMENT ONE

Services: Contractor shall review and tabulate 100 surveys conducted by Moff and provide a written summary to Moff of the number of responses in each category for each question on the survey as well as the mean and median for each question. *[This defines the work this contractor is performing. If there are additional details or analysis Moff desires it must be listed here. The end product of the work is a written summary. If Moff expected a presentation of the results it would not be required of the contractor under this description.]*

Term: From the Effective Date through March 1, 2009. *(This work would have to be completed by March 1, 2009 or the contractor would be in breach of this agreement.)*

Payment: On submission and acceptance of the written summary by Moff, Contractor shall be paid one hundred dollars ($100). *(This payment provision is written to benefit Moff because it conditions payment on completion of the work and completion to the satisfaction of Moff while relieving Moff of any firm date that Moff must either make the payment or accept the work. This means that Moff can delay payment as long as possible while holding the contractor to a high degree of performance because payment is contingent on the quality of the product.)*

Checklist for Contracts Where Your Company Is the Buyer of Services

- ❑ Correct legal name of parties
- ❑ Addresses of parties
- ❑ Effective date of contract
- ❑ Date services start, if different
- ❑ Definitions for capitalized terms
- ❑ Term of contract

- ❑ Detailed description of services to be provided:
    - What is to be done
    - How is it to be accomplished
    - When is it to be done
    - Where is it to be done
    - Are there specific qualifications for the worker who performs the services
    - Are there specific workers you want to name as required to perform this service
    - How will it be determined that the services were completed
    - What are the specifications for services
    - Deadlines for completion of services and individual steps
    - What specific labor and materials are supplied by service provider
    - What specific labor and materials are supplied by your company
    - Quality standards that must be met
- ❑ Agreement to follow company's existing or revised policies on security, safety, and smoking
- ❑ Assume risk of exposure to hazardous materials or dangerous conditions on site (identify)
- ❑ Documents created by service provider in performance of services belong to Company
- ❑ Payment terms
    - Retainer due—if so is this billed against or held until some date
    - Deposit due—when is it refundable
    - When is payment due and how is this calculated
    - Is an invoice sent or amount due automatically
    - If invoice what are the invoice intervals
    - What details must invoice contain
    - What is payment amount
    - In what currency
    - How is payment to be made—cash, check, electronic funds transfer, or other
    - Out-of-pocket expenses reimbursable, if so on what basis and when
    - No right of deduction or set-off

- ❑ Relationship is that of independent contractor
- ❑ No joint venture, agency, partnership, trust, or association
- ❑ Contractor responsible for all taxes, compliance with employer duties
- ❑ Confidential information
  - Will provider or its employees have access to confidential information
  - If so, do provider's employees sign confidentiality agreement with provider agreeing to maintain customer's confidentiality
  - Identify and define your company's confidential information
  - What are acceptable uses and disclosures
  - Term of confidentiality obligations
  - Duties towards confidential information
- ❑ Exceptions to duties of confidentiality
- ❑ No solicitation of employees
  - Length of restriction
- ❑ Alternative dispute resolution
  - Negotiation
  - Mediation
  - Arbitration
  - Is alternative exclusive or required before litigation
  - Who pays for alternative
  - Who specifically is required to participate in alternative
  - Qualifications of neutral party officiating over the alternative
  - What is the time frame for alternative
  - Where does alternative dispute forum occur
  - What rules govern alternative dispute forum
  - If neutral party renders a decision is it binding
- ❑ Assignment/subcontracting permitted
  - Preclude partial or complete assignment but allow subcontracting
  - Preclude subcontracting but allow partial or complete assignment
  - Allowed with consent not to be withheld unreasonably
  - Allowed with consent at your company's sole discretion
  - Allowed if a party is sold
  - Allowed if a party is transferred to an affiliate or subsidiary

- If subcontractors permitted will sub be required to maintain company confidential information

❑ Recovery of prevailing party's expenses in litigation
- Attorneys fees
- Legal costs
- Expert witness fees
- Investigation costs

❑ Choice of law to interpret contract

❑ Choice of venue for litigation

❑ Compliance with laws
- Requirement to obtain permits and licenses

❑ Conflicting language between agreements is resolved in what manner

❑ Rights provided in contract are cumulative or exclusive

❑ Publicity
- Allow with other party's written consent not to be unreasonably withheld
- Allow for your company at its discretion
- Prohibit entirely
- Allow use of customer's name in advertisements

❑ Force Majeure—consider inclusion of fire, accident, acts of public enemy, terrorism, severe weather, acts of God, labor disruption, flood, failure of suppliers to deliver, difficulty obtaining supplies, epidemics, nuclear strike, government intervention, government or freight embargo, quarantine, difficulty obtaining transportation
- Notice required if event occurs
- Right to terminate if event lasts specified amount of time

❑ Indemnity
- Service provider provides indemnification
- To your company, officers, employees, consultants, directors, agents, parent company, subsidiary
- For claims, liabilities, losses, damages, costs, charges, attorneys' fees, legal costs, liens, death, personal injury, accidents, property damage
- Arising out of actual or alleged defects in material and workmanship,

negligence, gross negligence, breach of the contract, claims of liens, or encumbrances

- ❑ Integration (or Entire Agreement) provision
  - All documents making up the agreement referenced
- ❑ Requirement to obtain and maintain insurance
  - Specific amounts
  - Insurance certificates required to be produced
  - Your company a "named insured"
- ❑ Limitation on liability
  - Consequential damages—special, indirect, incidental, exemplary
  - Limit liability to gross negligence
  - Limitation on remedies and if so is word "exclusive" included
  - Limitation on amount of damages
  - Limitation on liability provision conspicuous
- ❑ Notice provision
  - Is address for notices included
  - Acceptable ways to make delivery specified
  - Time that the other party is deemed to have received the notice specified
- ❑ Severability—illegal or otherwise unenforceable provisions can be severed
- ❑ Successors and assigns—agreement binding on
- ❑ Survival—certain terms of the agreement may survive termination
- ❑ Termination provision
  - How much notice is required before contract terminates
  - For cause
- ❑ Is right to cure default provided
  - Any breach or material breach
  - For convenience–
    - If elected by either party, does any party have a right to damages
  - Insolvency
    - Bankruptcy
    - Assignment for benefit of creditors
    - Receiver appointed

- Initiates reorganization
- Closes business
- Stops operating

- What must be returned or provided to your company if the contract is terminated

❑ Waiver—waiver of breach not agreement to waive all breaches

❑ Warranty

- How long and for what

❑ Written modification—all modifications in writing and signed

❑ Correct signature blocks

❑ Agreement signed and each page initialed by both parties

Chapter 10

The following agreement is a simple purchase order in which the buyer has decided to adopt the provision of the UCC plus the terms set forth below. The terms of purchase covers provisions the UCC does not cover but that are important to reduce the risk for the buyer. Although this agreement does not specifically state that the terms of the UCC are being adopted, the UCC automatically applies unless a written agreement states otherwise.

TERMS OF PURCHASE

Indemnification. Each Party shall indemnify and hold harmless the other, its parent, subsidiaries, affiliates, successors, assigns, employees, officers, directors, agents, or subcontractors from and against any and all suits, claims, losses, forfeitures, demands, fees, damages, liabilities, costs, expenses, obligations, proceedings, or injuries, of any kind or nature, including reasonable attorneys fees that party may hereafter incur, become responsible for, or pay out as a result of the other party's breach of any term or provision of this Agreement, or a claim of lien or encumbrances made by third parties.

[This provision is mutual—covering both the buyer and the seller. If the seller sent a purchase order with an indemnification provision covering only itself, this provision and that

provision would probably cancel each other out. In that case the warranties provided for in the UCC would provide coverage for many of the potential losses your company, the buyer, would be covered for here.]

Assignment. Neither party may assign or otherwise transfer this Agreement without the prior written consent of the other.

[Transferring this agreement to another company is not a subject provided for in the UCC, and contracts are presumed assignable unless there is an agreement otherwise. As the buyer your company probably does not want the seller to assign the right to ship products to your company to another seller who sells similar products.]

LIMITATION OF LIABILITY. IN NO EVENT SHALL EITHER PARTY BE LIABLE IN CONTRACT, TORT, OR OTHERWISE FOR INCIDENTAL OR CONSEQUENTIAL DAMAGES OF ANY KIND, INCLUDING, WITHOUT LIMITATION, ECONOMIC DAMAGE OR LOST PROFITS, REGARDLESS OF WHETHER EITHER PARTY SHALL BE ADVISED, SHALL HAVE OTHER REASON TO KNOW, OR IN FACT SHALL KNOW OF THE POSSIBILITY.

[This precludes either party from recovering any indirect damages resulting from a claim or litigation. An example would be where a bookcase falls on someone. The broken arm would be direct damage. The cost of a nonrefundable cruise the person missed because they had to have surgery on the arm would be consequential damages.]

Forum and Legal Fees. Should legal action arise concerning this Agreement, the prevailing party shall be entitled to recover all reasonable attorneys' fees and related costs, in addition to any other relief that may be awarded by any court or other tribunal.

[This provision avoids forum selection—where a lawsuit may be filed—as well as choice of law—what state law would be applied in a lawsuit. It merely provides that whoever prevails in a lawsuit or other court proceeding can recover the fees and costs they incurred in the process such as attorneys fees, expert witness fees, and court filing fees. Some states allow this recovery in a contract dispute under state law but some do not. In the states where no statute provides for recovery of the prevailing party's legal fees, this contract provision has the same effect.]

The parties agree that prior to initiating any legal proceedings against the other, the parties will engage a neutral mediator who will be charged with assisting the parties to reach a mutually agreeable resolution of all contested matters. The mediation shall take place in

Ingut, Noodle, USA and will be conducted in the English language. The mediator shall be chosen by mutual agreement of the parties and the mediator's fees shall be borne equally by the parties. In the event that a mediator cannot be agreed on by the parties, each party shall chose a mediator and the two mediators shall together chose a third mediator who will conduct the mediation. The costs of the two mediators chosen to choose the third mediator shall be borne equally by the parties. The parties agree to participate in the mediation in good faith.

[This provision requires that the parties mediate a dispute prior to filing a lawsuit in a court of law. Read these provisions carefully. Some require that you mediate and give up your right to file a lawsuit. Some, as this one does, require mediation prior to accessing the court system but still allow litigation if the mediation fails. Seriously consider whether your company wants to give up its right to access the court system. However, mediation is often a positive step in dispute resolution. If your company chooses to include a mediation provision, include as much detail as possible, because if this provision is used, the parties will usually not have a good enough relationship at that point to iron out these details then. Include things like where the mediation will take place, who will pay for the mediator, and the rented mediation location if any, and who is required to attend the mediation—the president of the company, or is the sales representative enough?]

Severability. If any provision of this Agreement is held by a court of law to be illegal, invalid, or unenforceable, that provision shall be deemed amended to achieve as nearly as possible the same economic effect as the original provision, and the legality, validity, and enforceability of the remaining provisions of this Agreement shall not be affected or impaired.

[Where the law changes, making a term in a contract unenforceable or even illegal, the entire contract may be void because it contains the now illegal or unenforceable term. Where the parties agree to a provision like this one the court may simply delete the term, leaving the rest of the contract to stand as it is. Whether a court will do that is a matter of state law, but it's wise to have this sentence in case the state court does allow striking only the offending provision.]

Waiver. No term or provision hereof will be considered waived and no breach of this Agreement excused unless such waiver or consent is in writing. The waiver or consent to a breach of any provision of this Agreement shall not operate or be construed as a waiver of, consent to, or excuse of any other or subsequent breach.

[This provision states that even if your company ignores a breach of contract once—which would have to be in writing according to this provision— it doesn't mean your company has decided to ignore all future breaches. By including this provision, if your company, for example, accepts a late delivery without claiming a breach of contract, it would not be forever waiving its right to claim a breach of contract for other late deliveries.]

Conflicts between Documents. These terms shall control over any conflicting terms in any other document that might be exchanged related to this transaction.

[It's a good idea to include a provision like this, but whether a court will decide your company's terms take precedence over similar terms in the seller's sales terms is unclear. There are many sellers using poorly written terms of sale agreements and in those cases, a provision like this will provide an advantage to your company.]

Force Majeure. Neither party shall be held responsible for any delay or failure in performance of any part of this Agreement to the extent such delay or failure is caused by fire, flood, explosion, terrorism, war, embargo, government requirement, civil or military authority, act of God, or other similar causes beyond its control and without the fault or negligence of the delayed or non-performing party. The party so affected shall notify the non-affected party in writing within ten (10) days after the beginning of any such cause that would affect the party's performance.

[The UCC excuses non-performance under the contract for commercial impracticability, but in order to provide an excuse for delay or non-performance for specific circumstances they should be listed here. The UCC does not require notice be given to the other party if a force majeure event occurs, so if your company desires to receive a notice it must require it in its contracts. Your company may also want to provide for a right to terminate the purchase if the event lasts a certain amount of time.]

Successors and Assigns. The Parties intend this Agreement to bind any and all of the Parties' successors, heirs, and assigns.

[To assure that when this agreement is transferred it is binding on the person or company it is transferred to, your company contracts need to specifically state the binding nature of the transfer. Otherwise because the party the agreement is transferred to is not a party to

this agreement, this contract may not be enforceable.]

Survival. All provisions that logically ought to survive termination of this Agreement shall survive.

[When a contract ends, either because it expires, is terminated, or when all the duties in the contract are performed, the terms of the contract no longer have any enforceability unless there is a provision in the agreement providing that certain provisions are meant to continue after the contract ends. These provisions are typically the indemnification, limitation of liability, choice of law, dispute resolution, and warranty provisions.]

Entire Agreement. This Agreement supersedes, terminates, and otherwise renders null and void any and all prior written or oral agreements or understandings between the parties relating to the subject matter of this Agreement. Except as otherwise provided in this Agreement, only a written instrument signed by both parties may modify this Agreement.

[This provision means that these terms of sale completely set forth the agreement the parties have entered into concerning the purchase and sale of products and that no other written or oral agreement may be considered part of the agreement the buyer and seller have entered into. If a dispute occurs a court would not allow any other oral or written agreement to be admissible to determine what the party's agreement was. This provision would even void the order between the parties that stated what exactly the buyer was purchasing, how many, when delivery was expected, and at what price. Because that's probably not a good idea, this provision should reference these order categories as being part of this agreement.]

Checklist for a Buyer's Purchase Order

- ❑ Definitions for capitalized terms
- ❑ Limit right to take actions affecting agreement to authorized buyer and member of management
- ❑ Order acceptance
  - On written acceptance from seller
  - On expiration of time period
  - On shipment
  - Payment not final acceptance
  - Acceptance not waiver of latent defects

   - Testing and inspection at any time during and after manufacture
- ❑ Products
   - Must meet specifications
   - No substitutions without consent
- ❑ Seller may not manufacture in advance of buyer's needs
- ❑ Buyer has right to require progress reports on orders
- ❑ Product rejection
   - At buyer's option may return for credit or replacement, halt at plant for correction, or keep if adjustment in price
- ❑ Buyer's changes to order
   - Process for initiating changes
   - Changes at any time
   - Changes can be specifications, delivery date, drawings, designs, packaging, destination, schedule, inspection, quantities, and suspension of manufacture
   - Notification of additional charges
   - Notification of additional time for delivery
- ❑ Price
   - As stated in buyer's PO
   - No extra charges
   - No greater than lowest prevailing price offered to any customer
- ❑ Invoices
   - What is to be included in invoice detail
   - Cash discount and how calculated
   - When time period for determining cash discounts begins
   - Payment due dates
   - Invoice intervals
   - Payments in what currency
   - Payments to be made by cash, check, electronic funds transfer, or other
   - Buyer has right to set off any amounts owed by seller
- ❑ Shipping
   - Notification of drop shipment
   - Notification of actual or expected delay

- Title and risk of loss passes at delivery to buyer
- Designation of carrier
- Packaging and labeling requirements
- No advance delivery
- If advance delivery, returned or stored at seller's cost
- Seller to pay rush delivery if needed to meet delivery date

❑ Time of essence to buyer only

❑ Returns—process

❑ Warranty

- Passed on to buyer's customer
- Free from defects in design, workmanship, and materials
- Conforms to specifications, drawings, samples, advertising literature
- Warranty period—period of time, period of use, or period of performance
- Warranty period for repaired products
- Warranty period for refurbished products
- Merchantable
- Fit for intended purpose
- Free of defects in title
- Does not infringe any patent, copyright, mask work, or other intellectual property right
- Packaged to protect from damage
- Remedies for breach of warranty at buyer's option
- Remedies include repair, replace, refund, or buyer may fix and charge seller
- Remedies not exclusive

❑ Buyer expressly objects to any conflicting terms in seller's PO

❑ Corrective action plan required on notice by buyer

❑ No credit hold without notice

❑ Taxes included in price

❑ No gratuities to staff or families of staff

❑ Patent Infringement

- Indemnification for all products
- Includes claims of unfair competition

   - Retain right to defend and settle
   - Seller must procure for buyer right to use product
   - Seller must modify product to become non-infringing
   - Seller must replace product with non-infringing product
   - Seller must refund price
- ❑ Termination provision
   - For cause
     - Any breach or material breach
     - Fails to perform
     - Performs unsatisfactorily
     - Fails to make progress
     - Right to cure period
   - For convenience
     - At any time
     - Work stops immediately
     - If partial cancellation, work continues on remainder of order
   - Amount of payment to seller for cancellation of custom products by period of time between cancellation and delivery date
     - ❑ Amount of payment for cancellation of stock products if any
     - ❑ Limit on time to claim payment for a cancellation
   - Insolvency
   - Bankruptcy
   - Assignment for benefit of creditors
   - Receiver appointed
   - Initiates reorganization
     - ❑ Closes business
     - ❑ Stops operating
     - ❑ Buyer has right to manufacture if seller ceases business
- ❑ Conflicting language between agreements resolved in what manner

  Confidential information
   - How defined
   - What are acceptable uses and disclosures

- Term of confidentiality obligations
- Duties towards confidential information
- Exceptions to duties of confidentiality

❑ No implied licenses to buyer's information or property

❑ Alternative dispute resolution

- Negotiation
- Mediation
- Arbitration
- If don't want any of these include provision specifically rejecting
- Is alternative exclusive or required before litigation
- Who pays for alternative
- Who specifically is required to participate in alternative
- Qualifications of neutral party officiating over the alternative
- What is the timeframe for alternative
- Where does alternative dispute forum occur
- What rules govern alternative dispute forum
- If neutral party renders a decision is it binding

❑ Indemnity

- Seller to provide
- To buyer, officers, employees, consultants, directors, agents, parent, subsidiary
- Claims, liabilities, losses, damages, costs, charges, attorneys' fees, legal costs, liens, death, personal injury, accidents, property damage
- Arising out of actual or alleged defects in material and workmanship, negligence, gross negligence, breach of the contract, claims of liens, or encumbrances

❑ Limitation on liability

- Consequential damages—special, indirect, incidental, exemplary
- Limit on damages

❑ Requirement to obtain and maintain insurance

- Contract liability, comprehensive, general, automobile liability, workers' compensation, product liability.
- Insurance certificates required to be produced

- Named insured

❑ Compliance with laws
- Requirement to obtain permits and licenses
- Comply with OSHA, hazardous materials laws

❑ Safety
- Label hazardous materials
- Provide material safety data sheet on any chemicals
- If hazardous materials in products, inform in writing
- If defects become known must inform buyer

❑ Publicity
- Allow with other party's written consent not to be unreasonably withheld
- Allow for your company at its discretion
- Prohibit entirely

❑ Choice of law to interpret contract

❑ Recovery of prevailing party's expenses in litigation
- Attorneys fees
- Legal costs
- Expert witness fees
- Investigation costs

❑ Severability—illegal or otherwise unenforceable provisions can be severed

❑ Waiver—waiver of breach not agreement to waive all breaches

❑ Assignment/subcontracting permitted
- Preclude partial or complete assignment but allow subcontracting
- Preclude subcontracting but allow partial or complete assignment
- Allowed with consent not to be withheld unreasonably
- Allowed with consent at other party's sole discretion
- Allowed if a party is sold
- Allowed if a party is transferred to an affiliate or subsidiary
- If subcontractors permitted will sub be required to maintain company confidential information

❑ Choice of venue for litigation

❑ Rights provided in contract are cumulative or exclusive

- ❑ Force Majeure—consider inclusion of fire, accident, acts of public enemy, terrorism, severe weather, acts of God, labor disruption, flood, failure of suppliers to deliver, difficulty obtaining supplies, epidemics, nuclear strike, government intervention, government or freight embargo, quarantine, difficulty obtaining transportation
  - Notice required if event occurs
  - Right to terminate if event lasts specified amount of time
- ❑ Integration (or Entire Agreement) provision
  - All documents making up the agreement referenced
- ❑ Notice provision
  - Are both parties' addresses included
  - Acceptable delivery methods
  - Time that the other party is deemed to have received the notice specified
- ❑ No joint venture, agency, partnership, trust, or association
- ❑ Successors and assigns—agreement binding on
- ❑ Survival—certain terms of the agreement may survive termination
- ❑ Written modification—all modifications in writing and signed
- ❑ If terms on back of a form, does the front call attention to the terms
- ❑ Will Buyer provide tooling or otherwise have its own property at seller
  - Seller must insure it, label it as buyers', separate it from other property, return it in good condition, and secure it
  - Buyer may enter and inspect it at any time

Index